Statesmen, Scoundrels, and Eccentrics

Statesmen, Scoundrels, and Eccentrics

A Gallery of Amazing Arkansans

TOM DILLARD

The University of Arkansas Press
Fayetteville
2010

Copyright © 2010 by The University of Arkansas Press

ISBN-10: 1-555728-927-1
ISBN-13: 978-1-555728-927-2

14   13   12   11   10   5   4   3   2   1

Designed by Liz Lester

⊛ The paper used in this publication meets the minimum requirements of the American National Standard for Permanence of Paper for Printed Library Materials Z39. 48-1984.

LIBRARY OF CONGRESS CATALOGING-IN-PUBLICATION DATA

Dillard, Tom W.
     Statesmen, scoundrels, and eccentrics : a gallery of amazing Arkansans / Tom Dillard.
          p.   cm.
     Includes bibliographical references.
     ISBN 978-1-55728-927-8 (pbk. : alk. paper)
     1. Arkansas—Biography. 2. Arkansas—History. I. Title.
     F410.D55   2010
     920.0767—dc22
                              2009041227

Dedication

This book is dedicated to my wife, Mary Frost Dillard,
a daughter of Arkansas who always seeks to know and to give.

CONTENTS

Foreword xi

Acknowledgments xiii

Introduction xv

CHAPTER I
Natives, Explorers, and Early Settlers

Hernando de Soto 3

Saracen 8

Jean Laffite 11

William E. Woodruff 14

Matthew Lyon 17

Hiram A. Whittington 20

Jacob Wolf 23

Antoine Barraque 26

Friedrich Gerstaecker 29

Davy Crockett 32

CHAPTER II
Antebellum Politicians

Robert Crittenden 37

Gov. George Izard 40

Chester Ashley 43

Augustus H. Garland 46

Robert Ward Johnson 49

CHAPTER III
Postbellum Politicians

Gov. Powell Clayton 55

Sen. Stephen W. Dorsey 61

William H. Grey 65

Isaac T. Gillam 68

Gov. James H. Berry 71

CHAPTER IV
Twentieth-Century Politicians

Gov. John S. Little 77

Sen. Joseph T. Robinson 80

Gov. Charles H. Brough 85

Sen. Thaddeus Caraway 89

Sen. Hattie Caraway 92

Rep. Claude A. Fuller 95

Rep. Clyde T. Ellis 98

Gov. Winthrop Rockefeller 101

Lt. Gov. Maurice "Footsie" Britt 104

CHAPTER V
The Law

Nelson Hacket 109

John R. Eakin 112

Mifflin W. Gibbs 115

Judge Isaac C. Parker 118

Scipio A. Jones 121

CHAPTER VI
Entrepreneurs

Nathan Warren 127

Scott Bond 129

Green Thompson 132

Conrad Elsken 136

Ben Pearson 139

CHAPTER VII
Artists and Writers

Edward Payson Washbourne	145
John Hallum	148
Alice French	151
Dionicio Rodriguez	155
Brewer Family	158
Vance Randolph	161
Miss Lily Peter	165

CHAPTER VIII
Education, Science, and Medicine

Dr. Charles McDermott	171
J. C. Corbin	174
Ida Joe Brooks	177
Anna P. Strong	180
Dr. William Baerg	183
Keller and Marian Breland	187
Samuel Lee Kountz	190
Harold Alexander	192

CHAPTER IX
Entertainers and Performers

Scott Joplin	197
Norm McLeod	200
Broncho Billy Anderson	204
Lum and Abner	207
Louis Jordan	210
Emma Dusenbury	213
Hazel Walker	216

CHAPTER X
Religious Leaders

Rev. Cephas Washburn	221
Bishop Edward Fitzgerald	224
Rev. Hay Watson Smith	228
Rabbi Ira E. Sanders	232

CHAPTER XI
Seers, Spiritualists, and Skeptics

Caroline Dye	237
Lessie Stringfellow	239
Bernie Babcock	242
Harold M. Sherman	246

CHAPTER XII
Eccentrics, Frauds, and the Inexplicable

William Hope "Coin" Harvey	251
King Crowley	254
Old Mike	258
Dr. John R. Brinkley	261
Ted Richmond	264

FOREWORD

How many people out of a hundred know that an Arkansas slave pushed the British Empire into helping runaway slaves from the United States?

Remember the Alamo? How many people know that Davy Crockett caroused his way across Arkansas (where he described the men as "half horse half alligator") as he headed toward San Antonio for his final rendezvous?

Can you guess why Jean Lafitte came to Arkansas? He claimed to be a spy, but people recognized the famous pirate everywhere he went and wanted to stop for a chat.

For years, Tom Dillard has been a persuasive public voice for Arkansas history: the teaching of it, the importance of it, the plain necessity of it if we hope to know what we have been and therefore what we are. Mr. Dillard has now put his history where his mouth is. This collection of essays is not concerned with dates, battles, and the political back-and-forths of Arkansas through its centuries of recorded events. It is rather a series of brilliant profiles of scores of the state's most interesting people. All of these essays first appeared as weekly columns in the *Arkansas Democrat-Gazette.*

You don't have to be a dead warrior or a political big shot to attract Tom Dillard's attention. He is a demon researcher, and his eye is as likely to come to rest on a gangster or a con artist in the brittle old documents as it is on the first woman elected to the United States Senate or the famous member of Congress who pushed President Roosevelt's New Deal into law. I guess the scholars would call his selection process eclectic, but that sounds far too dull to describe these profiles. How can you stop reading if you dip into the first paragraph of the yarn about the fellow who thought Ozark people did not read enough and set himself up as a walking library, toting books in a tow sack through the hills and hollows? Or the one about John R. Brinkley, the famous goat gland doctor and con artist? Or the candid account of the career of Stephen W. Dorsey, a pioneer in the field of white-collar crime?

I thought I was reasonably well educated in my state's history, but I had never heard of William H. Grey until Mr. Dillard introduced me to him. Grey was one of the more effective black leaders in Arkansas's Reconstruction politics. Turned out he probably got a taste for politics because his supposed white father, Representative Henry A. Wise of Virginia, took the lad with him to the chambers of Congress every day to fold documents and listen to the speeches.

And that runaway slave who embarrassed the British Empire? His name was Nelson Hacket. He was a slave in Fayetteville when he stole his master's fastest horse and rode it to Canada, precipitating an international incident. In the course of his adventures he established a record of escapes that would be the envy of any jailbird and, if emulated today, would leave the nation's jails half empty all the time. Take a look at his chapter. Somebody ought to make a movie about him.

Roy Reed

ACKNOWLEDGMENTS

The debts owed by any author are extensive, but this is especially so in my case. Ferreting out obscure information on often little-known people means that I regularly called upon friends, relatives, historians, librarians, and archivists across the state—and sometimes outside. To all these unfailingly helpful folks, I extend my heartfelt thanks.

The University of Arkansas Libraries assisted me in many ways. I am especially grateful to Timothy G. Nutt, manuscripts and rare books librarian at the University of Arkansas Libraries special collections department, who is always helpful to anyone working on Arkansas topics. Other University of Arkansas library colleagues who lent assistance were Andrea Cantrell, research services librarian, and several of her staff, including Geoffrey Stark and Jim Wilhelm. Valerie Robertson assisted with illustrations. Todd Lewis shared his deep knowledge of Arkansas African American history. Beth Juhl, who is an amazingly productive librarian and student of Arkansas history, is good at locating the most obscure sources, and I thank her. Stephen Chism shared his knowledge of the Stringfellow family.

Russell P. Baker, state archivist at the Arkansas History Commission in Little Rock, helped me on several occasions. Independent consultant and log house restoration specialist Joan Gould of Fayetteville helped straighten out the details on Jacob Wolf and his famous log house at Norfork. Ann M. Early, state archeologist, helped me thread my way through the labyrinth of American Indian history.

Jimmy Bryant, director of archives at the University of Central Arkansas in Conway, was always helpful and cheerfully shared information and photographs. Professor James Willis at Southern Arkansas University was mighty helpful on diverse matters, and the same was true of Willis's colleague Professor Ben Johnson and his wife, Sherrel. Linda Pine, head of the archives and special collections at the University of Arkansas at Little Rock, shared information on Governor Winthrop Rockefeller and others.

Among the many individuals who assisted me were subscribers to the Arkansas History Discussion Group on the Internet. James J. Johnston of Fayetteville was a veritable gold mine of information on the north-central Ozarks, especially Searcy County.

My graduate school mentor, Professor Willard B. Gatewood of Fayetteville, was a source of inspiration as well as information. Judge Morris S. Arnold inspired me on many occasions, and on more than one helped me avoid pitfalls. My good friend Joe Beck of Little Rock eagerly shared information on his remarkable grandfather, Conrad Elsken of Logan County. Shirley Manning of Montgomery County was a helpful adviser on many topics, and George W. Gatliff of Malvern was always ready to share his extensive knowledge and experience in studying Arkansas's past.

I acknowledge with gratitude Griffin Smith, executive editor of the *Arkansas Democrat-Gazette,* who took a chance on me when he asked that I try my hand at writing a weekly column on Arkansas history. My editors at the newspaper have always been helpful, and I appreciate them. My long-suffering wife, Mary Frost Dillard, read most of these sketches more than once—and her suggestions as well as editing have made it possible for me to conceive, write, and submit a weekly historical essay while holding down a demanding job.

INTRODUCTION

This collection of biographical sketches got its start in 2002 when Griffin Smith, executive editor of the *Arkansas Democrat-Gazette,* asked me to write a weekly column on Arkansas history for his newspaper. I began the column with the firm belief that Arkansas history has relevance beyond narrow antiquarian appeal. A savvy politician once said "all politics is local," which meant, simply put, that voters react more to local political issues than to hot-button national or international causes. The same is true of history. While exceptions are apparent, one could argue that all history is local. In a democracy, decisions are often made based on local impact. Besides, state history is fun because it is local and specific to us.

Through the years I have kept a list of Arkansas characters, men and women who should be better known. Some of the folks in this collection are already fairly well known among Arkansans, men such as the "Hanging Judge," Isaac C. Parker of Fort Smith, or Hattie Caraway, the first *elected* female U.S. senator. But I want to share my fascination with little-known Arkansas characters such as Isaac T. Gillam, a slave who became a prominent politician in post–Civil War Little Rock, and Norman McLeod, an eccentric Hot Springs photographer and owner of the spa city's first large tourist trap.

Essays such as these cannot possibly tell a complete story, so I have included a reading list with each sketch. Most of the public libraries in Arkansas maintain collections about Arkansas, so the titles can usually be found without too much leg work; and modern interlibrary loan agreements allow libraries to share materials quickly.

While I hope this book can help educate new residents about Arkansas, a surprising number of native-born Arkansans know little about the state and its history. Citizens of our state, when fully aware of their heritage, can take pride in being Arkansans. That is not to say that our traditional backward image does not have some basis in fact, it is merely to affirm that our heritage is like that of any state—full of achievement and failure, with a great deal in between. Regardless of the prevailing image, Arkansans should define themselves rather than letting others.

Not all the people discussed in this book are admirable, and some might ask why I would include sketches on such charlatans as Dr. John Brinkley. While I am sensitive not to stereotype our state or its people, I do not see myself as an Arkansas booster. Our state has plenty of boosters. Our heritage is wonderfully complex, full of rhythm and discord, peopled by generations of hardworking men and women who have contributed much to our region and nation.

Over the nearly two centuries since Arkansas became a territory separate from Missouri, we have had just enough scoundrels and villains to make the mix interesting. Arkansas voters are sometimes bipolar in our selection of leaders. In a single election in 1968, Arkansans gave their vote to a liberal Republican governor, Winthrop Rockefeller; George Wallace, the rabidly segregationist third-party candidate for president; and an intellectual internationalist U.S. senator, J. W. Fulbright. When it comes to political leadership, we Arkansans do not always make the right decisions, but at least in the twenty-first century Arkansas compares favorably with most of its sister states.

Rather than boosting Arkansas, I want to serve up our history as if it were the offering at a barbeque joint on the White River: you might not want to eat the pig knuckles, but you have to admit they are interesting. If you come away from this book with nothing else, take time to celebrate the incredible variety of people who made up our wonderful little state during the three centuries since an Italian by the name of Henri de Tonty planted a small outpost on the lower reaches of a river they called the Arkansa.

CHAPTER I

Natives,
Explorers,
and Early Settlers

Hernando de Soto

The written history of Arkansas began with the arrival of Spaniard Hernando de Soto and his expeditionary force in 1541. Born of a noble but nearly impoverished family in western Spain around 1500, de Soto had to borrow money to come to the New World. Arriving on the sickly coast of Panama in 1514, the teenage Spaniard quickly became an outstanding soldier. De Soto took part in savage expeditions against Indians in Panama, Nicaragua, and Peru.

De Soto perfected his skill at killing Indians from none other than Hernando Pizarro during his conquest of the extraordinarily rich Incan empire of Peru. After two decades, de Soto returned to Spain and married Isabel de Bobadilla. After a few years in retirement enjoying the wealth that came from robbing and enslaving Indians, de Soto set about to explore mainland North America under a charter from King Charles V.

De Soto's army landed in the Tampa Bay area in 1539, and from there moved northward through modern Florida, Georgia, South Carolina, Tennessee, Alabama, and Mississippi. By the time the Spanish force, which originally numbered about six hundred soldiers, 220 horses, war dogs, and twelve priests, reached the Mississippi River, it had been reduced to a mere shadow of its glory. The previous October in modern Alabama, de Soto's force suffered many losses and wounds during the battle of Mauvilla—so they were ready to lick their wounds before figuring out how to get the remainder of the army across the vast Mississippi. Amazingly enough, some of the European women who accompanied the expedition lived to experience the endless trek about modern Arkansas.

The only portion of the Spanish party that held their numbers against the constant onslaught of Indian attacks were the hundreds of hogs that accompanied the expedition, and which were the personal property of de Soto. Only after de Soto died and his effects were auctioned did the pigs finally get eaten by the half-starved soldiers.

Tradition holds that escaped pigs from the Spanish herd became the ancestors of today's wild hogs. Pigs were not native to the New World.

The Mississippi River did not deter the Spanish. Interestingly, the various "chronicles" of the de Soto *entrada* do not record that their discovery of this vast river had much impact on the expedition. De Soto was a commander of a conquering army, neither a botanist nor naturalist of any kind, so rivers were seen as mere obstacles.

The de Soto trek was a string of bloody encounters with one Indian force after another, and it hung together because of de Soto's personal leadership. When the expedition came upon a wide brown river, he simply ordered his engineers to build rafts.

From the moment he arrived on the eastern shore of the Mississippi, de Soto faced daily attacks by Indian archers in giant painted canoes. He mounted a heavy guard and had his engineers erect a dry dock, where four large rafts were constructed and "caulked with hemp and flax." These were large vessels, capable of transporting fifty or sixty soldiers, horses, and baggage.

In keeping with his reputation for bold military leadership, de Soto launched the crossing at 3:00 A.M. In an amazing act of naval daring, de Soto got his whole expedition, pigs and all, safely across the river by about 7:30 the same morning. One biographer of de Soto has written of the remarkable crossing of the great river, "incredibly, not a single person was lost, not a horse nor piglet, though Ranjel [one of the explorers who left a written account] says the men all agreed 'nothing so difficult could ever be offered them again.'"

De Soto came to his position as leader of a huge military expedition into "Florida" as a hardened military commander, having fought with Pizarro in Peru, where he personally lead expeditions to lance fleeing Indians. (Within three hours of the surrender of the Inca, de Soto's men had created a cache of looted gold and other valuables worth 80,000 pesos. The Spanish had to keep their forges running at night in order to melt the huge amount of looted silver and gold objects.)

If rich civilizations like this could exist in places like Peru in South America, why not on the mainland north of the Florida coast? On May 18, 1539, de Soto sailed a small armada from Havana bound for the western coast of modern Florida. Drawing upon his ill-gotten riches from Peru, de Soto was able to take along a contingent of almost one hundred guards, servants, stable hands, secretaries, and even lawyers. Those employees made up about one-sixth of the entire force. They landed near modern Tampa Bay, where archeologists have found their discarded chain mail, and set off on a foray that took them the length of Florida, across parts of the Carolinas, and then through Alabama and Mississippi and finally into Arkansas. The entire torturous experience had yielded nothing more valuable than a small batch of fresh water pearls, small loot indeed for having killed and maimed thousands of Indians.

Historians, archeologists, and tourism promoters have argued for more than a century on the exact route taken by de Soto. He might have crossed the Mississippi near modern Helena, or perhaps much closer to modern Memphis. Charles M. Hudson at the University of Georgia mounted a huge effort to trace the route in the 1980s and 1990s. His conclusions differed markedly with the findings of a similar investigation led by famed ethnologist John R. Swanton, whose report was published in 1939, and on whose study team Arkansan John R. Fordyce had served.

Communities boast of being on de Soto's route, while local historians write about de Soto in the same spirit of those claiming "George Washington once slept here." For decades Hot Springs has claimed to have been on de Soto's route. Hudson's research has the Spanish exploring up the modern Fourche la Fave River rather than venturing into the modern valley of the vapors. The fierce battle with the Tula Indians probably occurred along the Fourche and not at modern Caddo Gap— where a marker claims to be the site of the Tula battle.

Almost all scholars agree that the site the Spanish called "Casqui" was on the St. Francis River at the modern city of Parkin, Arkansas. Here the Spanish erected a huge cross atop one of the major mounds located in the large city, which was surrounded by a protective moat and earthen wall. Archeologists have found de Soto–era artifacts at Parkin.

As was his practice, de Soto entered into a military alliance with the leader of the city of Casqui and attacked a nearby rival town. Other than food and furs, no valuables were found in this first attack on the Indians west of the Mississippi. De Soto, however, could not afford to give up and so pushed his forces farther west, with scouting parties sent into the Ozarks.

Upon arriving at the Arkansas River, the Spanish traveled along the river to the area near modern Russellville and then turned south across the river and into the rugged ridges of the Ouachita Mountains. After a disastrous confrontation with the Tula, de Soto sent scouts farther west but without result. Finally, the disappointed commander turned back east toward the Mississippi.

Near the modern town of Redfield, de Soto ordered his command into winter camp in October 1541. The weather was miserable, with heavy snows covering the ground for weeks. At the first hint of spring, the surviving army resumed its march to the Mississippi on March 6, 1542.

It was probably in the vicinity of modern Arkansas City, near the confluence of the Arkansas and the Mississippi rivers, where de Soto met his end. With his army a mere shadow of its former size, de Soto was forced to resort to claims of divinity in order to subdue the local Indians. But without his army the Spaniard's claim received a skeptical reply from the Indians—who asked de Soto to demonstrate his godhood by drying up the Mississippi River. Soon de Soto was in bed consumed with fever, which did not prevent him from raving about the insolent Indians.

On May 21, 1542, Hernando de Soto died at the age of forty-two. A few days before his death he assembled his close friends for a farewell. De Soto also named an old associate from his days in Peru, Luis de Moscoso, as his successor.

Even in death de Soto continued to deceive the local Indians. His body was secretly buried at night within the Spanish camp but then disinterred and buried in the brown waters of the Mississippi—apparently stuffed inside a hollow log. The tiny remnants of de Soto's *entrada* first tried to make their way overland to Mexico and possibly reached as far west as modern Dallas; but they eventually gave up and circled back to Arkansas, where they spent another winter, and then made their way down the Mississippi River to the Gulf and then onward to Mexico, where their arrival in September 1543 surprised local officials.

FOR MORE INFORMATION:

Mitchem, Jeffrey M. "Hernando de Soto (1500?–1542)." *The Encyclopedia of Arkansas History and Culture.* http://www.encyclopediaofarkansas.net/encyclopedia/entry-detail.aspx?search=1&entryID=1770.

Young, Gloria A., and Michael P. Hoffman, eds. *The Expedition of Hernando de Soto West of the Mississippi, 1541–1543.* Fayetteville: University of Arkansas Press, 1993.

Saracen

A Quapaw Indian, Saracen has been portrayed in Arkansas history as "the rescuer of captive children." During the Revolutionary War, a contingent of Tories and Chickasaws attacked Arkansas Post in retaliation for Spanish support of the American rebels. This little-known skirmish in the Revolution resulted in captives being taken, which were later freed by a party of Quapaw and Spanish troops. The rescue became the stuff of immediate legend. Old Arkansas history textbooks sometimes included a drawing depicting Saracen wearing war paint and brandishing a war club, looking very much like a character from a James Fennimore Cooper novel.

Judge Morris S. Arnold, the leading authority on colonial Arkansas, has depicted Saracen as a more complicated character, but still larger than life. He was probably the son of a Quapaw woman and Francois Sarazin, a French soldier at Arkansas Post who later became the post's interpreter. Common law marriages between French frontier colonials and Indian women were common and their children numerous.

The Quapaws and the French had a long and peaceful association, with the Quapaws being major actors in various colonial adventures. Not only did the French trade with the Quapaws, but they also used their warriors as proxy soldiers in their frequent confrontations with unfriendly Indians and the threatening English across the Mississippi River.

By the time the American Revolution erupted, Louisiana was under the control of the Spanish. The Spanish provided aid and shelter to the American rebels, which irritated the British. In 1779 the Spanish joined in the war against Britain, and colonial Arkansas was drawn into international intrigue and war.

Arkansas Post was not well prepared for warfare. Established in 1686, the Post never hosted a sizable garrison and sometimes as few as six soldiers staffed the fort. The British were in no position to send regular troops to attack the Post, but Tories from east of the Mississippi, along with their Chickasaw allies, harassed Spanish military and trade vessels on the river. Finally, before daylight on April 17, 1783, the British attacked the Post.

The attacking forces numbered no more than 120, including twelve or so Chickasaws. They were led by James Colbert, a Tory who had lived among the Chickasaws for many years. Colbert successfully eluded Spanish patrols and reached the walls of the fort before being turned back. A few Spanish troops were killed, and Colbert kidnapped a number of residents, including women and children as well as three black slaves. A Spanish-Quapaw counterattack quickly sent Colbert's band fleeing, with most of his hostages escaping in the melee.

Soon a large contingent of Quapaws and about twenty Spanish soldiers were in pursuit. They overtook Colbert before he could reach the safety of the Mississippi, and this is where Saracen enters the picture.

Saracen is not named in the official written reports of the battle, but the Spanish commandant wrote of a Quapaw who confronted the Colbert band and threw a tomahawk into their midst. Intimidated, Colbert surrendered his captives but was allowed to leave. Though the official records are silent as to the name of this courageous Quapaw, within a few years of the battle the post commandant referred to Saracen as "famous" for freeing the captives.

Saracen's fame spread after the United States acquired Louisiana in 1803. Eventually, the Americans considered Saracen a Quapaw chief, though he had no hereditary rights to that position. Still later, after Saracen died in Pine Bluff about 1832 at around ninety years of age, he became the stuff of local legend.

Being idealized by the white settlers did nothing to protect Saracen from the poverty and shame that came to almost all Indians living in Arkansas. Morris S. "Buzz" Arnold, a historian of colonial Arkansas, noted that Saracen's reputation "did not fare nearly so well among many of the Quapaws" as it did among his white neighbors. He wrote, "During the 1820s and 1830s, when the American government was treating the Quapaw tribe with a cavalier inhumanity, the Quapaws, now evidently numbering fewer than five hundred souls, became split into two groups, the one under the leadership of the traditional chief Heckaton, the other under Saracen, whom Governor James Miller of the Arkansas Territory had elevated to the position of 'chief,' despite his lack of hereditary right. In 1827, Saracen, some of his family having actually starved to death, and he himself being reduced by extreme poverty to begging the federal government for help, found it necessary to abase himself by assuring Governor Izard 'that he himself was half a white man by Birth and entirely white in Affection & Inclination.'"

This sort of groveling and tribal denial has tarnished Saracen's reputation, of course. But, one must recall that he was starving during the times he was pleading with white authorities. And, he had watched in horror as his mother's tribe was reduced to tattered survivors. Saracen was one of the chiefs who signed an agreement in 1824 removing the Quapaws to Caddo lands in what is now northwestern Louisiana.

Like most of his fellow tribesmen, Saracen was unhappy, but unlike the others the legendary chief was allowed to return to the Pine Bluff area. Upon his death in 1832, Saracen was buried in the Old Town Cemetery, but his body was not included when most of the graves were later relocated to the new Bellwood Cemetery in 1860. According to the late James W. Leslie, a noted Pine Bluff historian, Saracen's body was discovered in 1883 when the Altheimer brothers were excavating for a new building on Main Street. The body was moved to Bellwood and then to St. Joseph's Catholic Church cemetery in 1905.

A large tombstone marks his grave. At one time St. Joseph's had a window commemorating Saracen as "Friend to the Missionaries, Rescuer of Captive Children." It lay in storage for decades before being rediscovered in the late 1960s.

FOR MORE INFORMATION:

Arnold, Morris S. *The Rumble of a Distant Drum: The Quapaws and Old World Newcomers 1673–1804*. Fayetteville: University of Arkansas Press, 2000.

Leslie, James W. *Saracen's Country*. Little Rock: Rose Publishing Co., 1974.

Jean Laffite

North Little Rock was originally known as "Argenta." The word
argenta means "silver" in Latin, and at one time efforts were made to
mine silver on the north shore of the Arkansas River. While silver was
extracted from the area, the silver mines were begun as a ruse to cover
a Spanish espionage trip up the Arkansas in 1816.

At the end of the War of 1812, American settlers began pouring
into the lands recently opened by the Louisiana Purchase. The Spanish,
rightfully fearing the land lust of the Americans, were worried. They
viewed Arkansas as both a buffer and a potential route for more
Americans to move to the southwestern frontier. Since the Spanish
knew little about Arkansas, they devised a plan to send a party of spies
up the Arkansas River under the guise of mineral prospecting.

The expedition included three prominent men of the time, including Jean Laffite, a famed pirate (who insisted he was not a pirate but
"a corsair, a privateer"), as well as Maj. Arsene Lacarriere Latour and
Louis Bringier. Laffite was a strange choice for this assignment, for he
was a national hero after his valiant defense of New Orleans during
the War of 1812. He was recognized by many Arkansans and seems to
have made no effort to hide his identity. He might have been brought
along in part because of his fluency in French, English, and Spanish.

Louis Bringier was a more obvious choice for the venture since he
had previously lived in Arkansas. He was living at New Madrid in modern Missouri in 1811 when the area was struck by the great earthquake
of that year. The actual leader of the effort was Arsene Latour, widely
recognized as the best engineer and cartographer in New Orleans.

Such a band of miners would not seem out of place in early
Arkansas. A few years earlier a hunter named Trammel had supposedly
discovered gold in what is today northern Pulaski County. The hunter
sold the specimen, supposedly a nugget in a quartz matrix, to Frederick
Notrebe, an Arkansas Post merchant. Forwarded to an assayer in New

Orleans, the specimen was determined to be real and the city soon caught gold fever. The excitement provided a good cover for the spies.

We do not know exactly where the party visited during its eight-month sojourn up the Arkansas River. It is known that stops were made at Arkansas Post, as well as the present sites of Pine Bluff, Little Rock, Big Rock, Crystal Hill, Cadron, and Dardanelle Rock.

The large expedition was described by historian Margaret Smith Ross as "a large number of men of several nationalities." Most of the party were miners and boatmen. One source said the group traveled in "a splendidly fitted up barge," probably a flatboat.

While one early source says the spies prospected at the site where Little Rock would later develop, they soon moved their operation upstream and to the north shore, about where modern Kellogg Acres is in North Little Rock. Shafts were sunk, and even a smelter was built. Latour soon announced that no silver was found, and the party moved on upstream, turning from prospecting to trading with the Indians.

At Cadron and Dardanelle Rock the party did a little trading and land speculating, one of the main economic pursuits in early Arkansas. Mostly, though, the Frenchmen talked with local residents. Latour was particularly interested in learning about existing and proposed roads, postal routes, fords along the river, and how well the settlers were satisfied with the American government. By November 1816, the expedition was finished and they headed back to New Orleans. The following April, Latour submitted his written report to the Spanish, who were not at all pleased with the quality of the observations.

Laffite's visit to Arkansas was anything but secret, and it has provided an interesting tale about how early Arkansans orally transmitted their history. In the late 1800s, three men wrote of learning about the Laffite visit soon after they settled in early Arkansas. William F. Pope, author of a fascinating but often unreliable 1895 book, *Early Days in Arkansas,* claimed that he learned of the visit in 1833 from early settler James Pyeatt of Crystal Hill. Daniel T. Witter, also an early settler, wrote to the *Arkansas Gazette* in 1873 that he learned of the expedition soon after his arrival in 1820. But, because Arkansas did not have any sort of historical journal until World War II, biographers of Lafitte have considered 1816 to be a blank page.

Laffite left documentary evidence of his trip to Arkansas. On

Independence Day, 1816, a land transaction near Arkansas Post was signed by a witness named "Jn. Laffite."

Historian Margaret Smith Ross wrote, "over a period of years, tradition greatly embroidered the story of Jean Laffite in Arkansas." The fact that he was on a spy mission for the Spanish would never had been discovered had historians not discovered Latour's report in Spanish archives.

FOR MORE INFORMATION:

Hodges, Mr. and Mrs. T. L. "Jean Lafitte and Major L. Latour in Arkansas Territory." *Arkansas Historical Quarterly* 7 (Winter 1948): 237–56.

Ross, Margaret Smith. "Secret Mission to Arkansas." *Arkansas Gazette,* March 24, 31, 1957.

William E. Woodruff

William E. Woodruff, the founding editor and publisher of Arkansas's first newspaper, is one of those icons of history that even the most unconcerned schoolboy finds interesting. Woodruff, a Long Island native and trained printer, first tried newspapering in Nashville, Tennessee, before relocating to Arkansas in 1819, the year Arkansas became a territory. In the autumn of that year Woodruff set off by keelboat from Nashville, his vessel carrying not only a newly purchased secondhand Ramage press but also large bundles of paper, inkwells, printers' ink, and everything that would be needed to publish a newspaper on the frontier. Woodruff was able to reach Arkansas Post by water, which was fortunate, for little in the way of roads existed in the newly minted territory. On the last day of October, 1819, Woodruff arrived at the Post.

In a recent history of newspapering in Arkansas, historian Michael B. Dougan noted that Woodruff, in choosing to spell the new territory *Arkansas*—rather than Arkansaw, the spelling used by the newly appointed territorial governor—essentially established how the name of the new territory would be spelled. The first issue of Woodruff's newspaper, the *Arkansas Gazette,* was published on November 20, 1819.

Woodruff continued to put out his weekly newspaper for the next three decades. He was an eyewitness to the founding of Arkansas, and he recorded the entire political and partisan process in minute detail. It was not an easy career, though, and his newspaper probably contributed little to his early income. He was the postmaster at one time, and he probably made his wealth from dealing in land.

To some degree, Woodruff was one of many land speculators who haunted early Arkansas. Men like Moses Austin, father of the great Texas promoter Stephen F. Austin, cut their land-speculating teeth in Missouri and Arkansas before heading for Texas. Woodruff made a good deal of income by managing land for absentee owners. He also sold everything from vegetable seeds to books.

Woodruff encountered every conceivable shortage as he worked to get a reliable supply of paper, ink, and other necessities. During a two-year period during the 1820s, the enterprising editor missed only two issues, but he had to print 16 issues on half-sheets, 30 on smaller stock, 11 on stationery or book stock, and 6 on a light blue paper. A total of 65 issues out of 102 encountered production problems.

Fortunately for history, Woodruff distributed his newspaper far and wide. It is a truism in the field of state history that the early history of the Arkansas Gazette *is* the history of Arkansas. If it were not for the issues mailed to the Library of Congress in Washington—as well as the personal collection of an early Gazette printer, Hiram A. Whittington—a complete run of the newspaper would not be extant.

Through Woodruff's paper, we are able to witness the birth pangs of Arkansas politics. It recorded the 1821 relocation of the territorial capital from the flood-prone and sickly Arkansas Post area to the "point of rocks," where Little Rock would emerge.

The early pages of the paper often told of duels, bloody shootings involving prominent men such as Pulaski County Clerk Robert C. Oden; Fontaine Pope, the nephew of Gov. John Pope; and C. F. M. Noland, a humorist and political satirist. Even the great Whig journalist, legal genius, and Masonic thinker Albert Pike engaged in a duel, but without loss of life to either combatant.

Editor Woodruff knew the great organizer of territorial Arkansas, Robert Crittenden. Appointed territorial secretary at the age of twenty-two, Crittenden basically took it upon himself to organize the new territory when the newly appointed governor, Gen. James Miller, was tardy in getting to Arkansas. When the governor finally arrived, his boat carried a large banner that read "Arkansaw."

Woodruff and Crittenden lost little time in becoming suspicious of each other, and soon they were in opposite and very hostile camps. From time to time, Crittenden managed to deny Woodruff access to official territorial printing work, but in 1821 Woodruff got the contract to produce the first book in Arkansas, *Laws of the Territory of Arkansas.*

Crittenden recruited Albert Pike to manage a newspaper, the *Arkansas Advocate,* to challenge Woodruff. This resulted in Arkansas's first newspaper war, a battle that involved the publication of harsh political attacks that often veered into personal matters too. Then, suddenly, there was a third newspaper, the *Times*. As a town of only a few hundred residents, Little Rock had a richness of newspapers.

Woodruff married Jane Eliza Mills in 1827 in Little Rock. They had eleven children. The Woodruff home was a beautiful brick structure, with formal gardens on two sides. Woodruff hired a European gardener to maintain his showplace home.

In 1838 Woodruff sold the *Gazette,* but he owned it off and on until 1853, when he retired to enjoy "employments better suited to my taste and disposition." During the Civil War the legislature named a county after Woodruff, but he was expelled from Little Rock after the city fell to Union troops in September 1863.

After the Civil War, he resumed his land business. He died in 1885 and was buried in Mount Holly Cemetery in Little Rock.

FOR MORE INFORMATION:

Dougan, Michael B. *Community Diaries: Arkansas Newspapering, 1819–2002.* Little Rock: August House, 2003.

Ross, Margaret Smith. *Arkansas Gazette: The Early Years, 1819–1866.* Little Rock: Arkansas Gazette Foundation, 1969.

Matthew Lyon

Matthew Lyon serves as an inspiration for older Arkansans. In 1822, at the age of seventy-two, Lyon captained a flatboat full of cargo from well up the Arkansas River to New Orleans and then returned with a cotton gin. That journey merely hinted at Lyon's force of will, for he brought the same determination to practically every aspect of life.

Today few people recognize the name Matthew Lyon, but when he arrived in the new Arkansas Territory in 1821 to assume control of the Indian trading post at Spadra Bluff on the Arkansas River near modern Clarksville, he was recognized throughout the young nation. His notoriety came from serving Vermont for six years in the U.S. House of Representatives, where he became a leading Jeffersonian Democrat in opposition to the Federalist Party.

Born in 1750 in Wicklow County, Ireland, Matthew was only twelve years old when his father was put to death by the British government for insurrection. He arrived in America penniless and indentured for his passage. He had learned book binding in Ireland, but he secured employment with the Ethan Allen Iron Work, Salisbury, Connecticut, and later married Allen's niece. The extended family moved to Vermont, where Lyon joined the "Green Mountain Boys" in defense of local land ownership claims. He served in the convention that created the state of Vermont in 1777.

Lyon was astonishingly hard working. His homestead near Lake Champlain contained a sawmill, gristmill, tannery, iron smelter, and slate mill. His later pulp paper mill was possibly the first in the country. He purchased a printing press from Benjamin Franklin, cast his own type, and printed his own newspaper. One historian noted Lyon's penchant for integrating his assets: "Lyon wrote, printed, and bound books in fine sheepskin from the backs of his own sheep, tanned in his tannery, with tannic acid from his barkmill."

Like many veterans of the American Revolution, Matthew Lyon took his politics seriously. Lyon, who was first elected to Congress in

1796 after four failing efforts, was a fierce opponent of Federalist President John Adams. Lyon spat in the face of Federalist Congressman Roger Griswold of Connecticut during a heated debate in January 1798, and a few days later Griswold avenged his honor by attacking Lyon on the floor of the House. Although taken by surprise, Lyon managed to grab a pair of fireplace tongs and a melee resulted. (The brawl generated vast public discussion. In 2006 a rare book dealer offered for sale an original 1798 cartoonlike rendering of the fight; the price for the seven-by-nine-inch drawing was $650.)

Lyon was a leading opponent of the alien and sedition acts of 1798, and "Matt, the democrat" was the first victim of the new laws. He was sent to jail for a year for writing that President Adams was power hungry and had "an unbounded thirst for ridiculous pomp, foolish adulation, and selfish avarice." He won reelection while occupying a tiny jail cell.

Lyon did not seek reelection in 1800, for he was on the move again. He purchased land in Kentucky and laid out the town of Eddyville. Despite having been born in poverty in Ireland, Lyon was a natural businessman and he established extensive business activities in Kentucky, including a shipyard on the Cumberland River. He also served in the Kentucky legislature and represented the state for eight years in the U.S. House of Representatives. He was defeated for reelection in 1810, and two years later he relocated to Missouri, where he narrowly lost another Congressional campaign.

The War of 1812 as well as natural disasters destroyed Lyon's fortune. President James Monroe took pity on Lyon and named him as the government "factor" for the Cherokee Indians in Arkansas—which even Lyon must have considered a minor reward. As the agent of the national government, Lyon's job was to provide trade goods to the Indians in exchange for various hides and other products.

The Cherokees, who had long had contact with European settlers and had developed a taste for manufactured goods, purchased items such as hardware, needles, scissors, and cloth—the most commonly sought items. Among the food items purchased by the Cherokees were salt, sugar, and coffee.

His new government position in a new frontier territory did not in the least deter Lyon from his habitual political involvement—nor did it dull his sharp tongue. Within months of settling at Spadra, Lyon was sending biting letters to the *Arkansas Gazette,* criticizing everyone from territorial governor James Miller to the U.S. secretary of war. Residency requirements were unheard of in 1821, so the newly arrived Lyon announced his candidacy for Congress from Arkansas. He lost by sixty-one votes to James Woodson Bates, the man after whom the city of Batesville was named.

Never stopping to lick his wounds, the seventy-two-year-old Lyon spent the winter of 1821–22 building a flatboat to transport to New Orleans the hides and other products he received in trade with the Indians. The bulk of the cargo consisted of almost nine thousand pounds of deer hides, worth an estimated sixteen hundred dollars. The most valuable hides, however, were the 106 beaver pelts valued at more than two dollars each. The single buffalo hide was valued at a paltry fifty cents.

On his return from New Orleans, Lyon stopped in Little Rock, where he visited with *Gazette* editor William E. Woodruff. Woodruff was astonished by Lyon's voyage, and he published an account in his newspaper, noting that "during this long journey, he has undergone more bodily fatigue than could have been expected of a man at his advanced age, but we could not discover that it had in the least affected his health. On the trip down the river his boat ran aground several times, when he was always the first man to jump in the water, to shove her off."

Soon after returning to Spadra, Lyon learned that Congress had abolished the Indian trading post system, and he was out of a job. He died soon after and was buried at Spadra. Despite the fact that the family moved Lyon's body to Kentucky, descendants of Lyon can still be found in Arkansas.

FOR MORE INFORMATION:

Montagno, George L. "Matthew Lyon's Last Frontier." *Arkansas Historical Quarterly* 16 (Spring 1957): 46–55.

Worley, Ted R. "Starting Anew in Arkansas, Lyon at 71 was Still a Rebel." *Arkansas Gazette,* November 11, 1956.

Hiram A. Whittington

The Whittington family was among the most prominent in early Arkansas. The Whittingtons settled in Arkansas during the early territorial period, making their homes in early Hot Springs and later Montgomery County. The Whittingtons go back practically to the founding of Salem, the Montgomery County seat, later renamed Mount Ida.

The patriarch who brought the Whittington family to Arkansas was Hiram Abiff Whittington, who, along with his younger brother, Granville, moved to frontier Arkansas from long-settled Massachusetts. Hiram was born in January 1805, in Boston, the son of a middle-class family with deep Puritan roots.

At the age of fifteen, Hiram apprenticed as a printer, ultimately training further under Alden Spooner of New York, who mentored William E. Woodruff, the first printer and journalist in Arkansas Territory. Woodruff offered Whittington a printing job, and on Christmas Day, 1826, the twenty-one-year-old made his way into Little Rock, still a bit shocked by the five days it took to travel from Arkansas Post.

After working with Woodruff for a few years, Hiram journeyed to Dwight Mission, the Cherokee settlement near modern Russellville, where he sought to become editor of a planned tribal newspaper. When this did not come to pass, he relocated to Hot Springs in 1832, where he engaged in the grocery business, served as postmaster, won election to several public offices, helped develop the whetstone industry, and became something of a land speculator. He died in May 1890 and was buried in a small family cemetery. Whittington Avenue in Hot Springs is named for him.

Students of Arkansas history owe Hiram's younger brother Granville Whittington a special thanks, for he preserved the early letters his brother wrote back home telling of the wonders of frontier

Arkansas. Hiram himself also deserves special recognition for carefully preserving early copies of the *Arkansas Gazette,* which is an indispensable source for historians.

Hiram's early letters did not portend good things for this Yankee immigrant. He complained about the heat, the insects—especially ticks, partisan politics, drunkenness, and the local women. In his first letter from Arkansas Territory, he referred to "this little rock on the bank of a dirty river." Little Rock was less than a decade old in 1827 when Hiram wrote his brother: "The town, and I believe the whole territory, is inhabited by the dregs of Kentucky, Georgia and Louisiana, but principally from the former, and a more drunken, good for nothing set of fellows never got together."

Hiram did not find local women to his liking either, even complaining that he had to undress in front of them when he traveled and boarded with settlers: "I did not take my pantaloons off, however, until I had got between the sheets." He found frontier women to be far too natural for his New England tastes, noting especially that "if the girls feel a tick biting them at a party, and even if they are on the floor dancing, they immediately stop and unpin and scratch themselves until they find it." Perhaps not surprisingly, Hiram went back to Boston to find a wife, whom he married in 1836. She died after fifteen years of marriage and the birth of six children. Hiram never remarried.

With the assistance of Little Rock merchant John McLain, Whittington established a small store in Hot Springs soon after arriving. In one of his letters home, he described a lazy afternoon: "I have no customers, no official business. . . . I live here in a little cabin of logs about 10 feet square, with an adjoining room of about seven by nine feet. The larger room is my store. The smaller is my private apartment, sitting room, drawing room, clerk's office, post office and bed chamber."

Though Hiram comes across as a bit fussy and critical in his early letters, over time he found Arkansas much to his liking. He built a large home in Hot Springs, which was often filled with family and friends. Intellectually curious despite his lack of formal education, Hiram compiled a large library in his home. He gave land for both the St. Mary's Catholic Church and First Presbyterian Church in Hot Springs. By the outbreak of the Civil War in 1861, Hiram was writing letters referring to "the fanatical vandals of the North." His son William served in the Confederate army, surviving the battles of Elk Horn Tavern, Corinth, and the losing effort to defend Atlanta.

Hiram's interesting contributions to documenting Arkansas history did not become apparent until long after his death in 1890. His collection of *Arkansas Gazette* newspapers covered sixty years, and they were crucial to compiling a full set for microfilming. His letters, compiled and bound by his bookbinder brother Granville, lay in an attic in Granville's Mount Ida home until 1913, when they were discovered as the building was being demolished.

FOR MORE INFORMATION:

Hudgins, Mary D. "Hiram Abiff Whittington—Arkansas Anachronism." *Record* 1 (1960): 15–22.

McLane, Bobbie Jones, Charles W. Cunning, and Wendy Bradley Richter. *Observations of Arkansas: The 1824–1863 Letters of Hiram Abiff Whittington.* Hot Springs: Garland County Historical Society, 1997.

Ross, Margaret S., ed. *Letters of Hiram Abiff Whittington: An Arkansas Pioneer from Massachusetts, 1827–1834.* Bulletin Series. Little Rock: Pulaski County Historical Society, 1956.

Jacob Wolf

Major Jacob Wolf was one of those larger-than-life settlers on the Arkansas frontier. His economic good sense and willingness to work hard made him a prosperous man, which in turn allowed him to attain considerable political power. The Wolf House, located at Norfork in Baxter County, is generally recognized as the state's oldest surviving public building.

Wolf was born in Rowan County, North Carolina, the son of Pennsylvania German descendants. Educational opportunities were few, and Wolf spent little time in school. The family moved to Kentucky in 1799, and Jacob married there in 1809, the first of his three marriages. After his wife died, Wolf moved to Arkansas around 1820. In 1823 he married his second wife, Elizabeth Lantz Saunders, and they had ten children before Elizabeth died about 1846.

On November 15, 1824, Wolf filed a claim for seventy-six acres of land lying immediately below the juncture of the White and Big North Fork rivers. On a height overlooking the beautiful White River, Wolf built his home, which he envisioned to be the first in a town named Liberty. Wolf secured a license to operate ferries across the White and Big North Fork rivers, and a settlement gradually grew up around Wolf's homestead. A post office opened in 1826.

Izard County was created in 1825, and the following year Wolf won election to the territorial legislature. He succeeded in pushing through legislation to locate the permanent county courthouse in Liberty, and he donated land for a courthouse. He also got the contract to build the building. Thus, the Wolf House was constructed not as a residence but as Izard County's first seat of justice.

Joan Gould, author of the entry on the Wolf House in the *Encyclopedia of Arkansas History and Culture*, described the new structure as "a two-story log house with a central breezeway on the first level, typically called a dogtrot, to serve as the courthouse. The large upper-level room that extends over the breezeway served as the courtroom."

Large yellow pines were felled to build Wolf's house. Pines practically disappeared from the river valleys of the Ozarks later in the nineteenth century, but they were considered inexhaustible when Wolf was building the courthouse.

Liberty prospered for a time. When writer and editor C. F. M. Noland visited the site on a trip up the White River in 1830, he found a tavern and inn (probably in Wolf's dwelling, as was typical of the time), a store, and blacksmith shop, situated on an "elevated and commanding" location. Among the county officials housed in the courthouse at Liberty was John P. Houston, brother of famed Texan Sam Houston.

Additional counties were created from Izard County, and by 1835 Liberty was no longer conveniently located and the county seat was moved to the now disappeared town of Athens. Still a legislator, Wolf secured the return of the land he donated for the courthouse. Thus, Wolf moved his family of sixteen children and five stepchildren into the structure. Over time additional structures were added, including two cabins for slaves. A large barn and stable completed the homestead of a successful businessman and politician.

Wolf was obviously moving up the ladder of frontier political and economic power. Described as a "large, brawny man with clear blue eyes crowning a strong brave countenance," Wolf looked the role of patriarch. Shortly after his arrival in Arkansas, he was commissioned a major in the Arkansas Territorial Militia—thereby earning Wolf a title that followed him the rest of his life. He worked as a blacksmith, a trade that was dear to him, as well as a carpenter and storekeeper. In 1844 the post office at Wolf's home was renamed North Fork, and Wolf was appointed postmaster, a post he held until his death.

An ardent Baptist, Wolf helped organize the White River Baptist Association in 1840 and served as its treasurer. His religious convictions did not prevent him from owning slaves, of which he had fifteen in 1850. A peek into Wolf's values came when he sat for a photograph a few years before he died on the first day of 1863. He insisted on having three props included in the photo: his hammer and anvil, a Baptist hymnal, and a Bible.

The Wolf House was sold in 1865, and it remained in private hands (including occupation and ownership by two of Wolf's sons during the post–Civil War era and early twentieth century) until the late 1930s, when it became public property and was maintained by local supporters. In 1999, the Arkansas Historic Preservation Program awarded a restoration grant to bring the structure back to its appearance as a courthouse. The house was restored under the careful oversight of the prominent Little Rock restoration architect Tommy Jameson, with the assistance of historic preservation consultant Joan Gould of the Fayetteville area. The project involved extensive archeological excavations as well as the use of tree-ring analysis to settle the debate on its age. It was built in 1829, making the Wolf House the oldest public structure in Arkansas.

FOR MORE INFORMATION:

Baker, Russell P. "Jacob Wolf." *Arkansas Historical Quarterly* 37 (Summer 1978): 182–92.

Gould, Joan. "Jacob Wolf House." *The Encyclopedia of Arkansas History and Culture.* http://encyclopediaofarkansas.net/encyclopedia/entry-detail.aspx?search= 1&entryID=2113.

Jameson, Tommy, and Joan L. Gould. *The Jacob Wolf House, 16 January 2004: Historic Structure Report.* Little Rock: Jameson Architects, P.A., 2004.

Antoine Barraque

Among the rugged immigrants to early Arkansas was Antoine Barraque, a soldier, fur trader, Indian agent, and planter who lived an outsized life and died the patriarch of a large family. Born in 1773 in the French department of Gascoigne, near the Pyrenees Mountains, Barraque must have come from a prosperous family, for he was educated in Paris and surviving examples of his writing show that he had a good command of formal French.

Barraque served in Napoleon's army, fighting at the battles of Marengo, Austerliz, Jena, Lodi, and in the Moscow campaign, where he lost his only brother. The late James Leslie of Pine Bluff, a fine local historian, wrote that Barraque migrated to the United States after the Battle of Waterloo, "fearing imprisonment."

After spending a short time in Philadelphia for reasons unknown, the forty-three-year-old Frenchman relocated to Arkansas—which was then a part of Missouri Territory. Settling in Arkansas Post in 1816, Barraque lived with the family of Joseph Dardenne, a wealthy merchant.

Almost immediately Barraque began trading with the Quapaws, which indicates that he probably came to Arkansas with some financial means. Within a year of his arrival, he married Marie Therese, Dardenne's daughter. This marriage probably bolstered his economic and social ties to the Quapaws.

With Dardenne's assistance, Barraque began buying land and established a plantation on the north side of the Arkansas River. Named "New Gascony" after his former home in France, Barraque's plantation became an early center for cotton cultivation and ginning. Barraque also became a business partner of Frederic Notrebe, another French immigrant and veteran of Napoleon's army, who was a prosperous merchant and plantation owner.

In the autumn of 1823 Barraque came close to losing his life while on a commercial hunting expedition to the Red River country of southwest Arkansas. His hunting group, which included a slave as well as a mixture of whites and Quapaws, was attacked by as many as 100 Osage warriors. Seven of Barraque's party were killed, including his slave, and hides, provisions, and horses were stolen. The fact that Barraque was out hunting at the time of the attack probably saved his life.

Though Barraque was highly regarded by the Quapaws and had done business with them since his arrival in the area, he was a party to their removal from their ancestral homeland in Arkansas. The fact that the Quapaws had always maintained friendly relations with the French and later the Americans did nothing to prevent the taking of their lands.

In 1818 the Quapaws signed a treaty at St. Louis that took all their lands north of the Arkansas River, though they retained a large reservation that stretched from the edge of Little Rock (hence the "Quapaw Quarter") all the way to Arkansas Post. Within a few months residents of the new Territory of Arkansas were clamoring for the complete removal of the Quapaws. Finally, in 1824 the Quapaws signed another treaty, this one requiring their removal to the Red River area, where they were expected to share lands traditionally held by the Caddo Indians. Barraque signed the treaty as a witness.

Barraque, at the request of Quapaw chief Heckatoo, was appointed a "subagent" to escort the tribe, which now numbered only 455 individuals, to the Red River. Jim Leslie has estimated that as many as one-third of the Quapaws died during and immediately after the trek to the Caddo lands in 1826–27. Barraque, who wrote a detailed account of the removal in French, unsuccessfully tried to intercede with state authorities on behalf of the Quapaws.

Barraque next appears in the public record in 1832, when he took possession of the records of the newly created Jefferson County and moved them from the new town of Pine Bluff to his own New Gascony farm. This action resulted in an election, in which the voters selected Pine Bluff as the county seat. Barraque henceforth devoted his considerable energy to business.

He sold his New Gascony plantation and bought about 1,200 acres where White Bluff is today. George W. Featherstonhaugh, an English traveler who found little about Arkansas to his liking, visited Barraque's plantation in 1835 and was impressed with both the family and the farm. He later wrote that the Barraque farm "is one of the best cotton plantations on the river," and "Mons. Barraque's family were all French, and occupied a house containing two large and very comfortable rooms, neatly and sufficiently furnished."

The Barraque household was a large one, including eleven children, at least ten of whom apparently survived to adulthood. Most of his children established families in the Pine Bluff area. A photograph of Barraque as an old man shows an obviously prosperous man with a full head of silver hair, his hand resting on a fancy cane and a stoic look on his still handsome face. Antoine Barraque died in 1858, at the age of eighty-six. When Pine Bluff was platted, the first street south of the courthouse was named for Barraque.

FOR MORE INFORMATION:

Ashcraft, Ginger L. "Antoine Barraque and His Involvement in Indian Affairs of Southeast Arkansas, 1816–1832." *Arkansas Historical Quarterly* 32 (Autumn 1973): 226–40.

Leslie, James W. "Barraque, Antoine." In *Arkansas Biography: A Collection of Notable Lives,* ed. Nancy A. Williams and Jeannie M. Whayne, 18–19. Fayetteville: University of Arkansas Press, 2000.

Teske, Steven. "Antoine Barraque (1773–1858)." *The Encyclopedia of Arkansas History and Culture.* http://encyclopediaofarkansas.net/encyclopedia/entry-detail.aspx?search=1&entryID=2962.

Friedrich Gerstäcker

Friedrich Gerstäcker was a keen observer of nineteenth century Arkansas, and his books and stories about his vagabond days in Arkansas before the Civil War were sincere and complicated accounts. His appeal is manifold, especially his unstinting admiration for Arkansas and early Arkansans. This was quite unusual among early visitors to the state. Gerstäcker also knew how to tell a good story. His *Wild Sports in the Far West* (1846) documented antebellum Arkansas in appealing detail.

Researchers from the Gerstäcker Museum in Braunschweig, Germany, made a trip to Arkansas in the mid-1990s to identify some of the locales described by Gerstäcker. (This sort of intense interest is not surprising since Gerstäcker is still read in Germany and Austria. An Internet search turned up 378 citations on Gerstäcker, including the fact that one of his pieces of fiction has recently been turned into a musical script.)

Born in 1816 in Hamburg, Germany, to opera singer parents, Gerstäcker grew up with a fascination for foreign adventure. As James W. Miller, author of the entry on Gerstäcker in the *Encyclopedia of Arkansas History and Culture,* noted, "His imagination had been fired as a boy by the works of James Fenimore Cooper, and he idealized the American frontier as a place of ultimate freedom." At the age of twenty-one he left for the United States, where he traveled across the young nation, walking much of the journey. Between 1838 and 1842 Gerstäcker spent as much time as possible in Arkansas, which he depicted as a virtual paradise for hunters like himself.

University of Arkansas historian Evan Bukey summarized Gerstäcker's Arkansas as "a land just back from the cutting edge of the frontier, uninhabited by Indians but populated by a group of rugged-individualistic, hard-drinking, somewhat lazy and often violent backwoodsmen. It is not a bucolic existence, but is one that Gerstäcker admired, for it was *natural.*"

Gerstäcker was pleased to discover a variety of German immigrants living in Arkansas. He stayed for a time with Gustavus Klingelhoeffer, the leader of a German colony located in Perry County. He hunted along the Fourche La Fave River, finding huge flocks of turkeys, vast numbers of deer, and his favored quarry, large black bears.

Gerstäcker is appreciated by historians of frontier Arkansas because of his close observations and good writing skills. For example, here is how the German visitor described a hog-killing in west-central Arkansas: "The weather set in very cold, and we resolved to kill and salt the pigs. . . . A young American . . . cut down a large sassafras tree, and hollowed out half a dozen troughs, five for the meat, and one for the lard. The neighbors were called in to help, the pigs driven into the enclosure, shot, stuck, scalded, cleaned, and carried into the house. Not having any large caldron to scald them, it was done Arkansas fashion. A cask with the head out was half sunk in the earth, and filled with cold water, and a large fire was made close by and covered with stones. When these were hot enough, they were thrown into the water, and the cask covered with a blanket. The water was soon hot enough for our purpose: the pigs were dipped once or twice in the water, and five or six pairs of hands soon removed all the bristles. By evening all was finished, and part of the fat laid aside, out of reach of the dogs, for making soap. The good people who came to help us, now set-to to drink . . . so that in the course of an hour and a half, none of them knew exactly whether he was standing on his head or his feet."

In December 1841, Gerstäcker and a friend traveled into the Ozark Mountains, where he lived with a settler and hunted bears. In one instance, Gerstäcker and a companion named Erskine engaged in a harrowing fight with an enraged bear. Both hunters emptied their single-shot rifles but only wounded the snarling beast. Gerstäcker's dog, "Beargrease," led a pack of hounds against the bruin. Both hunters then attacked with their knives. "At the third slash from my knife, the bear turned and I saw its blow aimed at me. I tried to dodge, but felt a sudden, blinding pain."

Gerstäcker lost consciousness, to be greeted by a scene of destruction when he awoke. "My dog was licking the blood from my face . . . Almighty God, the scene that was spread around me. The body of the bear lay almost against me. Not farther than three feet away was the body of Erskine, stark and cold. . . . Around him lay five of the best dogs." Erskine was buried in a shallow grave covered with large stones.

Not long after, Gerstäcker returned to Germany, where he was surprised to discover that his letters home had been published to wide acclaim. He proceeded to become a popular writer, which gave him the financial means to fulfill his wanderlust.

In 1867, a quarter century after his first visit, Gerstäcker returned to Arkansas. He found a state ravaged by Civil War, many of his old friends having been killed by "Jayhawkers." He visited the homesteads of his old hunting friends and was left melancholy when he discovered most of them abandoned wrecks. His diary tells of a lost era, a youth lived with discovery and adventure. He recalls, "Arkansas—there I spent the best years of my youth; there for the first time I felt free and independent and found a home in the virgin forest. For me the name was magic."

In a few years Gerstäcker was dead, but his reputation has lived on as succeeding generations of German readers have discovered some of his seventy books and 425 articles.

In 1950 an Oklahoma college professor by the name of Clarence Evans undertook to locate some of the places Gerstäcker visited. He calculated that the great bear hunt, and thus Erskine's grave, must be somewhere near the Madison County community of Combs.

FOR MORE INFORMATION:

Evans, Clarence. "Friedrich Gerstäcker, Social Chronicler of the Arkansas Frontier." *Arkansas Historical Quarterly* 6 (Winter 1947): 440–49.

Miller, James W. "Friedrich Wilhelm Christian Gerstäcker (1816–1872)." *The Encyclopedia of Arkansas History and Culture.* http://encyclopediaofarkansas. net/encyclopedia/entry-detail.aspx?search=1&entryID=1656.

Miller, James W., ed. *In the Arkansas Backwoods: Tales and Sketches by Friedrich Gerstäcker.* Columbia: University of Missouri Press, 1991.

Davy Crockett

In the autumn of 1835, the citizens of Little Rock, Arkansas Territory, hosted a dinner in honor of David Crockett, the frontiersman-politician who literally became a legend in his own time. Crockett was already a major cultural and political figure when he passed through Little Rock on his way to Texas and martyrdom at the Alamo.

Crockett was born in 1786 in eastern Tennessee, the son of a tavern owner. As a boy of twelve, he was hired out to a cattle herder. Crockett probably never spent more than a few months in school, but he was literate—despite atrocious spelling. Though jilted by a young woman in 1805, Crockett recovered quickly and married Mary (Polly) Finley. Crockett was given to wandering. He cajoled Polly into moving from one home to the next. The couple had two sons.

Crockett was never much of a farmer, but he was attracted to military service and politics. He joined the militia in 1813, saw action as a scout, and participated in Gen. Andrew Jackson's savage revenge attack on a Creek Indian town. He later served again under Jackson in the Florida campaign against the Seminole Indians. This military experience makes it difficult to understand why Crockett would later split with President Andrew Jackson, in part over Crockett's opposition to the president's policy to remove the eastern Indians to what is now Oklahoma.

The fluid nature of frontier society allowed Crockett to move quickly into partisan politics. Even as a young man, David had a gregarious personality. His growing reputation as a sharpshooter, hunter, and teller of tall tales did not hurt his political chances. He served as a justice of the peace, a town commissioner, and in the Tennessee state legislature. He later served in the U.S. House of Representatives, though he was defeated as often as he was elected. Often, Crockett would conclude a political speech by saying that if defeated, his constituents "can go to hell, and I will go to Texas."

Crockett lost his seat in Congress in 1835 and set off for Texas on

November 2, 1835, after spending a night drinking in Memphis. He took a steamboat down the Mississippi River to the Arkansas River, and then up that muddy stream to Little Rock. Here is how the *Arkansas Gazette* described Crockett's arrival in Little Rock: "A rare treat: Among the distinguished characters who have honored our City with their presence, within the last week, was no less a personage than Col. David Crockett— better known as Davy Crockett—the real critter himself."

The *Gazette* was a rabidly Jacksonian newspaper, so it must have galled the editor, William E. Woodruff, to note that "the news of the arrival rapidly spread, and . . . hundreds flocked to see this wonderful man, who, it is said, can whip his weight in wild cats, or grin the largest panther out of the highest tree." Woodruff did not attempt to contain his contempt for a dinner in honor of Crockett that "several anti-Jackson men" organized at the Jeffries Hotel.

In a purported autobiography published after Crockett's death, Davy was at first reluctant to accept the invitation to dinner in Little Rock. Then he got a look at the hotel's larder and changed his mind. After being conducted to a shed in the yard, "I beheld, hanging up, a fine fat cub bear, several haunches of venison, a wild turkey as big as a young ostrich, and small game too tedious to mention." Crockett's speech must have been a challenge since it followed thirteen whiskey toasts, but he managed to hold forth against the president and his cronies.

The speech is lost to history, but Crockett's performance in a shooting contest is a well-known episode in Arkansas folklore. Upon arriving in Little Rock, Crockett did what most travelers did at the time—he made his way to a tavern. While there, he was invited to engage in a shooting contest. Crockett accepted and with his rifle put a bullet through the absolute center of a target. The amazed crowd called for a second shot, and Crockett complied. When no hole appeared in the target, the crowd assumed he had missed altogether. With a confident smile on his lips, Crockett demonstrated that the second bullet had followed the exact path of the first. Indeed, Crockett found a second bullet in the hole. In his purported autobiography, Crockett admits that he slyly pushed the second bullet into the hole by hand while examining the target.

Crockett's biography has him "gratified with the hospitality and kindness of the citizens of Little Rock." He concluded: "There are some first-rate men there, of the real half horse half alligator breed." The *Gazette* editor noted that Crockett and his party, "all completely armed and well mounted, took their departure on Friday morning for Texas, in which country, we understand, they intend establishing their future abode, and in the defense of which, we hope they may cover themselves with glory."

The editor's wish came to pass four months later when, on March 6, 1836, David Crockett was killed during the battle at the Alamo in San Antonio. Crockett was well on his way to immortality before he died, but his death served to speed up the process. Indeed, some Crockett scholars contend that Crockett might have stayed at the Alamo because, as Richard B. Hauck has written, "he was determined to live up to his legend."

Crockett has been an enduring American hero, an icon of the frontier. Any boy who grew up in the late 1950s, when Walt Disney presented Fess Parker as Davy Crockett on weekly television, can recall wearing a coonskin cap. The Disney Company was still promoting Davy Crockett as recently as 2004 when it released "The Alamo," a film in which Malvern native Billy Bob Thornton played a hero resigned to his tragic fate.

FOR MORE INFORMATION:

Derr, Mark. *The Frontiersman: The Real Life and the Many Legends of Davy Crockett.* New York: William Morrow & Co., 1993. See especially chapter 10.

Lofaro, Michael A., ed. *Davy Crockett: The Man, the Legend, the Legacy, 1786–1986.* Knoxville: University of Tennessee Press, 1985.

Arkansas Gazette, November 17, 1835.

CHAPTER II

Antebellum Politicians

Robert Crittenden

In the era of term limits, a thirty-year-old state senator might be referred to as a "veteran" legislator. Robert Crittenden, the man who essentially created the government of Arkansas in the first place, was only twenty-two years of age when he took office as the territorial secretary, the number two official in the new territory, in 1819.

Within the meteor that was Robert Crittenden can be found so many of the unusual characteristics that composed Arkansas's messy frontier democracy. Born in 1797 into a politically powerful Kentucky family, Crittenden's brother, John J., was an influential U.S. senator.

Young Robert joined the U.S. Army in 1814 and served through 1818, when he commenced the study of law. With the considerable political assistance of his brother the senator, Crittenden was named secretary of the newly created Arkansas Territory in 1819, a position akin to being both secretary of state and lieutenant governor.

Robert Crittenden was not the only ambitious young man in Arkansas. Andrew H. Scott, named a territorial judge the same year as Crittenden's appointment, was all of thirty years old. William E. Woodruff, who was so small of stature that he was called "Little Billy," was a mere twenty-four when he established the first newspaper in Arkansas. Robert C. Oden was appointed Pulaski County clerk in 1819 but had to surrender the office when it was discovered that he was a minor.

The Federal legislation that created Arkansas Territory took effect on July 4, 1819, and Crittenden lost no time in relocating to Arkansas Post, the territorial capitol. In contrast, the newly appointed governor, War of 1812 hero Gen. James Miller, did not arrive until the end of the year.

In the absence of the governor, Crittenden assumed the duties of acting governor and set about to create a governmental structure for the new territory. The acting governor convened the federally appointed territorial legislature, which soon adopted laws establishing a governmental infrastructure. When the legislature adjourned and the governor was still nowhere in sight, Crittenden began filling positions in state government. He also named all officials in the territory's five counties.

Crittenden's most significant move as acting governor was issuing a decree that recognized Arkansas as a territory of the second class, a gesture that allowed the territory its own legislature and delegate to Congress—and set Arkansas on a fast tract to statehood. Crittenden immediately called a special election to select the legislature and congressional delegate.

Governor Miller finally made his arrival in Arkansas Post on December 26, 1819, landing at the wharf in a large barge draped in flags. He was surprised and peeved to discover that acting governor Crittenden had already created a state and local governmental system and in the process had become the most powerful politician in the state.

Crittenden's power grew so strong that the various presidentially appointed governors were little more than figureheads. Gov. George Izard had the misfortune of arriving in Little Rock when Secretary Crittenden was out of town, and he was unable to get a briefing on territorial affairs until the secretary returned. Enemies referred to Crittenden as the Cardinal Wolsey of Arkansas politics, referring to King Henry VIII's conniving lieutenant.

Crittenden inspired intense loyalty from a wide spectrum of Arkansas residents. Albert Pike was a lowly frontier schoolteacher when Crittenden met him in 1833 and immediately brought the young educator under his wing. Years later, Pike wrote of Crittenden: "He was a man of fine presence and handsome face, with clear bright eyes, and unmistakable intellect and genius, frank, genial, one to attach men warmly to himself, impulsive, generous, warm-hearted, an abler man, I think, than his brother John J. Crittenden [Kentucky governor, five-time U.S. senator, and U.S. attorney general under three presidents]."

The fluid nature of frontier politics allowed for flexible political loyalties. Congressman Henry W. Conway, the thirty-one-year-old scion of a large and powerful frontier family that included the shrewd and ambitious William Rector and Ambrose Sevier, was a loyal Crittenden lieutenant at first but later became Crittenden's arch enemy. In 1827

Secretary Crittenden and Congressman Conway met on the east bank of the Mississippi River in a duel that resulted in Conway's death.

Crittenden's political power waned with time, especially after losing the support of the only newspaper in the state. His killing of Congressman Conway turned many of his old supporters against Crittenden. President Andrew Jackson replaced both Robert Crittenden as territorial secretary and John J. Crittenden as U.S. district attorney in Kentucky.

Crittenden then set about to create a more formal political movement. Creating his own newspaper, the *Arkansas Advocate*, Crittenden recruited the brilliant young Albert Pike as its editor. In 1833 Crittenden made his only campaign for public office, being decisively defeated by the incumbent U.S. Senator Ambrose Sevier. He retired from politics, aggressively practiced law, and died in Mississippi in 1834, at the age of thirty-seven.

Robert Crittenden was the first political boss of Arkansas. And although he died young, his political faction evolved into the Whig Party. Crittenden County in eastern Arkansas, with West Memphis as its major city, is named for the young man from Kentucky who left such a profound mark on early Arkansas.

FOR MORE INFORMATION:

Bird, Allen W. "Robert Crittenden (1797–1834)." *The Encyclopedia of Arkansas History and Culture.* http://encyclopediaofarkansas.net/encyclopedia/entry-detail.aspx?search=1&entryID=2270.

Hallum, John. *Biographical and Pictorial History of Arkansas.* Albany: Weed Parsons, 1887.

White, Lonnie J. "The Election of 1827 and the Conway-Crittenden Duel." *Arkansas Historical Quarterly* 19 (Winter 1960): 293–313.

Gov. George Izard

Territorial Governor George Izard should have been a good governor for Arkansas. He was well educated, honest, and strong willed. Arkansas's second territorial governor, Izard worked hard to bring order and development to frontier Arkansas. Though he ultimately failed, he was a stabilizing force in a tiny western jurisdiction, where the politicians were famed for killing each other in duels.

Izard was born October 21, 1776, in London, England, where his parents were living temporarily. The family name was pronounced with the emphasis on the second syllable. His father was a wealthy South Carolina businessman, diplomat, and member of the Continental Congress and later U.S. senator. Izard was one of twelve children. The family relocated to Paris in 1777, as London became an unsafe place for colonials of dubious loyalty.

Without a doubt, Izard was one of the better-educated governors in Arkansas history. He had the kind of education that a family of great wealth and power could offer its offspring. Wes Goodner of Little Rock, a keen student of Governor Izard and author of the governor's entry in the *Encyclopedia of Arkansas History and Culture,* reports that young George began his education at the College de Navarre in Paris.

In 1780 Mrs. Izard and the children sailed for America to rejoin her husband in South Carolina. When his private tutor died, George was sent to a boarding school in Charleston, and later he studied at Columbia University and the College of Philadelphia, taking a bachelor's degree in 1792, at the tender age of sixteen.

Izard continued his studies in Europe, first in Britain, then in Germany, and finally in France, where he enrolled in the École du Génie. While in Paris, Izard was offered a lieutenancy in the U.S. Corps of Artillerists and Engineers, and he assumed the post in 1797. He later oversaw construction of Fort Pinckney in South Carolina. Despite his youth, Izard held prominent posts in the army, including as aide de camp to

Gen. Alexander Hamilton. Later he became commander of the post at West Point, but he grew bored and resigned his commission.

The War of 1812 brought Izard back into the army, and he was quickly promoted to colonel and then brigadier general. On a cold day in January 1814, Izard was promoted to major general and given command of the Northern Army on Lake Champlain. The Canadian front was a daunting assignment, and Izard proceeded cautiously. His retreat to winter quarters brought criticism, and again Izard resigned his commission. In 1816 he published a detailed response to his critics.

Izard had to be convinced to accept the governorship of a small territory just organized on the western frontier—Arkansas. He had hoped for a diplomatic post. Izard's predecessor, James Miller, had been the first governor of territorial Arkansas. Miller was no match for the twenty-two-year-old territorial secretary, Robert Crittenden, who arrived in the state to find the governor missing and proceeded to assume control over the territory. Governor Miller spent much of his time back home in New Hampshire, finally resigning on the last day of 1824.

Territorial Arkansas was a political briar patch. For such a tiny place (the 1820 population was 14,255), territorial Arkansas was overrun with ambitious young politicians who practiced warfare that involved taking no prisoners. Fist fights often broke out over trivial affronts, and Arkansas had its first duel in 1820—only a year after the territory was created. Historian Michael B. Dougan has described it as "the era of personal politics."

Izard arrived in Arkansas in May 1825. He was not happy with what he found. The territorial government was a shambles, with little in the way of records—and the acting governor, Secretary Crittenden, was back home in Kentucky. The two men were destined to become political foes, and it certainly did not help that Izard found the territory in such a sorry state.

Izard was nothing if not an organizer, and he set about to bring some sort of order and development to the rugged territory. The governor sought federal funding for roads, then practically unknown in Arkansas. He worked hard to organize the territorial militia, for he feared that removal of eastern Indians through Arkansas would endanger the state. While the militia had a large roster of distinguished officers, it was more form than fact.

Izard's unbending nature put him at odds with much of the political infrastructure in the territory. He especially ruffled feathers when he charged two Indian agents with corruption. In 1828 Governor Izard called a special session of the legislature, and when legislators responded slowly to his program, he questioned their diligence. The legislature reacted angrily, accusing Izard of wielding "dictatorial power."

Izard and Crittenden were as different as two men could be, and from the beginning they did not get along. Izard adroitly co-opted much of Crittenden's political power by courting the political elite, including awarding militia colonelcies to Henry Conway, Ambrose Sevier, and Chester Ashley.

A man of education and broad interests, Izard studied Arkansas's natural history as well as "aboriginal inhabitants." He was a member of the American Philosophical Society of Philadelphia, and the group published Izard's reports on the territory. He also sent a "small collection of reptiles and insects," and his most extensive submission was a Quapaw Indian vocabulary.

Mrs. Izard, who stayed in Philadelphia and never moved to Arkansas, died in 1826. Governor Izard died on November 22, 1828, and was buried in Little Rock in a cemetery near where the Federal Building on Capitol Avenue now stands. His remains were later moved to Mount Holly Cemetery, where he was interred in the plot of Sen. Chester Ashley.

FOR MORE INFORMATION:

Bolton, S. Charles. *Territorial Ambition: Land and Society in Arkansas, 1800–1840.* Fayetteville: University of Arkansas Press, 1993.

Dougan, Michael B. *Arkansas Odyssey: The Saga of Arkansas from Prehistory Times to Present.* Little Rock: Rose Publishing Co., 1994.

Goodner, Wes. "George Izard (1776–1828)." *The Encyclopedia of Arkansas History and Culture.* http://encyclopediaofarkansas.net/encyclopedia/entry-detail.aspx?search=1&entryID=3662.

White, Lonnie J. "Arkansas Territorial Politics, 1824–1827." *Arkansas Historical Quarterly* 20 (Spring 1961): 17–39.

Chester Ashley

Chester Ashley was one of the great political titans of early Arkansas. His life in Arkansas was brief, but like many of his contemporaries, he lived it in an outsized way. Ashley was one of the most successful founding fathers of Arkansas. An early settler in territorial Arkansas, he practiced law with the firebrand Robert Crittenden, made a fortune as a land speculator, built a mansion, and died a U.S. senator. He was referred to as the "Talleyrand of Arkansas" in deference to his diplomatic skills.

The thing that really makes Ashley interesting is his duality. He was rich and successful, but, like many of his contemporaries, Ashley was something of a rogue. Historians are challenged to interpret him neatly, though Michael B. Dougan has described Ashley as a "wily speculator and devious politician . . . this prince of speculators, whose land deals were both legendary and dubious." There is undoubtedly more to his life than Dougan allows, but one would never describe Ashley as one dimensional.

The legendary Little Rock lawyer and founder of the law firm that bears his name, U. M. Rose, wrote a biographical sketch of Ashley in 1911 describing "a man of great breadth of view and versatility of mind" who succeeded due to "superior abilities, great industry, and wise foresight." A definitive history of Ashley is yet to be written, but that is not due to a lack of an interesting subject.

Born in 1791 in Amherst, Massachusetts, the Ashley family moved to Hudson, New York, when Chester was only six. He grew up in Hudson, was educated at Williams College in Massachusetts, and then attended Litchfield Law School in Connecticut, graduating in 1814. He was among the better educated of Arkansas's political leaders of all eras.

After briefly practicing law in Hudson, Ashley, like many young men of his era, moved to the western frontier, settling in southern Illinois. From there he moved to Missouri, but in 1820 Ashley showed up in Arkansas Territory. The following year, he married Mary Watkins Worthington Elliott of St. Genevieve, Missouri.

Little Rock was a mere collection of log cabins when Ashley arrived on the scene. Arkansas Post, the territorial capital on the lower reaches of the Arkansas River, was not well suited as the seat of government because of frequent flooding. Little Rock was being considered as a new capital. The problem was that two sets of rivals claimed ownership of the "point of rocks," as the area was commonly known.

Ashley was the attorney for one set of claimants, the investors who based ownership on certificates issued by the federal government to compensate victims of the New Madrid earthquakes of 1811–12. The other claimants were led by William Russell, a famous St. Louis land speculator who held a preemption claim, which took precedence due to being based on actual settlement. The legal and political maneuvering was intense.

Ownership of the site of Little Rock was finally reached in a compromise of November 22, 1821, with Ashley signing on behalf of the New Madrid claimants and Russell acting for the preemptioners. Thus, in a very short time after his arrival, Chester Ashley went from hanging his shingle to owning a large part of the future capital of a new territory.

Ashley rose quickly in business, political, and social circles. Historian Walter L. Brown has noted that as the best trained lawyer in early Arkansas, Ashley was known for being cool, unexcitable, and professionally aloof—yet thoroughly read in the law. As a young man, Ashley was tall and handsome, his blue eyes piercing. Photographs show he turned gray early and put on weight. Fellow lawyer Albert Pike thought Ashley too portly to deserve the title "Colonel," which came from his early service in the militia.

Ashley's public record was severely damaged by being heavily involved in the great banking fiasco of the 1830s. Ashley, along with his close ally William E. Woodruff, owned stock in the Arkansas State Bank, and Ashley served as a director. The State Bank, along with the Real Estate Bank, ultimately failed, with corruption being one obvious cause. Ashley's reputation also suffered by being the attorney for John Bowie in a prominent land dispute and was indicted for suborning a jury.

Ashley might have been the richest man in Little Rock before the Civil War. He built one of the grand homes of the state. Occupying a whole block bounded by Markham, Second, Cumberland, and Scott streets, the Ashley home started out as a story-and-a-half building, but it grew as Ashley's career prospered. In the early 1840s Ashley had the house remodeled to better reflect his growing political standing. The expanded Ashley home became two-story and sported an imposing Greek Revival portico held up by six huge columns. (After capturing Little Rock in 1863, Civil War Union Gen. Frederick Steele chose the Ashley home as his headquarters. The house later became the Oakleaf Hotel and was demolished around 1900.)

Despite his high profile, Ashley did not seek public office until 1844 when he was a Democratic Party presidential elector. That same year he was chosen by the Arkansas legislature to complete the term of U.S. Senator William S. Fulton, who died in office. Though a freshman, Ashley served as chairman of the Senate Judiciary Committee. He was generally acknowledged to be one of the better legal minds in the senate.

Ashley was reelected in 1846 but died on April 29, 1848, after an illness of five days. His grave is in Mount Holly Cemetery on land he donated for that purpose many years earlier. The legislature named a new county in southeast Arkansas after Ashley within months of his death, and both Chester and Ashley streets in Little Rock honor him.

FOR MORE INFORMATION:

Foster, Lynn. "Chester Ashley." *The Encyclopedia of Arkansas History and Culture.* http://encyclopediaofarkansas.net/encyclopedia/entry-detail.aspx?search=1&entryID=1274.

Ruple, Susan H. "The Life and Times of Chester Ashley, 1791–1848." Master's thesis, University of Arkansas, 1983.

Rose, U. M. "Chester Ashley." *Publications of the Arkansas Historical Association.* Vol. 3. Fayetteville: Arkansas Historical Association, 1911.

Augustus H. Garland

Garland County was named in honor of Augustus H. Garland, one of the great figures of nineteenth-century Arkansas history—in politics, the law, and the Confederacy. His appointment to the cabinet of President Grover Cleveland was a first for an Arkansan.

Born in Tipton County, Tennessee, in June 1832, Garland was only a few months old when his parents moved to Lost Prairie on the Red River in modern Miller County, where his father operated a store. His father died within a year, and the family relocated to nearby Spring Hill and later to Washington in Hempstead County. Young Augustus was educated in a local academy and attended college in Kentucky, where many members of the early Arkansas elite educated their children. After a brief stint as a teacher, Garland began studying law and was admitted to practice in 1853. He relocated to Little Rock in 1856, where he practiced law.

As was typical on the frontier, Garland found politics an appealing adjunct to the practice of law. He was a Whig, as was his law partner in Little Rock, Ebenezer Cummins, who had formerly practiced with Albert Pike. In the presidential election of 1860, Garland was an elector for John Bell, the nominee of the Constitutional Union Party. Like many of his fellow Whigs, he opposed the secession of Arkansas during the Civil War. He was elected to represent Pulaski County in the 1861 convention called to consider secession, and he fought joining the Confederacy until hostilities were imminent.

As war drew near, Garland threw his support to the new Confederate States of America and later served in both the Confederate House and Senate. He helped surrender the state archives to Unionist governor Isaac Murphy after the war.

With the return of peace, the thirty-three-year-old Garland was anxious to resume his law practice. In July 1865 he received a presidential pardon for his Confederate service but was unable to practice before federal courts due to his inability to take the "Ironclad Oath," a promise that he never bore arms against the United States nor served in a hostile government. Garland argued that the oath was ex post facto law and unconstitutional and that it abridged the pardoning powers of the president. In a 5–4 decision known as *Ex parte Garland,* the Supreme Court agreed and thereby freed many former Confederates across the South to regain their political rights.

Garland was elected to the U.S. Senate, but he was not seated because Arkansas had not been readmitted to the Union. During the Reconstruction period Garland put most of his energies into building his law practice. But, when the Reconstruction leaders fell into the internecine conflict known as the Brooks-Baxter War, Garland gave his support to the more conservative Baxter.

The Brooks-Baxter War ended Reconstruction in Arkansas, and the Democrats nominated Garland for governor, a post he won easily. He was a progressive governor who worked hard to bring reconciliation to a state left divided by the Civil War. He was a racial moderate, and he implemented legislation to build a black college in Pine Bluff. He succeeded in reducing considerably the state debt of $17 million.

Garland emphasized the importance of immigration to Arkansas, and he was the first governor to try to deal with the state's image problem. At his urging, the state participated in the Centennial Exposition in Philadelphia in 1876, building an impressive exhibit hall to tout Arkansas's natural resources and agricultural products. The fountain from that building now stands in front of the Old State House in Little Rock.

Garland did not run for reelection in 1876 but was elected the following year to the U.S. Senate. As a senator, Garland promoted civil service reform, federal aid to education, and preservation of the gold standard. As a "sound money" man, Senator Garland opposed the "Greenback" movement—though his brother Rufus was a leader of the Greenback Party.

In 1885 Garland resigned his Senate seat to become President Grover Cleveland's attorney general, the first Arkansan to serve in a presidential cabinet. His cabinet service was marred by charges of a scandal over telephone patents. His tenure as attorney general ended when Cleveland was defeated for a second term. Garland stayed in Washington, where he resumed the practice of law. He died on January 26, 1899, after collapsing while arguing a case before the U.S. Supreme Court. He was buried in Little Rock's historic Mount Holly Cemetery.

Garland was a remarkable man, but his life was filled with personal tragedy. Several of his children, including both sons who carried his name, died in childhood. His wife died on Christmas Eve 1877, leaving him to raise four surviving children. His daughter Daisy later committed suicide, while his son Will died of a cocaine overdose in 1906.

Personal tragedies aside, Augustus Hill Garland was, especially in the aftermath of the Civil War, the perfect leader for imperfect times in Arkansas history.

FOR MORE INFORMATION:

Schlup, Leonard. "Augustus Hill Garland: Gilded Age Democrat." *Arkansas Historical Quarterly* 40 (Winter 1981): 338–46.

Watkins, Beverly. "Augustus Hill Garland (1832–1899)." *The Encyclopedia of Arkansas History and Culture.* http://encyclopediaofarkansas.net/encyclopedia/entry-detail.aspx?search=1&entryID=106.

Watkins, Beverly Nettles. "Augustus Hill Garland, 1832–1899: Arkansas Lawyer to United States Attorney General." Ph.D. diss., Auburn University, 1985.

Robert Ward Johnson

One of the great antebellum leaders of Arkansas, Robert Ward Johnson, was appointed to the U.S. Senate by Gov. Elias N. Conway on July 6, 1853. It was only natural that Conway would appoint Johnson. In addition to Johnson's prior service in Congress, they were related by marriage and were members of what was called the "Family" or the "Dynasty"—the small group of men within the Democratic Party who ruled the state before the Civil War. "Bob" Johnson was among the most prominent Arkansans during the decade-long run-up to the Civil War.

Robert Ward Johnson was born in 1814 in Kentucky. His family had found great political and business success in frontier Kentucky, and two of Johnson's uncles represented Kentucky in the U.S. House of Representatives, while another uncle, Richard Mentor Johnson, served as vice president of the United States during the presidency of Martin Van Buren.

Bob Johnson came to Arkansas in 1821 when his father, Benjamin, was appointed superior judge for Arkansas Territory. With no educational opportunities available in territorial Little Rock, young Bob attended St. Joseph's Academy in Bardstown, Kentucky. He took a law degree from Yale in 1835.

Before returning to Little Rock to practice law, Johnson married Sarah S. Smith of Louisville, Kentucky. They had six children, though only three lived to adulthood. When Sarah died in 1862, Johnson married her sister, but they had no children.

After practicing law for a short period, Johnson became Pulaski County prosecuting attorney in 1840. After two years, he won election as state attorney general, and in 1846 was elected as the state's sole member of the U.S. House of Representatives. During his three terms in the House, Johnson was low key—though he was a major supporter of federal aid for railroad construction and served as chairman of the House Committee on Indian Affairs. He declined to run for reelection in 1852.

Johnson's respite from Congress was brief, for in 1853 he was drafted to succeed Arkansas's U.S. Sen. Solon Borland, who newly elected President Franklin Pierce had named minister plenipotentiary to Central America and stationed in Nicaragua. In 1855 Johnson was selected to serve a full term. Thus, Johnson was caught up in the maelstrom surrounding the great debate on the future of slavery in America.

Johnson already had a reputation as a hardliner when it came to defending slavery. During his terms in the House he had worked to rouse concern among Arkansans for what he viewed as a sustained attack on the slave economy. In 1850 Congressman Johnson issued an "Address to the People of Arkansas" in which he startled his constituents with the alarming news that the national union is "a matter that might be seriously questioned!"

Johnson's early efforts to arouse sectional sentiment in Arkansas failed, but as time passed he gained assistance from Congressman Thomas Hindman and others. He was a stout opponent of regular Democratic presidential nominee Stephen A. Douglas in 1860, throwing his support behind John C. Breckinridge of Kentucky, the southern candidate. When Republican Abraham Lincoln emerged victorious in 1860, Johnson issued a public letter to the people of the state calling for "sympathy with the seceding states" and refusal to "submit to . . . the great powers and forces . . . directed toward their subservience and subjugation."

In his last address before departing Congress, Johnson admitted that dissolution of the Union would be sorrowful: "I know from the bottom of my soul that I am not averse to the continuation and preservation of the present Union of States . . . and I feel from the bottom of my heart whenever it shall be divided it will be given up for petty causes . . . irritations and misapprehensions, to the consequences of war and the contingencies of blood and disaster."

When Arkansas finally seceded in May 1861, Johnson was one of five Arkansans elected to the Provisional Confederate Congress. He was later selected by the state legislature to serve as one of Arkansas's two Confederate senators. Serving on the rebel senate's powerful Military Affairs Committee, Johnson was an ally of Confederate president Jefferson Davis.

The Civil War proved a disaster for Johnson and his family. He lost his plantations and the enslaved people used to work them. After fleeing to Galveston, Texas, in preparation for moving to South America, Johnson changed his mind and returned to Arkansas, where he opened a law practice with his old political enemy, Albert Pike. His new law practice caused his temporary relocation to Washington, D.C.

Before departing for Washington, Johnson was feted at a banquet at which he bade farewell and commented on what he saw as a defect in state life: "a state pride has been needed. The state that cherished no distinct 'state pride' must have a meager and barren history, if not actually [be] disgraceful in the great American future. Her people, without it, will have few incentives to honor, toleration and noble efforts. Her children will grow up without memories or proud ambitions, as it were without a home, like the children of a 'poor house,' to be fed and clothed and turned out on the world as a given age, 'atoms valueless in oceans of atoms.'" This is probably the first time Arkansans openly discussed what would become known in the modern era as the "Arkansas inferiority complex."

FOR MORE INFORMATION:

DeBlack, Thomas A. "The Family [Political Dynasty]." *The Encyclopedia of Arkansas History and Culture.* http://encyclopediaofarkansas.net/encyclopedia/entry-detail.aspx?search=1&entryID=2666.

Lewis, Elsie M. "Robert Ward Johnson: Militant Spokesman of the Old South-West." *Arkansas Historical Quarterly* 13 (Spring 1954): 16–30.

Woods, James M. "Robert Ward Johnson (1814–1879)." *The Encyclopedia of Arkansas History and Culture.* http://encyclopediaofarkansas.net/encyclopedia/entry-detail.aspx?search=1&entryID=1682.

CHAPTER III

Postbellum Politicians

Gov. Powell Clayton

In the summer of 1868 former Union army commander Powell Clayton was sworn in as the first Republican governor of Arkansas. He won the governorship because many Democratic voters had been disfranchised by provisions of the Reconstruction Acts of 1867. Traditionally, historians have portrayed Clayton as little more than a thief, or a "thieving poltroon," as one of Clayton's many enemies called him. In more recent decades historians have tended to acknowledge that Clayton at least brought railroads to the state, that he deserves some credit for founding the University of Arkansas, and that he essentially destroyed the Ku Klux Klan. He was too complicated to be easily categorized, though everyone conceded that Powell Clayton was a brilliant commander of cavalry forces.

Clayton was born in Bethel Township, Pennsylvania, on August 7, 1833. His father was a carpenter and orchardist. He received a good education, including attending the Partridge Military Academy in his home state. He also studied civil engineering for a time in Delaware. Like many young and ambitious men of his time, Clayton sought his fortune on the frontier, settling in Leavenworth, Kansas, in 1855.

Working as a surveyor and doing a little land speculating on the side, Clayton soon made a place for himself in the small Kansas town. In 1861, when the Civil War commenced, Clayton was named commander of a light infantry company in the First Kansas Infantry. Within three months of being sworn in, Clayton was tested under fire at the battle of Wilson's Creek near Springfield, Missouri. The First Kansas was in the thick of the fight, losing forty-nine of seventy-four troopers, and Clayton was commended for his leadership.

Clayton worked his way up the command structure with speed and agility. In February 1862, he was promoted to lieutenant colonel, and only a month later he was promoted to colonel of the Fifth Kansas Cavalry. In this capacity Clayton came to Helena, Arkansas, an important port town on the Mississippi River. When Confederates mounted

Powell Clayton, Reconstruction governor and U.S. senator. *Photo courtesy of Prints and Photographs Division, Library of Congress.*

an attack on Helena on Independence Day 1863, Clayton played a major role in defending the city.

After participating in the capture of Little Rock in the fall of 1863, Clayton was sent to command a post at Pine Bluff. On October 25, 1863, a large force of Confederate forces attacked the city. Clayton's outnumbered men fought off the rebels, with the considerable help of recently freed slaves. Later, Clayton was promoted to brigadier general. He was mustered out in August 1865, ready to start a new life in Arkansas—a state that had been a battleground so recently.

Even before the war ended, Clayton invited his twin brothers, Union army veterans William Henry Harrison Clayton and John Middleton Clayton, to join him in Jefferson County and purchase a plantation. He soon married a woman from Helena, Adaline McGraw. Clayton seemed to like being a planter, for he never sold his plantation and ultimately accumulated over forty thousand acres of land.

At first Clayton refused to involve himself in politics, but he later changed his mind, claiming that confrontations with ex-rebels convinced him that Unionists needed protection. After the adoption of the federal Reconstruction Acts of 1867, Clayton helped organize the Arkansas Republican Party. He was nominated for governor in 1868, but over the opposition of a native Unionist from north Arkansas, James M. Johnson, who would become a continuing thorn in Clayton's side. With many former rebels now disfranchised under the Reconstruction Acts, which denied the vote to anyone who had fought for or otherwise served the Confederacy, Clayton won the governorship.

It was a hot July 2, 1868, when governor-elect Clayton and outgoing Gov. Isaac Murphy rode in an open carriage to the statehouse on Markham Street in Little Rock. Clayton's formal attire, including white gloves, puzzled Gov. Murphy. Why would anyone wear "dude gloves" on a hot day. Clayton, in perhaps his only recorded humorous statement, commented that he would "take off the gloves" considering the task he was undertaking.

Clayton became governor at a time of violence and uncertainty. The Ku Klux Klan moved into Arkansas from its base in Tennessee, and before long the new governor was receiving reports of freedmen being lynched and white Unionists being threatened. Republican Congressman James Hinds was murdered in October, and Clayton declared martial law in fourteen counties on November 4, 1868.

Clayton's decisive leadership in sending the militia into Ku Klux Klan strongholds—such as at Centre Point in Howard County— probably broke the back of that terrorist organization. Clayton also started a public school system in Arkansas, created the Arkansas School for the Deaf, and used state bonds to build over six hundred miles of railroads. There is no doubt that Clayton was heavy-handed, that corruption ran rampant, and that public debt grew dramatically during his tenure. Still, Powell Clayton dragged Arkansas, kicking and screaming every step of the way, into the modern world. In January 1871, the Republican-controlled state legislature elected Clayton to serve in the U.S. Senate.

Clayton wanted to take his seat in Washington immediately, but he could not, for doing so would have meant that his arch enemy, Lt. Gov. James Johnson, would ascend to the governorship. More than any other governor, excepting perhaps Bill Clinton, Powell Clayton was a lightning rod for discord. The state Republican Party was a contentious lot from its birth in April 1868, quickly breaking into feuding camps of native Unionists versus recent arrivals. Clayton was impeached on one occasion, but the trial was never held. Threats against his life were common.

Powell Clayton was nothing if not a man of compromise, and soon he worked out a deal that provided the lieutenant governor with the more prominent post of secretary of state—thereby allowing a Clayton ally to become lieutenant governor. The legislature dutifully elected Clayton to the Senate again in March 1871, and he departed for Washington, D.C.

Clayton's tenure in Congress was not particularly notable. He worked hard to get funding for a bridge across the river at Little Rock, as well as many other improvements. However, it was in the area of civil and political rights for blacks that Senator Clayton spoke out most forcefully and eloquently. In one widely reported confrontation Clayton interrupted Democratic Sen. Augustus S. Merrimon of North Carolina, who was in the middle of a lengthy indictment of Reconstruction racial policies. Clayton supported national civil rights legislation to protect blacks in the future, asking on one occasion, "Are we to turn over to ... the Ku Klux Klan ... the colored people of this country?"

At the end of his six-year term in 1877, Senator Clayton was turned out of office by the now-Democratic state legislature. He left Washington for Little Rock, where he went into business and maintained his control over the state Republican organization. Clayton was chairman or national committeeman of the Arkansas GOP for nearly forty years. He constantly had to do battle against insurgencies within the GOP, which he fought with the same intensity he exhibited leading cavalry into battle. As William H. Burnside, the primary biographer of Clayton, has written, "Authoritarian both in philosophy and personality, he did indeed deserve the title 'Boss Clayton.'"

Politics alone could not contain the energy and drive of a man like Powell Clayton. From his initial introduction, Clayton saw Arkansas as "a land of opportunities." He invested in a number of Arkansas businesses, but his most impressive venture was building the Crescent Hotel in Eureka Springs.

Reading that 15,000 tourists and invalids were visiting the hamlet of Eureka Springs every year to take advantage of the numerous mineral springs that bubbled from its rocky cliffs, Clayton jumped into action. He convinced three prominent businessmen—Missouri railroad tycoons Richard C. Kerens and Arthur H. Foote, and Little Rock banker Logan H. Roots—to join him in forming the Eureka Springs Improvement Company.

Clayton recognized that a railroad connection was necessary before Eureka Springs could prosper. He organized the Eureka Springs Railway Company, which built an eighteen-mile line to Seligman, Missouri. Soon, Clayton had quarries opened to provide the large limestone blocks needed to construct the sprawling Crescent Hotel. With 100 rooms and large lobbies and dining rooms, the Crescent was one of the most imposing hotels in the south. The hotel was opened in a grand celebration on May 20, 1886, with none other than former presidential candidate James G. Blaine delivering the dedicatory address. The Crescent still functions as a hotel, although it has gone through periods of neglect.

From 1897 to 1905, Clayton served as the U.S. ambassador to Mexico, a major political plum paid to a party loyalist who always managed to deliver the convention delegates if not the support of the voters. Growing old, Clayton settled in Washington, D.C., after he left Mexico City in 1905. However, he continued to run the Arkansas GOP from Washington, though he later transferred power to his loyal lieutenant, Harmon L. Remmel. Clayton died on August 25, 1914, at the age of eighty-one. He was buried in Arlington National Cemetery.

Clayton's descendants all lived in Europe. Of Clayton's five children, only one had offspring of their own. While living with her father in Mexico City, Charlotte Clayton met and married the Belgian minister to Mexico, Baron Ludovic Moncheur. Possessing a charm that her famous father never had, Charlotte was a vivacious and popular woman in the various posts where her husband served. They had three children, one of which, Charles Moncheur—Powell Clayton's only grandson—carried on the family tradition of military service when he served as a bomber pilot for the Royal Air Force during World War II.

FOR MORE INFORMATION:

Burnside, William H. *The Honorable Powell Clayton.* Conway: University of Central Arkansas Press, 1991.

Clayton, Powell. *The Aftermath of the Civil War, in Arkansas.* New York: Neale Publishing Co., 1915.

Moneyhon, Carl H. "Powell Clayton (1833–1914)." *The Encyclopedia of Arkansas History and Culture.* http://encyclopediaofarkansas.net/encyclopedia/entry-detail.aspx?search=1&entryID=94#.

Sen. S. W. Dorsey

Cleveland County in southern Arkansas was created in the Reconstruction legislature of 1873 and named for Republican U.S. senator and railroad promoter Stephen W. Dorsey. Dorsey, who left Arkansas not long after his one term in the Senate, was loathed by the Democrats —and they ultimately took revenge. The county name was changed to Cleveland in 1885 to commemorate the election of the first Democratic president since the Civil War.

Stephen Wallace Dorsey was born in Vermont in 1842, but the family soon moved to Oberlin, Ohio, where their young son attended public schools. He served in the Union army during the Civil War. After the war, he settled in Sandusky and became president of a small tool company.

Dorsey moved to Arkansas to develop one of the many railroad companies being chartered in the aftermath of the Civil War. Prior to Reconstruction, Arkansas was almost bereft of railroads, and Reconstruction leaders viewed the rumbling steam-powered trains as the key to developing the state.

Settling in Helena, Dorsey was quickly drawn into the maelstrom of Reconstruction politics. In 1872 he was elected to the U.S. Senate by the Republican-controlled legislature—as senators were selected in those days. His election was not assured because Dorsey was not an ally of Powell Clayton, the Reconstruction governor and boss of the state Republican organization. The legislature spent five days casting ballots to fill the senate seat, but finally Dorsey won a majority when Democrats who had been supporting Augustus H. Garland switched to Dorsey.

No sooner had Dorsey taken his senate seat than internal bickering within the ruling Reconstruction Republican Party escalated into outright political warfare. In 1874 the situation imploded in what is known as the Brooks-Baxter War. Both Senators Clayton and Dorsey sided with Joseph Brooks in his attempt to evict Governor Elisha Baxter.

Stephen A. Dorsey, Reconstruction senator and Western cattle tycoon. *Photo courtesy of Prints and Photographs Division, Library of Congress.*

Dorsey turned against the governor when Baxter refused to issue additional state-guaranteed railroad-aid bonds to Dorsey's Arkansas Central Railroad Company. Baxter, who had been a Unionist lawyer before the Civil War, incurred the wrath of most Republicans when as governor he had named prominent Democrats to many important state positions. In the end, President Grant sided with Baxter, and this ended not only the struggle but Reconstruction itself. In 1874, resurgent

Democrats adopted a new constitution and Republicans were reduced to minority status for the next century.

Though the stoutly-built and bewhiskered Dorsey looked the role of a senator, his tenure in Congress was not productive. Given that Democrats held a huge majority in the Arkansas legislature, Dorsey stood no chance of being reelected, and his term ended in March 1879.

While many Republican leaders—such as Powell Clayton—stayed in Arkansas when Reconstruction ended, Dorsey quickly left the state and settled in New Mexico. He established a huge cattle herd, and his mining enterprises extended to Colorado and other states. He constructed a huge home at Mountain Springs, Colfax County, New Mexico, which is on the National Register of Historic Places. He also developed the town of Clayton, New Mexico, which he named for his son.

Like many entrepreneurs of dubious reputation, Dorsey was known as a charming and lavish host. His New Mexico log and masonry home, according to Dorsey's obituary in the *Arkansas Gazette,* cost $100,000, and the wine cellars were stocked with $10,000 worth of "the choicest wines and liquors." A spring-fed reservoir high on a mountain provided running water. One startled visitor noted that "he had water all over his house, and the pressure was sufficient to keep a large fountain playing continually in front of the big porch." One visitor recalled attending a party at the Dorsey mansion, where the "suave Senator" dispensed hospitality that was "the marvel of New Mexico."

Relocation to the far west did not keep Dorsey out of trouble. He was charged with a host of crimes. Indeed, his biography is titled *Rogue! Being an Account of the Life and High Times of Stephen W. Dorsey, United States Senator and New Mexico Cattle Baron.* Dorsey's legally questionable ventures were not limited to New Mexico, however. He gained national notoriety in the "Star Route" scandals of the Garfield presidential administration. Dorsey and other conspirators were involved in illegally awarding postal delivery contracts and taking kickbacks. Still, he avoided jail, though he died in near poverty in 1916. He was buried in Denver, Colorado.

In March 1885, the Arkansas legislature changed the name of Dorsey County. Two other counties named to honor Reconstruction

Republicans also received new names, including Sarber (which became Logan) and Clayton (shortened to Clay), both renamed in 1875. The Reconstruction-era counties of Sharp, Grant, Boone, Nevada, Lincoln, Baxter, Garland, Faulkner, Lonoke, Lee, Howard, and Stone all retain their original names.

FOR MORE INFORMATION:

Caperton, Thomas J. *Rogue! Being an Account of the Life and High Times of Stephen W. Dorsey, United States Senator and New Mexico Cattle Baron.* Santa Fe: Museum of New Mexico Press, 1978.

"Mr. Stephen W. Dorsey's Hospitality." *New York Times*, August 11, 1895.

"Stephen W. Dorsey, Reconstruction Senator." *Arkansas Gazette*, March 22, 1916.

Turner, Don. *The Life and Castle of Stephen W. Dorsey: The Hard-Working Vermont Boy Who Became a Senator from Arkansas, a Cattle Baron in New Mexico and the Key Figure in a National Political Scandal.* Amarillo: Humbug Gulch Press, 1967.

William H. Grey

One of the remarkable black leaders of nineteenth-century Arkansas was William H. Grey of Helena. A dynamic and forceful speaker, a leader who commanded the respect of his constituents, and an advocate for racial equality, Grey's star burned brightly in the Arkansas political firmament before paralysis prematurely stole his health.

Like many of the black leaders who came to Arkansas after the Civil War, Grey did not grow up in slavery. Grey's exact birth date and birthplace are unknown, but he was probably born in the late 1820s—in the Washington, D.C., area. There is considerable circumstantial evidence that Grey was the son of Henry A. Wise, a Virginia congressman and later governor. We do know that Wise only freed one of his slaves during his lifetime, and that was a woman named Elizabeth Gray and her two children, Mary Jane and William Henry. We also know Grey was a mulatto.

Contemporary accounts told of Congressman Wise bringing young William into the House of Representatives almost every day, where, as Wise's biographer has written, the young boy "folded documents at [Wise's] desk, and heard the speeches." Later, Grey became a Methodist minister, married, and had a number of children.

The end of the Civil War presented many opportunities for aggressive young black men who wanted to make a mark. Likewise, the end of slavery opened the south as a new frontier for political involvement, especially after the Reconstruction Acts were adopted. Growing up in the political whirlwind that was Washington, D.C., during the decade leading to the Civil War, Grey must have developed a considerable interest in politics. Whatever the cause, Grey moved to Helena, Arkansas, soon after the war.

After opening a grocery store and bakery in Helena, Grey successfully ran for the 1868 Constitutional Convention, the body charged with writing the Reconstruction constitution for the state. The convention was controlled by the Republican Party, which had been organized in Arkansas only a few months earlier.

The convention convened on January 7, 1868, in the state House of Representatives chamber, which, ironically, was the location of the Confederate secession convention seven years earlier. Grey was one of eight black members, a sizable minority among the seventy active delegates.

Widely recognized as one of the more able delegates, Grey emerged as the leading opponent of a proposal to ban "miscegenation," as interracial marriage was called. Grey, who could have pointed to his own mixed race as an example, spoke eloquently about how white men were responsible for the presence of so many mulatto freedmen, noting "the purity of blood . . . has already been somewhat interfered with in this country." He concluded, "when you place in your Constitution a provision of this nature, you at once create an inequality." In the end, Grey was successful, but conservative newspaper editors all over the state railed against the "miscegenationist" constitution.

At the end of the convention, Grey ran for and won election to the 1868 state House of Representatives. In 1874, at the end of Reconstruction, he was elected to the state Senate. Grey earned a good reputation during his legislative service, with one newspaper commenting that he "cuts as good a figure as any of them in the hall." His final elective service was as county clerk of Phillips County.

During the presidential campaign of 1868, while Grey was in the legislature, he was selected to serve as a delegate to the Republican national convention. Four years later he again served as a delegate to the GOP national convention, this time to second the nomination of President U. S. Grant. His 1872 speech was the first occasion for a black citizen to address a major political convention.

While serving in the legislature, Grey developed an interest in promoting immigration to the state of Arkansas. In 1872 he was elected Commissioner of Immigration and State Lands, a statewide political office. Among the many leading blacks he encouraged to move to Arkansas was Mifflin W. Gibbs, who later became the dean of Arkansas black leaders. He also promoted German immigration. He was removed from office in 1874 when the conservative Democrats finally brought an end to Reconstruction.

In September 1878, Grey was struck with paralysis. He was bedfast for the remaining ten years of his life. He died in November 1888, leaving a wife, several children still at home, and a very small estate.

FOR MORE INFORMATION:

Dillard, Tom W. "Three Important Black Leaders in Phillips County History." *Phillips County Historical Quarterly* 19 (1980–81): 10–23.

Palmer, Paul C. "Miscegenation as an Issue in the Arkansas Constitutional Convention of 1868." *Arkansas Historical Quarterly* 24 (Summer 1965): 99–119.

St. Hilaire, Joseph M. "The Negro Delegates in the Arkansas Constitutional Convention of 1868: A Group Profile." *Arkansas Historical Quarterly* 33 (Spring 1974): 38–69.

Isaac T. Gillam

Despite his birth as a slave, Isaac T. Gillam arose quickly on the political scene in post–Civil War Little Rock. Though he died early, Gillam crammed a great deal of political activity into a few years.

Isaac Taylor Gillam first entered the public record on September 15, 1863, when the young black man joined the U.S. Army, which had captured Little Rock only five days earlier. His exact birthday is unknown for he was a slave, and birth records were not kept of slaves. It is believed that Gillam was brought to Little Rock by his Tennessee owner, who was fleeing the federal army. Being a skilled blacksmith, Gillam was valuable property and worth transporting to another state.

After three years, Gillam left the U.S. Army as a sergeant and opened a blacksmith shop. As a sideline, he raised horses. For a time he also served as a city jailer and policeman, but those were political positions and subject to abrupt change.

Gillam was active in the local Republican Party during Reconstruction. During the Brooks-Baxter War, an armed conflict that arose from the contested gubernatorial election of 1872 and which brought an end to Reconstruction, Gillam served on the losing side as a captain in the Brooks militia. In 1877 he won election to the Little Rock City Council as a Republican, representing the heavily black Sixth Ward.

The Little Rock City Council, like much of the country at that time, was divided among three parties, with the insurgent Greenback Party holding the balance of power. Gillam, while a nominal Republican, often aligned with the Greenbackers to beat the Democrats. In one instance, Gillam and his fellow Republicans entered into a coalition with the Greenbackers to elect their candidate for police chief, though it took 102 ballots to do so.

Later Gillam switched to the Greenback Party and was elected under their banner to the state legislature in 1878, thereby simultaneously serving as a Republican city councilman and a Greenback legislator. He continued his political transformation in 1882 when he was

Isaac T. Gillam, a former slave who gained broad political experience after the Civil War. *Photo courtesy of University of Central Arkansas Archives, Conway.*

elected Pulaski county coroner as a Democrat. Gillam completed his metamorphosis in 1890 when he ran again for coroner, this time as the nominee of another insurgency, the Populist Party.

Gillam died in 1904, a decade after the state legislature disfranchised black voters. His contributions to society, however, continued through his widow, Cora Gillam, and children. Of the seven Gillam children to reach adulthood, five were teachers.

Many of the children attended Shorter College in North Little Rock, which the devout African Methodist Episcopal family helped create. While sisters Mary, Annie, and Leah were elementary teachers, Isaac T. Gillam II was among America's most noted black educators.

Graduating from Howard University, the younger Isaac Gillam later studied at Yale University and a number of other schools. While at the University of Cincinnati, he studied under the famous John Dewey. He retired from the Little Rock Public Schools after a long career, fifty years as principal at Gibbs High School alone.

Not all the educators coming from the Gillam family were able to stay in their place of birth. One of Isaac Jr.'s children, Dorothy Gillam, made her mark in education by teaching French in Cincinnati, Ohio. The Little Rock public schools had dropped foreign languages from the black schools around 1910 in order to stress "manual arts." Upon her retirement, Miss Dorothy Gillam moved back to Little Rock, settling into the family home near Philander Smith College. She maintained the family archives, including her grandfather's original commission naming Isaac T. Gillam as a major in the Joseph Brooks militia.

The Gillam family's most recent contribution to American leadership is the role Isaac T. Gillam IV played in American aviation and aerospace history. Gillam, a Korean War pilot and later an official at NASA, oversaw production of the shuttle program. He was inducted into the Arkansas Aviation Hall of Fame in 1996.

Families like the Gillams were able to do remarkable things, perhaps the most amazing being their success in reducing African American illiteracy from nearly 100 percent at the end of the Civil War to 40 percent in thirty-five years.

FOR MORE INFORMATION:

Dillard, Tom W. "The Gilliam [sic] Family, Four Generations of Black Arkansas Educators." *Journal of Arkansas Education* 45 (1973): 19, 22.

Dillard, Tom W. "Isaac Gillam: Black Pulaski Countian." *Pulaski County Historical Review* 24 (Spring 1976): 6–11.

Hagg, Beulah Sherwood. "Mrs. Cora Gillam." In *The American Slave: A Composite Autobiography,* ed. George P. Rawick. Westport, CT: Greenwood Publishing Co., 1972.

Gov. James H. Berry

Any Arkansan who lived in the later part of the 1800s would have recognized the name J. H. Berry, but he is not well known to modern Arkansans. A Civil War hero with a reputation for honesty, Berry rose from the state legislature to the U.S. Senate—only to be brought down by the unrestrained tactics of Gov. Jeff Davis.

James Henderson Berry was born in Jackson County, Alabama, on May 15, 1841, to James M. and Isabelle Orr Berry. In 1848 his parents, along with other relatives, moved to Carrollton, Arkansas, then a flourishing town and the seat of Carroll County. Along with his nine siblings, young Berry worked on the family farm. His mother's early death brought an end to Berry's formal education.

When the Civil War erupted in 1861, the twenty-year-old Berry enlisted in the Confederate army. He was elected second lieutenant of Company E of the Sixteenth Arkansas Infantry and fought in battles at Pea Ridge in Arkansas and at Iuka and Corinth in Mississippi. At the latter battle Berry suffered a severe leg wound and was captured. Federal surgeons amputated his right leg above the knee and paroled him.

Settling in Ozark, Berry taught school for a short time. He married Lizzie Quaile, the daughter of a local businessman, and the newlyweds relocated to Carrollton, where Berry immediately entered politics. Despite his youth, Berry was elected to the state House of Representatives in 1866 as a Democrat.

After serving only one term in the legislature, Berry moved to Bentonville, where he opened a law office with Sam W. Peel, his brother-in-law. He was elected again to the legislature in 1872, this time representing Benton and Washington counties. Two years later he was elected Speaker of the House. He was elected to a circuit judgeship in 1878, where he served until resigning to run for governor in 1882.

Berry's previous political service, his large circle of friends, and his Civil War record made him a formidable candidate. Ultimately, all his Democratic opponents withdrew from the campaign and Berry rolled over his Republican opponent, W. D. Slack, by a huge majority.

Berry's two-year term as governor produced mixed results. He was successful in taxing railroads, which had previously been exempt. He also worked to prosecute former state officials for corruption, though few convictions resulted. The legislature refused to cooperate with Governor Berry's efforts to reform the inhumane state prison system, though he was successful in establishing a State Hospital for Nervous Diseases.

In 1883 racial violence erupted along the Howard-Hempstead county line, with four blacks and a single white man killed. Governor Berry immediately sent the adjutant general of the state militia to the area and calm was restored. A large number of black defendants were arrested, several sent to prison, and one executed. Berry eventually pardoned one of the black defendants, a humane act that came back to haunt him during a campaign many years later.

After a single term as governor, Berry unsuccessfully sought a seat in the U.S. Senate in 1885. However, later that same year Sen. Augustus H. Garland resigned to become President Grover Cleveland's attorney general, and the legislature tapped Berry for the vacancy. (Berry's cousin Campbell Polson Berry represented California in the U.S. House of Representatives from 1879 to 1883.)

Berry's record in the senate was mixed. According to biographer Joe Seagraves, "as a senator, Berry was diligent but not prominent or dynamic." While he supported such progressive legislation as railroad and trust regulation, a graduated income tax, and the direct election of U.S. senators (which were then elected by the various state legislatures), he opposed civil service reforms and extending the vote to women.

Berry served four terms in the senate, and he was expected to be reelected in 1906. However, the 1906 election was the first to be determined by a direct vote of the people rather than by the legislature, and Governor Jeff Davis had other plans. Davis was immensely popular with poor farmers, of which Arkansas had legions. Davis was able to shape the debate, and he had the considerable advantage of seeming immune to public censure—even when his public drinking provoked the Second Baptist Church to expel Davis from church membership.

Davis attacked Berry as aloof, as a tool of trusts, and he reminded voters that as governor, Berry had pardoned a black murder defendant. The *Arkansas Democrat* called the election "the vilest and meanest state campaign ever witnessed in Arkansas."

Berry was simply not prepared for the rough-and-tumble nature of modern elective politics. While Davis did not shy away from making direct attacks on the incumbent senator, Berry usually relied upon supporters to come to his defense. Davis made 225 speeches during the campaign, appearing in every county. As Seagraves noted, Berry's defeat "marked the passing of the old order, for he was the last Confederate veteran to represent Arkansas in the Senate."

In his essay on Berry in the definitive reference book *Governors of Arkansas* (1995), Seagraves described Berry as a man of hard work but little in the way of major accomplishment: "For over half of his adult life Berry served his state and its people in various public offices. Whatever the office, he worked hard to fulfill its responsibilities. Yet, his record of achievement was neither brilliant nor remarkable." Seagraves concluded: "Those who knew him respected him less for his accomplishments than for his loyalty, honesty, and faithful service."

Berry retired to Bentonville, where he died in January 1913. He was buried in Bentonville City Cemetery and was survived by his wife, two sons, and two daughters.

FOR MORE INFORMATION:

Berry, James H. "Autobiography of James H. Berry." *Carroll County Historical Quarterly* 1 (October 1956): 1–6.

Mulhollan, Paige E. "The Public Career of James H. Berry." Masters thesis, University of Arkansas, 1962.

Seagraves, Joe T. "James Henderson Berry, 1883–1885." In *The Governors of Arkansas: Essays in Political Biography,* ed. Timothy P. Donovan, Willard B. Gatewood, and Jeannie M. Whayne, 77–82. 2nd ed. Fayetteville: University of Arkansas Press, 1995.

CHAPTER IV

Twentieth-Century Politicians

Gov. John S. Little

Gov. John S. Little reached the apex of political leadership in Arkansas in 1906, only to quickly fall ill shortly after his inauguration and disappear from the political landscape altogether. Though little remembered a century after his death, Governor Little was an important leader in his day and a close ally of the lightning rod governor and senator Jeff Davis.

Born of pioneering settlers Jesse and Elizabeth Tatum Little in 1851, John Sebastian Little received his middle name to commemorate being the first male white child born in the newly created Sebastian County. Known to his friends as "Bass," he grew up on the family farm near the hamlet of Jenny Lind, south of Fort Smith. After a brief stint at Cane Hill College in Washington County, Little taught school for three years while reading law in his spare time. It was not unusual for bright young men to teach a few terms of country schools while reading law in a local law office. No less a politician than Senator Joe T. Robinson got his start teaching country schools. In 1874, Little began practicing law in Greenwood, the county seat of the southern part of Sebastian County, but soon moved his practice to Paris in nearby Logan County.

Little quickly moved into local Democratic Party politics, and within a year of moving to Logan County he was elected prosecuting attorney. In 1884 Little was sent to the state legislature, followed by election as a circuit judge two years later. He won election to Congress in 1894, and he was active in politics until illness cruelly took it all from him just as he reached the zenith of power. More on that later.

Jeff Davis was a decade younger than Little, being born May 6, 1862, the first anniversary of Arkansas's secession from the Union—and named in honor of Confederate President Jefferson Davis. His father, Lewis W. Davis, was a Baptist preacher-turned-lawyer who also ran a prosperous real estate business and served a term in the state legislature. Young Jeff lived a privileged childhood, capped off with attendance at the University of Arkansas, the Vanderbilt University Law

School, and Cumberland University. His father had to use political influence to get the minimum age rule waived so his nineteen-year-old son could be admitted to the bar.

Like Bass Little, Jeff Davis found the lure of politics beyond his resistance. He came of age politically in 1888 when he stumped the state for Democratic presidential nominee Grover Cleveland. In 1890 Davis, like Little, was elected a prosecuting attorney. In 1898 he won election as state attorney general after his main opponent died.

Like Bill Clinton many years later, Jeff Davis used his election as state attorney general to propel himself into the governor's office. Just as Attorney General Clinton fought against the unpopular Arkansas Power & Light Company, Attorney General Davis waged a loud and bitter war against a host of trusts, on one occasion filing suit against every fire insurance company in the state.

While Little was a good stump speaker, he was also known as a man of decorum. What Davis lacked in decorum he more than made up in energy, fiery oratory, virulent racism, and no small amount of demagoguery.

In 1900 Davis won the governor's office, trouncing a respected opponent. Like Clinton, Davis was a lightning rod—he was hated or adored—but his power rested on the thousands of small farmers who roared approval as Governor Davis railed against the "high-collared roosters in Little Rock."

Davis was the first Arkansas governor to be elected to three terms. But his power extended even further as he engineered the election of a supporter to the U.S. Senate. Then when Davis himself won election to the Senate in 1906, he helped Congressman John Sebastian Little win the governorship.

Little, like Davis, was opposed to big business trusts. On January 18, 1907, Little delivered a progressive inaugural address calling for more funding for public education, election reform, infrastructure investment, and abolition of the badly abused practice of convict leasing. Arkansans breathed a sigh of relief, thinking that the uproar of the Davis years was over.

Two days after his inauguration, Governor Little suffered a severe mental breakdown accompanied by a physical collapse. He never recovered, and Senate pro tempore X. O. Pindall completed Little's term. Little was to have been Senator Davis's proxy in Arkansas politics, but Pindall wrecked that scenario. X. O. Pindall was a bitter enemy of the newly elected Senator Davis and even had Davis's portrait moved from the capitol building reception room to the bathroom.

After Davis tried unsuccessfully in 1908 to engineer the election of his close ally William F. Kirby as governor, his political power declined as his once powerful machine grew rusty.

Davis died in 1913 at age fifty, before completing his Senate term, and was buried in Mount Holly Cemetery in Little Rock. Little lived on another three years, dying in the Arkansas State Hospital for Nervous Diseases in 1916. He was buried in City Cemetery in Greenwood.

FOR MORE INFORMATION:

Arsenault, Raymond. *The Wild Ass of the Ozarks: Jeff Davis and the Social Bases of Southern Politics.* Knoxville: University of Tennessee Press, 1988.

Gatewood, Willard B., Jr. "John Sebastian Little (1851–1916)." *The Encyclopedia of Arkansas History and Culture.* http://encyclopediaofarkansas.net/encyclopedia/entry-detail.aspx?search=1&entryID=112.

Sen. Joseph T. Robinson

Until Bill Clinton came along, Senator Joe T. Robinson was the Arkansan whose flame burned brightest on the national political scene. A precocious and ambitious young politician who, in less than a month in 1913, served as an Arkansas congressman, governor, and senator, Robinson rose to the pinnacle of American political power in 1933 when he became the majority leader of the U.S. Senate under the newly triumphant President Franklin D. Roosevelt.

Born on a farm near Lonoke in 1872, Joseph Taylor Robinson was the son of a country physician, farmer, and part-time Baptist preacher. Young Joe was not a very serious student, but his father had a large library, and young Joe usually read every night. After getting a teaching license at seventeen, he taught for two years while saving his meager earnings for college. In 1890, Robinson entered the University of Arkansas. After two years he returned to Lonoke County, where he read law under Judge Thomas C. Trimble. He also spent a brief time at the University of Virginia law school in 1895. Though not holding a degree, he was far better educated than the average lawyer of his day.

Barely twenty-one years of age, Robinson ran as a Democrat for the legislature from Lonoke County. He decisively defeated the Populist candidate in the general election, and thus from the very start of his political career Joe T. Robinson was seen as a stunningly successful political leader. He served only one term in the legislature but was noted for joining forces with reform elements who wanted to increase railroad regulation. The young state representative married Ewilda Gertrude Miller, also of Lonoke. They had no children.

After serving only one term, Robinson withdrew from politics and worked on his law practice for six years. By 1902 he was ready to reenter politics—this time as a candidate for the U.S. House of Representatives. He took a great chance in this campaign, for the favorite was a popular and long-serving prosecutor in Pine Bluff, Sam M. Taylor. Robinson, however, had a secret weapon in a cousin by the name of James P. Eagle.

Also a resident of Lonoke County, Eagle was a former governor and, more important, he was a high-ranking Baptist leader. Robinson decisively beat Taylor in what one newspaperman attributed to Robinson being full of "the vinegar of hopeful audacity."

Robinson served ten years in the U.S. House, but as a Democrat during a time of Republican ascendancy, he was forced to ally with progressive Republicans in usually futile attempts to regulate railroads, ensure pure food and drugs, adopt the graduated income tax, and allow voters to choose U.S. senators.

Obviously still full of the vinegar of hopeful audacity, Robinson announced in 1912 that he would run against U.S. Senator Jeff Davis, a rough-hewn but wildly popular former attorney general and governor who was completing his first term in the Senate. After taking an inventory of Davis's wide support, Robinson took a more conservative approach and ran against incumbent Gov. George Washington Donaghey, who was seeking a third term. Robinson and Donaghey were actually quite alike in being moderate progressives. Robinson won the Democratic primary in a landslide, perhaps in part because Arkansas voters have traditionally denied their governors a third term.

Before Robinson could be sworn in as governor, Senator Davis suffered a massive heart attack and died. The Arkansas General Assembly of 1913 elected Governor Robinson to succeed Davis in the Senate, but not before a deadlock developed that was eventually broken by the tiny delegation of Republicans who switched their votes from a favorite son to Robinson.

In less than two weeks, Robinson had left his seat in the U.S. House, been sworn in as governor, and then elected to the U.S. Senate. Robinson rose quickly through the Senate ranks. A strong supporter of Democratic President Woodrow Wilson, he was an internationalist and a partisan of reforms such as ending child labor. Like most Americans, Robinson was appalled by the global human losses resulting from World War I, and he became an ardent supporter of Wilson's proposed League of Nations. Robinson's biographer, Cecil E. Weller Jr., says Robinson earned "a reputation as a master tactician and excellent parliamentarian" during the League debates that later helped him be chosen as the chairman of the 1920 Democratic National Convention.

The 1920s were rough for Democrats in Congress. Republican

Warren G. Harding of Ohio led a resurgent GOP conquest of the White House that year, while the House and Senate saw large Republican majorities. This dark cloud, however, offered more than one silver lining for Joe T. Robinson, for he was above all a man of ambition. He attacked the reigning Republicans with glee, including withering denunciations of Sen. Henry Cabot Lodge of Massachusetts. The national press often covered these fiery speeches, and in 1923 Robinson's Democratic colleagues in the Senate elected him minority leader.

Robinson wasted no time in taking the fight to the Republicans when a variety of scandals shook the Harding administration, most particularly the Teapot Dome oil leases. Robinson was in the headlines almost daily attacking the Harding administration for "prostituting its authority" and other reprehensible acts. In 1924 Robinson was nominated as a favorite son candidate for president by the Arkansas delegation at the Democratic national convention. His national standing was such that Robinson was discussed as a serious contender after the convention failed to quickly select a nominee. After 102 ballots, the nod finally went to a Wall Street Lawyer, John W. Davis, who suffered defeat at the hands of Republican Calvin Coolidge that November.

Robinson, always the loyal Democrat, came out of the 1924 convention with renewed stature. Four years later, the Democrats chose Robinson as their vice presidential nominee, to run on the ticket with New York Gov. Al Smith. This was the first time an Arkansan had been nominated for national political office. It was also the first time a Roman Catholic had been nominated by a major party for president. Robinson was put on the ticket in the hope he could keep the South loyal to the Democrats. Robinson's work was cut out for him, for Smith was not only a Catholic but also a "wet," meaning he was against Prohibition. The Republicans nominated Herbert Hoover, a technocrat of considerable talent.

The 1928 presidential contest was one of bombast and vitriol, and Robinson represented Arkansas and the nation well during these harsh times. He struck out at the Ku Klux Klan and others who promoted religious bigotry, stating that America "must not imprison human thought." Warning that "terror and dread" were the fates of religious intolerance, Robinson fought to calm the fears of his fellow Southerners.

Joseph T. Robinson, U.S. senator and New Deal leader. *Photo courtesy of Special Collections, University of Arkansas Libraries.*

In the end, the Republicans carried the election, including some southern states—but, Robinson's star was still rising.

Hoover had barely settled in the White House before the Depression struck and the whole political scene began a rapid shift. The Republicans lost control of Congress in 1930, and suddenly, for the first time,

Robinson was majority leader of the Senate. Two years later the Democrats took the White House when Franklin D. Roosevelt thrashed Hoover in a landslide. Roosevelt, like the last Democratic president, Woodrow Wilson, found Robinson to be loyal and trustworthy.

Robinson was a rigid disciplinarian as majority leader, and he ensured that Roosevelt's legislative proposals were quickly adopted. He delivered Roosevelt's emergency banking bill from the Senate with a 73–7 margin and within eight hours of its introduction. Robinson also pushed through a raft of other seminal New Deal measures, including the Civilian Conservation Corps, various relief measures, and the Social Security Act.

Robinson was unable to deliver on one of Roosevelt's proposals— his efforts to lessen conservative control of the Supreme Court by enlarging the size of the high court. Dubbed the "court-packing bill," it would have added a new judge for every incumbent judge older than seventy. In private, Roosevelt promised one of the seats to Robinson, who then redoubled his efforts. Robinson maneuvered and cajoled, but the battle was tough and made worse by the torrid temperatures of July 1937 when the unair-conditioned Senate was sweltering.

The entire battle ended abruptly on July 14, 1937, when Sen. Joe T. Robinson died of an apparent heart attack. He was buried in Roselawn Cemetery in Little Rock. Robinson Auditorium in Little Rock, a New Deal project, was named for the senator, as was Joe T. Robinson High School in western Pulaski County.

FOR MORE INFORMATION:

Weller, Cecil E., Jr. *Joe T. Robinson: Always a Loyal Democrat.* Fayetteville: University of Arkansas Press, 1998.

Gov. Charles H. Brough

Gov. Charles H. Brough, Arkansas's only governor with a doctoral degree, was recognized as a leader in many fields in addition to politics, including education and religion. Brough gets high marks for his efforts to modernize Arkansas, especially his work on behalf of constitutional reform. A devout Baptist, Brough demonstrated that religious faith and modernization were compatible and he was a powerful counterweight to the growing fundamentalist movement within his denomination. He had the misfortune of being in office in the autumn of 1919, when a race conflict erupted in Elaine, Phillips County. His legacy has suffered from his inability to comprehend the scope or nature of the trials that followed the conflict, in which twelve black men were tortured into confessing.

Born in Clinton, Mississippi, on July 9, 1876, Charles Hillman Brough (pronounced "Bruff") was the son of Milton Brough, a Pennsylvania native who had served in the Union army during the Civil War and eventually settled in Utah. His mother, Flora Thompson Brough, was a native of Maine who had grown up in Mississippi. By the time the couple married and had their son, Milton Brough was already a prosperous mine owner and banker in Utah Territory.

The first six years of Charles's youth was spent in Utah, before his family sent him to live with relatives in Clinton to take advantage of the educational facilities there. Mrs. Brough became ill and died in 1885, leaving the nine-year-old Charles and his seven-year-old brother, Knight, to be raised by their relatives in Mississippi.

Charles was a bright child who entered Mississippi College, a Baptist men's school in Clinton, at the age of fourteen. He was an outstanding student, especially excelling in oratory, an important subject at that time. In 1894 he graduated with high honors and then enrolled in graduate school at Johns Hopkins University in New Jersey. At Johns Hopkins, Brough studied history under Herbert Baxter Adams, one of the fathers of modern historical study. Again he earned high marks, and in 1898 he received a Ph.D. degree in history, economics, and jurisprudence.

Immediately after receiving his degree, Brough began teaching at Mississippi College, his alma mater. Shortly thereafter, he left his professorship to enter the University of Mississippi law school, completing the two-year course in one year with high honors. Instead of practicing law, however, he immediately returned to teaching.

In 1903 Brough accepted a professorship in political economy at the University of Arkansas in Fayetteville. He was a popular professor. In the days before rigid academic specialization, Brough taught courses in economics, transportation, tariff history, sociology, and law. He helped organize the Southern Sociological Congress in 1912, and the following year he was elected president of the Arkansas State Teachers Association. A popular orator, he gave speeches throughout the state—including stumping for Democratic candidates during election contests. In 1908 he took time out to marry Anne Wade Roark of Kentucky. They had no children.

Gradually Brough was drawn into elective politics. In 1916, he defeated the popular Secretary of State Earle W. Hodges to become the Democratic nominee for governor in 1916. He was reelected in 1918, with the Republicans endorsing him over Socialist Clay Fulks.

Brough's tenure as governor was part of a larger national phenomenon known as the progressive movement. As historian Foy Lisenby has written, "Arkansas progressivism reached maturity during Brough's two terms." He was a strong advocate for improving Arkansas's abysmal educational system, including creating a stable funding source for the schools, accepting federal educational funds, fighting illiteracy, and adopting a state compulsory-attendance law. The school attendance law promised more than it delivered, for whole counties could opt out.

Brough got the legislature to provide for a state commission on charities and corrections, which improved juvenile courts and lent assistance to needy mothers with dependent children. Brough was also proud of convincing the legislature to create the Arkansas Corporation Commission, which was supposed to regulate public utilities. He pushed constitutional revision, prohibition, good roads, and extending the vote to women, although not with uniform success. Governor Brough was a strong supporter of President Woodrow Wilson, a fellow southern progressive with an academic background.

Perhaps the most serious blow to Brough's gubernatorial administration was his failure to ensure fair treatment of the black defendants convicted in the aftermath of the Elaine race violence of 1919. An educated man who believed that black citizens deserved fair, though segregated, treatment, Brough was still unable to overcome his deep-seated racism. He refused to pardon the twelve black men who received death sentences after the Elaine race murders, although it was clear the men had been denied fair trials.

Leaving the governorship in 1921, Brough took a job as publicity agent for the Arkansas Advancement Association, which was similar to a state chamber of commerce. He gave lectures far and wide, including a stint on the Redpath Chautauqua, a national lecture circuit immensely popular at that time. In his position with the Advancement Association, Brough was a tireless promoter and defender of Arkansas. Baltimore journalist and gadfly Henry Mencken was not a fan of the "miasmatic jungles" of Arkansas. Brough and Mencken frequently exchanged barbed letters and telegrams, with Brough often coming off as pompous and a bit sanctimonious.

A longtime Baptist lay leader, Brough became president of Central Baptist College in Conway in 1928. This brought about a period of intense controversy and discord, as 1928 was an election year, and the loyal Democrat Brough campaigned for Alfred E. Smith, the Democratic nominee for president. Smith was reviled by many Arkansas Baptists, for he was a Catholic who supported repeal of prohibition. Conservative Baptists were also appalled when Brough came out against a measure on the 1928 ballot to outlaw the teaching of evolution. Brough fought back tenaciously and directly, accusing the anti-Smith Baptists of religious bigotry and the anti-evolutionists of being narrow minded. Ultimately, he resigned from the presidency of Central Baptist College.

For a few years Brough worked as a public relations representative for the University of Arkansas. In 1932 he mounted an unsuccessful race for the U.S. Senate, losing to incumbent Hattie Caraway. In December 1935, Brough died of a heart attack in Washington, D.C., where he was chairing a federal commission charged with fixing the border between Virginia and the District of Columbia. After being eulogized as "Arkansas' ambassador of good will," he was buried in Roselawn Cemetery in Little Rock.

FOR MORE INFORMATION:

Dougan, Michael B. "Charles Hillman Brough (1876–1935)." *The Encyclopedia of Arkansas History and Culture.* http://encyclopediaofarkansas.net/encyclopedia/entry-detail.aspx?search=1&entryID=89.

Lisenby, Foy. *Charles Hillman Brough: A Biography.* Fayetteville: University of Arkansas Press, 1996.

———. "Brough, Baptists, and Bombast: The Election of 1928." *Arkansas Historical Quarterly* 32 (Summer 1973): 120–31.

Sen. Thaddeus Caraway

Thaddeus Caraway represented Arkansas in the U.S. Senate through-out the turbulent 1920s, yet his place in the pantheon of Arkansas history has been overshadowed by his more famous wife and successor, Sen. Hattie Caraway. Mrs. Caraway was the first woman to be elected to the U.S. Senate. When Professor Calvin R. Ledbetter published an article on Thaddeus a few years ago, he titled it "The Other Caraway."

Hattie Caraway deserves all the attention she gets as the first woman elected to the U.S. Senate. She also defeated a raft of prominent politicians during her day, including John L. McClellan—who later had a long career in Congress. Her husband, however, was a significant political leader in his own right.

Thaddeus Horatius Caraway was born on a farm near Spring Hill, Missouri, on October 17, 1871, to a country doctor, Tolbert F. Caraway, and Mary Scates Caraway. The family moved to Tennessee when Thad was a young child, and his father died soon thereafter. He attended the public schools and in 1896 graduated from Dickson Normal College in Dickson, Tennessee.

While in college, Thad worked as a cotton picker, a sawmill laborer, and a railroad worker. He also made time to meet, court, and become engaged to Hattie Ophelia Wyatt, who also graduated from Dickson in 1896. He delayed getting married until 1902 in order to study law and establish a practice in Craighead County, first at Lake City and later at Jonesboro.

A Democrat, Caraway made his first foray into politics in 1908 when he won election as prosecuting attorney for the second judicial district, in northeast Arkansas. In 1912 Caraway took a dramatic political gamble by challenging ten-year incumbent First District Congressman R. B. Macon of Helena.

From the start of his political career, Caraway described himself as sympathizing with the working class, and this strategy worked well. He attacked his opponent as out of touch and aloof, and he took advantage of regional rivalries within the First Congressional District, which comprised eleven counties. Caraway's base was in Craighead County in the north of the district, while Macon was from Phillips County in the southern part. On election day, Caraway received huge majorities in the northern part and carried the election with over 60 percent of the vote.

Caraway entered Congress in 1913, when Democrat Woodrow Wilson began his first term as president. He was an ardent supporter of Wilson's progressive reform measures, especially workmen's compensation legislation, child labor laws, and various bills to assist farmers. The creation of the Federal Land Bank in 1916 was in part a product of his efforts. He also supported constitutional amendments to prohibit the sale of alcohol and to extend the vote to women.

Perhaps Caraway's most far-sighted work was on behalf of President Wilson's ill-fated proposal for an international peace-keeping body, the League of Nations. He attacked the Republican opponents of the League, predicting that the defeat of the League might "plunge the world again into war."

In 1920 Representative Caraway embarked upon another risky political venture when he filed against incumbent U.S. Sen. William F. Kirby. Kirby, who was completing the term of Sen. James P. Clarke, who died in 1916, had been an Arkansas attorney general as well as a member of the state supreme court.

Kirby had incurred considerable public wrath when he opposed President Wilson's efforts to enter World War I against the Germans. Caraway used Kirby's reluctance to go to war as a defining issue in the Democratic primary and won with an amazing 63 percent of the vote. He even managed to tie the vote in Miller County, where Kirby lived.

After almost a decade in the House, Caraway settled quickly into the Senate, where his colleague from Arkansas, Joseph T. Robinson, would soon be minority leader. He served on several important committees, including Agriculture and Commerce.

Caraway was as fiercely critical of Republican presidents as he was loyal to Wilson. Employing what the *Arkansas Gazette* called "a sarcastic tongue and a quick wit," he soon became known as "Caustic Caraway." Even Joe T. Robinson conceded that Caraway's "command of sarcasm and irony sometimes inflicted wounds that were not quickly healed."

Perhaps Caraway's greatest passion was his lengthy and unsuccessful attempt to abolish trading in agricultural futures. However, it was

Thaddeus and Hattie Caraway, two distinctively different senators. *Photo courtesy of Prints and Photographs Division, Library of Congress.*

the Teapot Dome scandal during the administration of Republican President Warren G. Harding that gave Caraway a national profile. He led the successful effort in the Senate to nullify the oil leases that caused the scandal. Caraway also played a leading role in forcing the resignation of U.S. Attorney General Harry M. Daugherty, who was caught up in an ongoing scandal.

During the early years of the Great Depression, Caraway worked hard to convince the Republican Congress and President Herbert Hoover to provide emergency relief to destitute farm families. He also supported providing pensions for the elderly, and he called for increased benefits for veterans.

In October 1931 Caraway had a kidney stone removed, and eight days later the sixty-year-old senator died of a blood clot. He was buried at West Lawn Cemetery in Jonesboro. Two weeks later Caraway's widow was appointed as his successor.

FOR MORE INFORMATION:

Clements, Derek Allen. "Thaddeus Horatius Caraway (1871–1931)." *The Encyclopedia of Arkansas History and Culture.* http://encyclopediaofarkansas. net/encyclopedia/entry-detail.aspx?search=1&entryID=1611.

Ledbetter, Calvin R. "The Other Caraway: Senator Thaddeus H. Caraway." *Arkansas Historical Quarterly* 64 (Summer 2005): 123–45.

Sen. Hattie Caraway

While Arkansas might not have been a leader in many areas of human rights, the state has been remarkably progressive in relation to women's rights. Arkansas was among the early states in recognizing the legal rights of married women, and the suffragette movement took early root in the state. Any doubts about Arkansas's pioneering status in women's political rights came in 1932 when Arkansans elected the first woman to the U.S. Senate. Hattie Caraway suddenly arose on the political scene in 1931 when her husband, Sen. Thaddeus Caraway, died in office and Hattie was appointed to succeed him. The following year she not only won election in her own right, she also managed to overcome a phalanx of powerful political leaders who underestimated "the little woman."

Born in 1878 in Tennessee, Hattie Ophelia Wyatt met Thaddeus Horatius Caraway, her future husband, while both were students at Dickson Normal College in that state. They were married in 1902, not long after Thaddeus opened a law practice in Lake City near Jonesboro.

After a brief but successful career as a prosecuting attorney, Thaddeus won election to Congress in 1912, defeating an incumbent. After four terms in the House, he defeated another incumbent in 1920 to become a U.S. senator. An ardent Democrat with a sarcastic tongue, he was known as a reformer and a champion of the common citizen. He died suddenly in November 1931.

Gov. Harvey Parnell named Hattie Caraway to succeed her husband, and then she won a special election in 1932 to fill out the remaining year of her late husband's term. Everyone expected the diminutive widow to serve quietly and then retire. Everyone, that is, except Hattie —and Huey Long!

Hattie and Huey Long, the senator from Louisiana known as the "King Fish," were seatmates in the Senate, and they developed a political relationship over time. Hattie found herself agreeing with Huey's strident calls for a national "Share the Wealth" plan. When Hattie unexpectedly filed for a full term on May 9, 1932, only hours before the filing deadline, the stage was set for one of the great political showdowns in Arkansas history.

Arrayed against Hattie in the Democratic primary campaign was a Who's Who of political leaders, including O. L. Bodenhamer, an El Dorado businessman and American Legion leader; former governor and Baptist lay leader Charles H. Brough; former U.S. senator and state attorney general William F. Kirby; and two other lesser-known candidates.

While Hattie Caraway did not have much of a political base, she did have the ardent support of Senator Long. Historians have speculated on Huey's motive in supporting Caraway, with many believing that his major motivation was his hatred for Arkansas's other U.S. senator, majority leader Joe T. Robinson. Whatever his motivation, Huey Long spent the first week of August 1932 campaigning for "this courageous little woman."

One historian has described Long's whirlwind campaign for Caraway as "a circus hitched to a tornado." The Huey-Hattie foray signaled the introduction of modern political campaigning in Arkansas. Huey arrived from Louisiana with a whole caravan, including sound trucks, literature vans, and advance men who raced across the state arranging one speech after another.

Arkansans came out in the thousands to listen as Huey attacked the "moneyed interests" while simultaneously portraying Hattie as "a poor widder woman" who had been targeted for removal by "the big men of Wall Street." Huey's weeklong speaking tour started off in Magnolia, where he gave a blistering speech before a giant crowd. A local politician wired anti-Caraway forces in Little Rock, "A cyclone just went through here and is headed your way. Very few trees left standing and even these are badly scarred up." In seven days of campaigning Huey delivered thirty-nine speeches, covered 2,100 miles, and spoke before an estimated 200,000 people. His Little Rock speech alone attracted about 30,000 people, for many years considered the largest political gathering in Arkansas history.

On primary election day, August 9, 1932, while Huey was taking the train back to Louisiana, Arkansans voted overwhelmingly for Mrs. Caraway. She carried sixty-one of the seventy-five counties, garnering as many votes as all her opponents combined.

Senator Caraway's tenure in the Senate was quiet and mostly

uneventful. Hattie was not given to making speeches, but she did establish herself as a steady ally of newly elected President Franklin D. Roosevelt. She was the first female to preside over the Senate, the first to chair a subcommittee, the first female to become a senior senator, and the first to take part in a filibuster. Like most southern senators, she opposed civil rights legislation, though she did support a proposed constitutional amendment to grant equal rights to women. Not forgetting the rural state she served, Hattie also served on the Senate Agriculture Committee, an assignment she requested.

In 1938 Hattie continued her reputation as a giant-killer, defeating Congressman John L. McClellan of Camden in a tight race. Six years later, however, she was defeated by Congressman J. William Fulbright, coming in last in a field of four candidates.

Hattie stayed in Washington after her defeat, serving on the U.S. Employee Compensation Commission. In January 1950 she suffered a stroke, which left her partly paralyzed. She died in December 1950 and was buried next to her husband in Jonesboro's West Lawn Cemetery.

In 2001 the U.S. Postal Service released a postage stamp in honor of Mrs. Caraway.

FOR MORE INFORMATION:

Crawford, Julienne. "Hattie Ophelia Wyatt Caraway (1878–1950)." *The Encyclopedia of Arkansas History and Culture*. http://encyclopediaofarkansas.net/ encyclopedia/entry-detail.aspx?search=1&entryID=1278.

Kincaid, Diane, ed. *Silent Hattie Speaks: The Personal Journal of Senator Hattie Caraway*. Westport, CT: Greenwood Press, 1979.

Malone, David. *Hattie and Huey: An Arkansas Tour*. Fayetteville: University of Arkansas Press, 1989.

Towns, Stuart. "A Louisiana Medicine Show: The Kingfish Elects an Arkansas Senator." *Arkansas Historical Quarterly* 25 (Summer 1966): 117–27.

Rep. Claude A. Fuller

No single man changed the face of north Arkansas, but Congressman Claude A. Fuller of Eureka Springs certainly had a major impact through his support of damming rivers. Fuller, while a member of Congress during the 1930s, secured approval of legislation that created a string of huge lakes along the White River in north Arkansas. The lakes, however, are merely the most obvious of Fuller's endeavors; he was a political power for much of his life, a businessman with broad interests, and a popular member of the community.

Claude Albert Fuller was born January 20, 1876, in Springhill, Illinois, but his father moved the family to Eureka Springs to work as a carpenter while Claude was still a child. He attended the public schools in Eureka Springs before studying for two years at Kent College of Law in Chicago. After two more years of reading law in Eureka Springs, Fuller was admitted to the bar in 1898. During all those years Fuller worked at a variety of jobs, including shining shoes and driving a mule-drawn streetcar. Symbolic of his general success, he later owned the streetcar company.

The same year Fuller was admitted to the bar, he was elected city clerk of Eureka Springs—the first of many political positions he held over a long life. In 1902 he was elected as a Democrat to the state House of Representatives, where he served through 1906. As a leading legislator, young Fuller participated in hearings on the state penitentiary, and he helped draft legislation to reform the agency.

In 1906 Fuller was elected mayor of Eureka Springs, a post he held until 1910, and then again during 1920–28. He worked hard to extend the city water and sewerage systems, and he also helped build a new courthouse. During his second period as mayor, he oversaw construction of a city auditorium, a historic structure that still functions. Perhaps the citizens of Eureka Springs most appreciated Fuller's efforts to pave the city streets for the first time. After two terms as prosecuting attorney for Carroll, Madison, Benton, and Washington counties,

Fuller retired from politics for a few years—excepting his service on the Eureka Springs School Board during 1914–1928.

As a major campaign volunteer for successful gubernatorial candidate Charles H. Brough in 1916, Fuller built a lasting political power base. He later used his relationship with Governor Brough to get a prison labor camp established in Carroll County to help complete public highway construction.

Fuller's political career reached its zenith with his election to Congress in 1928, the year Republican nominee Herbert Hoover took the White House. With the economy riding high, the future seemed bright for the Republicans in control of Congress. The onset of the Depression in 1929 ushered in a political earthquake that changed the political landscape for many years to come. Fuller was a strong opponent of the Hawley-Smoot Tariff Act of 1930, which probably made the depression much worse. By the time Franklin D. Roosevelt entered the White House in March 1933, the Democrats were already in firm control of the House, and Representative Fuller was well positioned for political leadership. His role as a leader in the election of Speaker of the House Henry T. Raney helped ensure Fuller's appointment to the Ways and Means Committee, one of the most powerful in Congress.

With the coming of the New Deal, public works flowed to Fuller's district. He got millions of dollars in appropriations for the University of Arkansas, as well as equally large amounts for road construction. He received substantial credit for securing federal funding for a new Veterans Administration Hospital in Fayetteville. No doubt his close political affiliation with Sen. Joe T. Robinson, the majority leader in the U.S. Senate, helped Fuller secure federal largesse.

Fuller considered himself a loyal "New Deal Democrat," and he was a vigorous supporter of Roosevelt's Social Security proposal. In 1938 Fuller sponsored legislation to establish flood control dams along the entire White River Basin. This resulted in the dams at Norfolk, Bull Shoals, Table Rock, and Beaver.

Fuller was defeated for reelection in 1938 when a younger and far more liberal New Dealer, Clyde Ellis, waged a fierce campaign with the assistance of newspaper editor Roberta Fulbright of Fayetteville.

Fuller quickly adjusted to life back in Eureka Springs, pitching headfirst into business again. He invigorated his law practice, where he already had a reputation as a tenacious and successful defense attorney. He continued to dabble in real estate, including owning the Basin Park Hotel for many years. He remained a booster for Eureka Springs even into old age, including supporting Gerald L. K. Smith's controversial plan that built the "Christ of the Ozarks." Fuller's retirement was enlivened by his two grandsons, who lived in Eureka Springs. He served as president of the Bank of Eureka Springs from 1930 until his death in January 1968, only a few days short of his ninety-second birthday. He was buried in Odd Fellows Cemetery in Eureka Springs.

FOR MORE INFORMATION:

Beals, Frank L. *Backwoods Baron: The Life Story of Claude Albert Fuller.* Wheaton, IL: Morton Publishing Co., 1951.

"Third District Congressman in '30s Dies." *Arkansas Gazette,* January 9, 1968.

Rep. Clyde T. Ellis

Clyde T. Ellis did as much as any single individual to advance Arkansas: he can be given credit for bringing electricity to the state's vast rural areas. Harvey Couch, the visionary founder of Arkansas Power & Light Company, built his business by providing electricity to residents of more densely settled areas where return on investment was much higher. Ellis was ready and waiting when the New Deal's rural electrification program came on the scene.

Born in Benton County in 1908, Ellis grew up on a farm near Garfield. In his later years, Ellis recalled Garfield as a "fine community" with two doctors, a drug store, bank, depot, two garages, cafés, several stores, an elementary school, and a high school. After attending the University of Arkansas, he was employed as a teacher and superintendent of schools in Garfield. His unsuccessful efforts to get electricity for the school caused him to become a crusader for extending electrical power to rural areas.

In 1932 Ellis won election to the Arkansas House of Representatives, and two years later he was elected to the state senate. He immediately introduced and secured passage of legislation to create a rural electrification program in Arkansas through the use of cooperatives.

Only 10 percent of American farms had electrical power in 1935, and the power companies were reluctant to sink the vast sums needed to extend electrical transmission lines to rural areas. Ellis recalled in his autobiography, "Those of us who experienced what really happened ... know, first hand, of the sheer arrogance of utility executives in their dealings with rural people. I remember it well in my own state of Arkansas. I can remember the trips I made with my father to what is now the Southwestern Electric Power Company office [where] he literally pleaded with them to build lines into the hill country where we lived."

Buoyed by his success at the state level, Ellis ran for Congress in 1938 as a New Deal Democrat. After a campaign of 187 speeches, he defeated incumbent Congressman Claude Fuller by fewer than 200 votes. While he had an interest in a variety of reform initiatives, his passion remained rural electrification.

Working closely with such powerful congressmen as Lyndon Johnson of Texas and George W. Norris of Nebraska, Ellis pushed for the development of hydroelectric plants. He was able to amend the Flood Control Act of 1938 to get hydroelectric generation capacity included in flood-control dams being built along the White River. These were among the early hydroelectric plants built under federal legislation.

Ellis and his New Deal allies were much less successful in creating an Arkansas River equivalent of the Tennessee Valley Authority (TVA). Arkansas Power & Light Company worked through U.S. Senate Majority Leader Joe T. Robinson to keep the federal government out of power production in Arkansas.

Having grown up near the Pea Ridge Civil War battlefield, Ellis worked for years to have it recognized as a national park. Though his efforts failed, the park was authorized in 1956 with the support of his successor, Congressman James Trimble.

In 1942 Ellis entered the race for the U.S. Senate, but he was defeated by former Congressman John L. McClellan. He was then appointed general manager of the new National Rural Electric Cooperative Association (NRECA), a nonprofit group that promoted public power. He named Arkansas attorney Thomas B. Fitzhugh as NRECA legal counsel.

For the next twenty-five years Ellis used the NRECA to promote public utilities, frequently advocating consumer needs over corporate interests. The NRECA was especially crucial in organizing political support for the Federal Rural Electrification Administration (REA). His contacts in Congress were crucial to his success, with Lyndon Johnson and Sam Reyburn being especially supportive.

Ellis had the opportunity to be at his parent's farm in 1940 when their home was electrified. He recalled later that though the lights glowed dimly, his mother wept with happiness. In addition to lights, electricity made possible running water, refrigeration, radio, and a multitude of conveniences that transformed daily life—especially for women.

In 1966, shortly before his retirement, Ellis published a memoir titled

A Giant Step (Random House). He died in 1980. A World War II Navy veteran, he was buried at Arlington National Cemetery in Washington, D.C. When an electrical power generating station on the Arkansas River was built at Barling in 1988, it was named for Ellis, an honor that would undoubtedly have brought a broad smile to Clyde T. Ellis.

FOR MORE INFORMATION:

Chesnutt, Ed F. "Rural Electrification in Arkansas, 1935–1940: The Formative Years." *Arkansas Historical Quarterly* 46 (Autumn 1987): 215–60.

Ellis, Clyde T. *A Giant Step.* New York: Random House, 1966.

Gov. Winthrop Rockefeller

Winthrop Rockefeller had a profound impact on Arkansas—an impact that lives long after his untimely death. Today Arkansans vote for Republicans as if it is the most natural thing in the world, but such was not the case in 1966 when Rockefeller became the first GOP governor since Reconstruction. His tenure as governor changed Arkansas government forever. Politics aside, Winthrop Rockefeller's generosity changed Arkansas while he lived, and through his philanthropies his contributions continue.

Born on May 1, 1912, Rockefeller was the son of John D. Jr. and Abbey Aldrich Rockefeller. He grew up in unsurpassed affluence, attending prestigious private schools and Yale University, though he withdrew before graduation. Unwilling to immediately accept a post in the family businesses, Rockefeller went to Texas in 1936, where he took a job as an oil field roughneck. For the remainder of his life he spoke of that year in the oil fields as a wonderful experience. Almost a year before the attack on Pearl Harbor, he joined the U.S. Army as a private. Military life, which allowed him to avoid the crushing expectations and traditions of his family, suited him just fine.

W.R., as he would become known in his Arkansas circles, should have stayed in the military after World War II, for his return to the family business in New York resulted in a playboy lifestyle, followed by a brief marriage and highly publicized divorce. He looked around for an escape and found the antithesis of New York City—rural Petit Jean Mountain, Arkansas.

Rockefeller threw himself into work on behalf of his new community. His family had inculcated a philanthropic ethic in each of their children, and Winthrop was no exception. With the assistance of over $1 million in Rockefeller support, the Morrilton Public School District became a member of the Model School Program. He spearheaded an effort to open a medical clinic in neighboring Perry County, one of the poorest in the state. He helped steer Rockefeller Brothers Fund gifts to Arkansas institutions, including extensive support for mental health services. The arts benefited substantially from Rockefeller benevolence and interest, especially that of his second wife, Jeanette. Their money and leadership allowed the Arkansas Arts Center to hire a professional staff and sponsor meaningful exhibitions and education. They funded the "Arkansas Arts Mobile," a specially fitted bus that took the arts into the most remote schools.

At first Rockefeller was nonpolitical, even serving as Democratic Governor Orval Faubus's chairman of the Arkansas Industrial Development Commission. He is credited with attracting over six hundred industrial plants to the poor state during his tenure. Rockefeller and Faubus gradually grew apart, however, and in 1964 W.R., running as a Republican, unsuccessfully challenged the five-term incumbent governor. Two years later he won a narrow victory, followed by an even smaller success in 1968. Dale Bumpers, then a little-known lawyer from Charleston, defeated Rockefeller in 1970. In less than three years Rockefeller died of cancer.

With each passing year historians are able to evaluate Rockefeller's administration with more detachment and objectivity. His touted "Era of Excellence" might have promised more than it delivered, but he was acknowledged to be personally honest, a great believer in his adopted state, and a good father to his only child, Winthrop Paul Rockefeller, who served as lieutenant governor prior to his premature death in 2006.

It is likely that Rockefeller's greatest contribution to Arkansas history was his work bringing black Arkansans into the mainstream. The Rockefeller family had been active in civil rights for African Americans for decades, and Winthrop was personally committed to this work. Local Conway County residents must have been shocked when the newly arrived Rockefeller brought along a black friend from New York, Jimmy Hudson, to manage Winrock Farms. W.R. was active in the Urban League as well as the Arkansas Council on Human Relations.

Upon his election as governor, Rockefeller made more substantive changes. He began hiring blacks for positions other than the janitorial crew. African Americans were also appointed to boards and commissions in large numbers, including local draft boards. Even some of Rockefeller's close aides opposed his appointment of William L.

"Sonny" Walker to head up the Office of Economic Opportunity—the first African American to direct a state agency. On the day after Martin Luther King's murder in April 1968, the governor stood on the capitol steps and joined hands with black leaders to sing "We Shall Overcome." By the time he left office in 1971, Rockefeller had brought 1,500 black Arkansans into state employment, including 170 holding administrative posts.

Rockefeller's work for prison reform was one of his most significant, even though it probably cost him votes. Inheriting a prison system known throughout America for its brutality and corruption, Governor Rockefeller brought in professional criminologist Tom Murton to reform the prison system. Unfortunately, Murton was unable to work as a part of a team, and his theatrical shenanigans shortened his tenure and set back prison reform in the state.

Decades after his death, Winthrop Rockefeller still has a profound impact on Arkansas and much of the world. He left much of his great fortune to the Winthrop Rockefeller Foundation and the Winthrop Rockefeller Trust, both headquartered in Little Rock, and Winrock International, a philanthropy with an international focus and headquartered at Winrock Farms on Petit Jean Mountain for many years. In recent years Winrock Farms was donated to the University of Arkansas System, which developed the Winthrop Rockefeller Institute as an educational conference center.

Winthrop Rockefeller caused many Arkansans to walk a little taller, pleased in the realization that a sophisticated New York–born heir of great wealth had chosen to live in their small, struggling state.

FOR MORE INFORMATION:

Dillard, Tom W. "Winthrop Rockefeller." In *The Governors of Arkansas: Essays in Political Biography*, edited by Timothy P. Donovan, Willard B. Gatewood Jr., and Jeannie M. Whayne, 236–45. 2nd ed. Fayetteville: University of Arkansas Press, 1995.

Ward, John L. *The Arkansas Rockefeller*. Baton Rouge: Louisiana State University Press, 1978.

———. *Winthrop Rockefeller, Philanthropist: A Life of Change*. Fayetteville: University of Arkansas Press, 2004.

Lt. Gov. Maurice "Footsie" Britt

Maurice Britt was one of those men who could do anything. He was a star athlete, a World War II hero, and a successful businessman. In 1966 Britt was elected the first Republican lieutenant governor of Arkansas since Reconstruction.

Britt was born in 1919 near Carlisle on a rice farm. His father died when Maurice was only thirteen years of age. Nevertheless, he excelled at Lonoke High School, serving as class president on one occasion and as valedictorian in 1937. He won a number of essay contests and was recognized for achievement in both English and Latin. It was his classmates at Lonoke who bestowed the nickname of "Footsie" due to Maurice's size thirteen feet.

Young Maurice's athletic achievements were even more amazing. He ran track, was a shot-putter, and was also a pole-vaulter. During his senior year, Maurice was captain of the Lonoke Jackrabbits track, basketball, and football teams. He was immediately offered an athletic scholarship by the University of Arkansas, where he lettered in both basketball and football, in addition to maintaining an active academic life. During his senior year Britt was named an honorable mention All-American. He was sports editor for the student newspaper, the *Arkansas Traveler*. For almost a year he played professional football for the Detroit Lions, after graduating with a journalism degree in 1941. He was elected to the Arkansas Sports Hall of Fame in 1972.

Britt's professional football career was ended after a few months by World War II when he was drafted into the U.S. Army. By November 1942, Britt was aboard a ship bound for Morocco. He served as a company commander in the 3rd Infantry Division, fighting in battles in North Africa and Sicily before landing in Italy.

It was during the campaign to take Rome that Britt began to see real action and to demonstrate incredible bravery under fire. During a fierce fight on Mount Rontondo in Italy on November 10, 1943, Britt and a small company of men wiped out a large force of attacking

Germans. An American battalion was in danger of being surrounded when Britt sprung into action. He single-handedly led a counterattack that stopped the offensive. Britt was credited with killing eleven enemies and personally taking four prisoners. It was later reckoned that Britt threw thirty-two hand grenades during the attack. This was despite the fact that Britt had been shot in the side, and his chest, face, and hands were covered with grenade wounds.

Meantime, Britt was headed toward Anzio, where he led his company ashore. In February 1944, while taking shelter in an old farmhouse, Britt was severely injured by an artillery shell. He awoke in a military hospital, with his right arm amputated and his right leg badly wounded. Britt was on a hospital ship on his way home when he learned that he had been awarded a Congressional Medal of Honor for the earlier action on Mount Rontondo.

Britt was presented his Congressional Medal of Honor during the 1944 annual commencement at the University of Arkansas in Fayetteville. He was the first American soldier to be awarded the three highest honors bestowed by the nation—the Congressional Medal of Honor, the Distinguished Service Cross, and the Silver Star—in addition to the Bronze Star and Purple Heart.

After the War, Britt settled in Fort Smith, where he joined his wife's family business. Later he established his own business in Fort Smith, where he was a pillar of the community. In 1966, he announced that he was running for lieutenant governor on the Republican ticket. His Democratic opponent was a respected Hope lawyer and judge, James Pilkinton.

The election of 1966 was a watershed one for Arkansas. Perennial governor Orval Faubus did not seek reelection, and the Democratic Party nominated the last of Arkansas's old-time segregationists, Jim Johnson. The GOP gubernatorial nominee was Winthrop Rockefeller, a racial moderate, who reached out to newly enfranchised black voters and won the election. Footsie Britt won too, but the results were so close that the outcome was in doubt for days. Rockefeller and Britt were reelected in 1968, by even smaller margins. Britt did not run for reelection in 1970, and later President Richard Nixon named him district director of the federal Small Business Administration (SBA).

After retiring from the SBA in 1985, Britt made one last foray into politics. He ran for the Republican nomination for governor in 1986 but was defeated handily by former governor Frank D. White, who in turn lost to incumbent Gov. Bill Clinton.

After living a relaxed retirement filled with fishing trips to Lonoke County, Footsie Britt died November 27, 1995, at the age of seventy-six. He was buried in the Little Rock National Cemetery.

FOR MORE INFORMATION:

"Maurice Britt Obituary." *Arkansas Democrat-Gazette,* November 28, 1995.

Withers, Ellen E. "'Footsie' Britt (1919–1995)." *The Encyclopedia of Arkansas History and Culture.* http://encyclopediaofarkansas.net/encyclopedia/entry-detail.aspx?search=1&entryID=2459.

CHAPTER V

The Law

Nelson Hacket

An Arkansas runaway slave named Nelson Hacket fled Washington County in 1841, an odyssey that ultimately failed, but not before making an international impact. Hacket fled by way of Michigan to freedom in Canada, only to be extradited to Arkansas and the shackles of slavery again. The Hacket case resulted in an international incident, and ultimately the case galvanized the British abolitionists into successfully demanding that the British government refuse to extradite runaway slaves.

Nelson Hacket was about thirty years old when he became the possession of Alfred Wallace in June 1840. Wallace, a prosperous farmer and merchant in the Fayetteville area, owned four other slaves. Serving as a valet and butler, Hacket was a highly trusted and valued "servant," as polite society put it. This did not keep Hacket from planning a daring escape. In mid-July 1841, while his owner was in central Arkansas, Hacket made his move. He took a "fine beaver coat," a gold watch, and a comfortable saddle. Most important, he stole Wallace's fine race horse to carry him northward.

Roads were primitive in 1841, especially on the western frontier, but Hacket was smart enough to rest during the day and travel at night. He apparently had little to eat other than berries and other wild foods. At the Mississippi River, he had the good fortune to happen upon a ferry tended by a sympathetic African American. He received food, valuable information, and a ride across the swirling river. Eventually, he made his way across the Ohio River into Illinois.

Illinois was a free state, and Hacket was able to travel during the day. He received assistance from several sources as he journeyed across Illinois, Indiana, Ohio, and through Michigan to Detroit. After six weeks of hard riding, Hacket strode aboard the ferry across the Detroit River and then to a runaway settlement near Sandwich, Canada, about fifty miles from the American border. He thought himself free.

Alfred Wallace had other plans. Indeed, Wallace set out looking for Hacket within days of his flight. A Washington County official, probably a deputy sheriff, pursued Hacket to Ohio, where he learned of the runaway's destination. Wallace arrived in Windsor, Canada, only a week after Hacket. Wallace immediately filed an affidavit describing Hacket's thefts of his owner's horse, coat, and other items. The next day, Wallace and the deputy located Hacket, whom they beat "with the butt of a whip, and a large stick." The runaway was arrested and thrown into the local jail. Wallace then convinced Michigan authorities to request the extradition of Hacket as a fugitive criminal. The local Canadian attorney general refused to honor the extradition, pointing out that Hacket had never been tried by a court of law.

The scene now shifted back to Arkansas, where Wallace initiated criminal charges, and a Washington County grand jury indicted Hacket for grand larceny. Four days later, Arkansas Gov. Archibald Yell formally requested Canadian authorities to extradite Hacket for trial in Arkansas. Canadian authorities then capitulated, and Hacket was ordered returned to Arkansas for trial.

Despite protests by black residents, Hacket was secretly taken to Detroit, where he was jailed. Free blacks in the Detroit area rallied to his aid, and legal maneuvers kept the runaway in Michigan through the winter. In the spring of 1842 Hacket was shackled and secretly sent back to Arkansas, though at one point he made an escape, only to be recaptured after two days. On May 26, 1842, Nelson Hacket was restored to the ownership of Alfred Wallace, the first instance in which criminal extradition had been used to retrieve a runaway slave from Canada.

Hacket was returned to slavery, but he was in the process of making international history. Abolitionists in the United States, as well as Canada and Britain, were incensed that "nefarious proceedings" had returned a runaway to slavery. In June 1842, the leadership of the British and Foreign Anti-Slavery Society considered the Hacket case and then called it to the attention of the British Foreign Secretary, Lord Aberdeen. Then, abolitionists in Britain and Canada took their case to legislative bodies, with one British parliamentarian saying that the Hacket case resulted in making "ourselves runaway slave-catchers for the United States."

Ultimately, British authorities bowed to the abolitionists, and instructions were issued to provincial governors to enforce extradition carefully. A test case in the Bahamas resulted in the refusal to surrender escaped slaves. As historian Roman Zorn wrote in his pioneering 1957 study of the Hacket case, "a humble Arkansas slave became the subject of international discussion, and his return became an antislavery *cause celebre.*"

FOR MORE INFORMATION:

Zorn, Roman J. "Arkansas Fugitive Slave Incident and Its International
    Repercussions." *Arkansas Historical Quarterly* 16 (Summer 1957): 139–44.

John R. Eakin

John R. Eakin was one of those pioneer Arkansans who excelled in a number of fields, most especially in journalism and the law. He edited the *Washington Telegraph* newspaper in Hempstead County in the heated times leading up to the Civil War, as well as serving as something of a reformer in the Arkansas Supreme Court.

Eakin was born in Shelbyville, Tennessee, in 1822, the son of a Scottish immigrant who made a small fortune in a frontier mercantile business. Eakin was well educated for the times, having begun college at age eleven and later graduating from the University of Nashville. He studied history and read law at Yale University, finishing his legal educating by reading under the prominent Andrew Ewing of Nashville. He married the college-educated Elizabeth Erwin, related by marriage to Edgar Allan Poe, in 1848.

Eakin inherited considerable wealth when his father died in 1849, much of which he spent on agricultural experiments—especially in growing and breeding grapes. By 1868, Eakin was growing more than one thousand grape vines representing forty varieties and species. However, he was financially overextended. His circumstances reduced, Eakin relocated to Washington, Arkansas, in 1857 to practice law.

Arriving in Arkansas just as the nation was embarking on a great debate over the future of slavery, Eakin affiliated with the Whig Party and did his part to prevent the secession of Arkansas from the Union. After becoming editor of the *Telegraph* in 1860, Eakin "opposed secession and war with pen and on the stump," as the nineteenth century historian John Hallum later wrote.

Once hostilities commenced with the firing on Fort Sumter, South Carolina, in the spring of 1861, Eakin, like most antisecessionist leaders, immediately closed ranks with the new Confederacy. While a state convention was meeting to consider secession, Eakin wrote: "Filled with indignation—all our love turned to disgust—anxious only now for the glory and honor of the South, we cry for war." Indeed, over the next four years he became known as the most widely read Arkansas propagandist for the rebel cause. Michael B. Dougan, the author of the entry on Eakin in the *Encyclopedia of Arkansas History and Culture,* defended Eakin's editorial stance: "he believed the press should be 'controlled by men of conscience,' and he refused to print forged documents or intentionally misleading stories."

When Little Rock fell to Union troops in September 1863, the Confederate state government fled to Washington, where a new state government was established in the county courthouse. The *Telegraph* became the official organ of the Arkansas Confederacy during the final two years of the war. It was the only Arkansas newspaper to publish continually throughout the Civil War, which gave Eakin substantial influence.

When the guns finally fell silent in April 1865, Eakin was quick to bury his disgust and accept a presidential pardon for his role in the rebellion—a course he also urged on his readers. Then he promptly gave up the *Telegraph* and went into politics. (The newspaper itself survived for another century. The Etter family closed it in 1947, by which time the town of Washington had become a tiny village abandoned to history.)

Since the Whig party could not survive the Civil War, Eakin, like his fellow Washington Whig and future governor and U.S. senator Augustus H. Garland, joined the Democratic Party—though "of necessity, not of choice," as one of his contemporaries said.

In 1866 Eakin was elected to the state legislature, and in 1874 he served in the constitutional convention that wrote the charter under which Arkansas is governed today. Soon thereafter he was elected chancery judge, and in 1878 he was appointed to the Arkansas Supreme Court.

As a jurist, Eakin was something of a maverick. In several cases he voted to protect the rights of women. While his choice of words would later sound quaint, his sentiments were clear in 1881 when he wrote that it is "undoubted everywhere that men and children are safest under the moral influences and social surroundings which are approved by women."

Eakin realized that married women had received some legal protection in Arkansas since 1835. The state constitution, adopted in 1874, even contained a provision giving property rights to married women. The 1875 general assembly adopted legislation to ensure a whole range of rights for married women, including the right to own and transfer property, to own a business, and to sue or be sued. Until the adoption of this law, women essentially gave up their property rights upon marriage.

In an 1882 case, *Felkner v. Tighe,* Judge Eakin vehemently dissented from a decision that essentially prohibited women from making contracts. He wrote that common law was no protection for women, for it granted them "the same capacity as an idiot."

Eakin, the father of seven children and a widower for two years, died unexpectedly in 1885 at the age of sixty-four. Two years later, when John Hallum published the first book-length history of Arkansas, he wrote a touching tribute to Eakin, stressing the judge's "strong, striking and marked individuality."

FOR MORE INFORMATION:

Dougan, Michael B. "Jno Eakin (1822–1885)." *The Encyclopedia of Arkansas History and Culture.* http://encyclopediaofarkansas.net/encyclopedia/entry-detail.aspx?search=1&entryID=3238.

Hallum, John. *Biographical and Pictorial History of Arkansas.* Albany, NY: Weed, Parsons, 1887.

"Hon. Dan W. Jones' Eloquent Tribute before the Supreme Court to the Late Judge John R. Eakin." *Arkansas Gazette,* December 15, 1885.

Smith, Robert Freeman. "John R. Eakin: Confederate Propagandist." *Arkansas Historical Quarterly* 12 (Winter 1953): 316–26.

Mifflin W. Gibbs

Arkansas was the home to the first elected black municipal judge in the United States, M. W. Gibbs. In 1873 Mifflin Wistar Gibbs was elected Little Rock police judge, a post the Republican held for two years before being defeated in 1875, when Reconstruction came to an end and Democrats recaptured political power in the state. Though for the remainder of his life Gibbs would be referred to by both blacks and whites as "Judge," his tenure as an elected official was actually a minor part of a long life of varied interests and accomplishments.

Born in 1823 of free parents, Gibbs grew up in the expanding black sections of Philadelphia. His formal education ended after only one year when his father, a Methodist cleric, died. Gibbs apprenticed as a carpenter, and he worked on a number of large buildings, including Bethel African Methodist Episcopal Church—"Mother Bethel," as it is known to AME members everywhere. When not plying his trade, young Gibbs spent his free time reading in the libraries of the local black literary societies.

In 1849, after having accompanied Frederick Douglass on an antislavery lecture tour, Gibbs joined the gold rush to California. He found San Francisco a "chaos of board cabins and tents," but before long he opened a clothing store. He also helped establish the first black newspaper west of the Mississippi River, the *Mirror of the Times*, which he served as both publisher and occasional contributor.

California proved to be as racist as the states back east, and after being told to withdraw their children from public schools, some eight hundred San Francisco blacks migrated to Victoria, British Columbia, in 1858. Victoria was not free of racial conflict, but it was a paradise compared to California.

Among Gibbs's early acts after he immigrated to British Columbia was registering to vote, a right long denied American blacks. In 1866 he won election to the Victoria City Council and was the first black person to hold the office.

In Victoria, Gibbs again went into the retail trade, opening the Boot and Shoe Emporium; he also diversified into real estate and construction. In a breathtaking undertaking that was filled with risk and challenge, Gibbs made his fortune in the coal mining business, opening the first coal mine on rugged Queen Charlotte's Island north of Victoria and building the railroad to serve it. In May 1870, Gibbs sailed to Victoria, taking with him the first shipment of anthracite coal ever mined on the Pacific coast. He was received as a local hero, and he could justifiably claim to have fulfilled his goal of going west and "doing some great thing."

With his business success and growing political power, the thirty-six-year-old Gibbs must have felt ready to begin a family. He married Maria Alexander, a native of Kentucky and a student at Oberlin College in Ohio. She was certainly a suitable mate for the prominent and successful businessman. In quick succession the Gibbses had five children.

His finances secure, Gibbs returned to the United States in 1870 without warning, settling in Oberlin, Ohio, where his wife had gone to school and where his daughters were studying. He apparently read law while living there.

It is not clear exactly why the middle-aged Gibbs decided to relocate to Arkansas, but he left his family in Ohio and settled in Little Rock in 1871. His brother, Jonathan, was already serving as Florida secretary of state, and Gibbs probably saw the post–Civil War South as a new frontier of opportunities. Gibbs never lived with Maria again, though they apparently never divorced. He did keep up with his children, and in 1904 Gibbs purchased a building in Washington, D.C., to serve as a musical conservatory for his daughter Harriet.

For the next forty-four years Gibbs was the premier black leader and businessman in Arkansas. After his service as municipal judge, he practiced law, but most of his considerable energies were spent on Republican politics. He was a delegate to every Republican national convention but one from 1876 to 1904. From 1887 to 1897, Gibbs was secretary of the Arkansas Republican Central Committee.

Gibbs was an ally of Powell Clayton, the former Union army general and Reconstruction governor who ran the state GOP from its founding in 1868 until late in life, when he turned it over to his lieutenant, Harmon L. Remmel. Gibbs received several presidential appointments, including registrar of public lands in Little Rock and later as receiver of public monies in the capital city. President McKinley named Gibbs American consul to Tamatave, a city on the Indian Ocean island of Madagascar, an assignment he found less than rewarding, resigning in 1901. Though an old man, he still had big plans.

On the first day of 1903 Gibbs opened the second black-owned bank in Arkansas, the Capital City Savings Bank in Little Rock. (The first black bank in the state was founded a few months earlier in Pine Bluff.) Until the very day the bank folded, it appeared that Capital City Savings Bank was in good fiscal condition. By 1905, deposits amounted to $100,000. The bank's officers and board members were from the city's black elite. No one suspected mismanagement, but on June 18, 1908, angry depositors nervously waited to withdraw their money after hearing that the bank was insolvent. The recession of 1907 did not help matters.

Charges of mismanagement and corruption could be heard, and Gibbs was sued in circuit court seeking $28,000 in claims. The situation worsened in January 1909 when Gibbs was indicted by a grand jury, and his personal fortune, estimated at $100,000, was sequestered. Ultimately, he avoided prosecution by reaching an out-of-court settlement. He also managed to keep most of his fortune intact, but Gibbs could never again be called the Horatio Alger of the black race.

The closure of the bank must have been a bitter pill for Gibbs. In 1915, at the age of ninety-two, he died at home in Little Rock. He left money for the M. W. Gibbs Old Ladies Home, which operated until 1968. Today a Little Rock elementary school bears Gibbs's name, a reminder of the Canadian immigrant who was America's first black municipal judge.

FOR MORE INFORMATION:

Dillard, Tom W. "'Golden Prospects and Fraternal Amenities': Mifflin W. Gibbs' Arkansas Years." *Arkansas Historical Quarterly* 35 (Winter 1976): 307–33.

Gibbs, Mifflin Wistar. *Shadow and Light: An Autobiography.* Little Rock: Published by the author, 1902. Reprinted, Lincoln: University of Nebraska Press, 1995.

Judge Isaac C. Parker

Few individuals are better known in Arkansas history than U.S. District Judge Isaac Charles Parker of Fort Smith. Parker's district covered western Arkansas and Indian Territory, and there was no more violent nor ruthless jurisdiction in the nation. For more than two decades Parker presided from the federal courthouse in Fort Smith, and his many death sentence rulings earned him the nickname "Hanging Judge." He was a far more complicated figure than his popular moniker might imply.

Born the youngest son of Joseph and Jane Parker in Barnesville, Ohio, on October 15, 1838, young Charles worked on the family farm, but he also managed to spend time in school. After graduating from the private Barnesville Classical Institute, he taught school for a time while reading law in a local law firm. Licensed in 1859, he began practice with an uncle in St. Joseph, Missouri. In 1861 he married Mary O'Toole, and the couple had two sons.

Parker began his political career as a Democrat, but the coming of the Civil War forced him to rethink his political philosophy. Like most federal judges, Parker came to the judiciary through politics. He spent most of the Civil War years as the St. Joseph city attorney, though he did serve in the local Unionist home guard unit. In 1864 he was a presidential elector, casting his vote for the reelection of President Abraham Lincoln. In 1870 Parker was elected to the U.S. House of Representatives from Missouri but was defeated in a U.S. Senate campaign in 1874. Parker lobbied for and received an appointment from President Grant to sit on the bench in Fort Smith. The thirty-six-year-old judge presided over his first case on March 18, 1875.

The Western District of Arkansas and Indian Territory was an unusual jurisdiction because the Indian tribes had their own courts and police system. The Indian Territory, as well as adjacent western Arkansas, was known for its vast tracts of wilderness, areas that provided numerous havens for criminals. Interestingly, during much of Parker's tenure, his decisions from the Western District court could not be appealed to higher courts.

The district was also known for its corruption. In the years prior to Parker's arrival, the Fort Smith court was scandalously corrupt. Numerous investigations documented bribery and other financial irregularities, with the court costing almost $1 million over three years.

Parker set a frenetic pace. Facing a huge case load, the judge held court six days a week. He was also a stalwart in the growing city of Fort Smith. Like many other Northerners who settled in Arkansas after the Civil War, Parker decried the lack of a public school system. He helped establish the Fort Smith school system, which his children attended. He and Mrs. Parker were well regarded in the community.

Parker was never accused of corruption, but he was often charged with being bloodthirsty. Between 1875 and 1896, Parker's court handled more than 12,000 criminal cases, with nearly 9,000 convictions. Of those convictions, 160 defendants were given the death penalty, although only 79 of that total were actually hanged.

Parker's penchant for death penalty rulings made the front pages of newspapers across the nation, with one critic referring to "Parker's slaughter-house." Since there was no appeal from his rulings, he was often depicted as arbitrary. Actually, the judge held complicated views on the death penalty, saying once, "I favor the abolition of capital punishment . . . provided there is a certainty of punishment, whatever that punishment may be." Parker also stressed that penalties were specified by law and that juries actually found guilt and assessed punishment.

As the years went by, Parker's reputation as a "hangman" grew to the point that Congress ultimately removed Indian Territory from his jurisdiction. Many of his sentences were overturned after 1889 when Congress adopted legislation allowing appeals from his court.

During the 1890s the U.S. Supreme Court reviewed forty-four death-sentence convictions from Parker's court, reversing thirty-one of them. The judge was criticized for allowing inflammatory evidence as well as permitting prosecutors to make prejudicial remarks. The most serious charge made against Parker was that he guided jurors toward conviction verdicts. The aging judge reacted in rage, accusing the appellate process of contributing to crime by making "the most strenuous efforts . . . to see not when they can affirm but when they can reverse a case."

Judge Parker died on November 17, 1896, and was buried in the Fort Smith National Cemetery, only a few blocks from his courtroom. His tenure on the bench is recounted at the Fort Smith National Historic Site, which includes his courtroom as well as a reproduction of Parker's famed gallows.

FOR MORE INFORMATION:

Harman, S. W. *Hell on the Border: He Hanged Eighty Eight Men.* Fort Smith: Phoenix Publishing Co., 1898. Reprinted, Lincoln: University of Nebraska Press, 1992.

Radcliff, Maranda. "Isaac Charles Parker (1838–1896)." *The Encyclopedia of Arkansas History and Culture.* http://encyclopediaofarkansas.net/encyclopedia/entry-detail.aspx?search=1&entryID=1732.

Shirley, Glenn. *Law West of Fort Smith: A History of Frontier Justice in the Indian Territory, 1834–1896.* New York: Henry Holt, 1957.

Stolberg, Mary M. "Politician, Populist, Reformer: A Reexamination of 'Hanging Judge' Isaac C. Parker." *Arkansas Historical Quarterly* 47 (Spring 1988): 3–28.

Scipio A. Jones

Before his death in 1943, Scipio A. Jones was the foremost African American lawyer in Arkansas. He was also among the most prominent black leaders in the state and region.

Scipio's date and place of birth are not known. He was almost certainly the biological son of his mother's owner, not an uncommon occurrence during the slave regime. His mother, along with other slaves, was taken to Texas to escape liberation when Union troops marched into southwest Arkansas in the spring of 1864. He was probably born while the family was returning to Arkansas after the Union army was driven out of south Arkansas.

An infant when the war ended in 1865, Scipio was raised by his mother and her husband, Jemima and Horace Jones. The first written record we have on him is the 1870 census, which noted that young Scipio was the only literate member of the family.

At about the age of twenty, Scipio moved to what is today North Little Rock, where he eventually took a degree from Shorter College. He then taught school for a time while reading law during his free time in the offices of several prominent white attorneys.

Jones was authorized to practice law on June 15, 1889, after passing the required examination. In 1900 he was admitted to practice before the Arkansas Supreme Court, and in 1905 the U.S. Supreme Court recognized his credentials.

Jones practiced law until the end of his days, sometimes with a partner but often in a solo practice. Like many lawyers of his time, he also dabbled in various business investments. He owned considerable rental property, invested in a local ice company, and in 1908 he launched the Arkansas Realty and Investment Co., which Jones thought would "afford the race a better opportunity to develop . . . and grow prosperous."

Much of Jones's practice revolved around a variety of black fraternal organizations, including the Mosaic Templars of America. Founded in

Little Rock in 1882, the Mosaic Templars grew steadily through the years, and by 1924 the group had 80,000 members in more than 2,000 lodges in twenty-three states, South and Central America, and the West Indies. Jones served the group as its attorney general.

Jones reached the pinnacle of his legal practice in the aftermath of vicious race violence around Elaine in Phillips County in 1919. While the white leadership portrayed the violence as a black conspiracy to kill local white landowners, blacks claimed it resulted from white opposition to black sharecroppers organizing a union.

The violence resulted in the deaths of an unknown number of people, mostly blacks. Estimates range from twenty to more than eight hundred, but no accounting was taken at the time as far as is known. Among the more egregious murders was the killing of four middle-class black citizens, Dr. D. A. E. Johnston, a Helena dentist; Dr. Louis H. Johnston, an Oklahoma City physician, and two brothers in the automobile business, one of whom had been wounded in France during World War I. They were murdered while tied up inside an automobile after being taken off a train.

As soon as the guns grew silent a massive roundup of black men began, 122 being charged with a variety of offenses. No whites were prosecuted, though the bulk of the dead were black. Twelve black men were sentenced to death after they confessed. The problem was that the confessions were beaten out of them.

While the violence at Elaine has been a blot on Arkansas history, the legal effort to free the twelve condemned men is actually an uplifting though harrowing story. With assistance from the recently established National Association for the Advancement of Colored People, several prominent white attorneys were hired to appeal the death sentences. Former state attorney general George Murphy, a veteran of the Confederate army, took on the case for the NAACP. When Murphy died suddenly, his partner Edgar McHaney took charge of the defense. Black Arkansans also raised enough money to hire Scipio Jones to work on the case. By 1919, Jones had appeared seventeen times before the Arkansas Supreme Court, an amazing record for a black attorney.

Neither Governors Charles H. Brough nor Thomas C. McRae would budge from their hands-off attitude. But, McHaney and Jones made a formidable team, and with a little help from Judge John E.

Scipio A. Jones, a famed black lawyer. *Photo courtesy of University of Central Arkansas Archives, Conway.*

Martineau and others, they were able to delay the executions and take their appeals all the way to the U.S. Supreme Court. Black leader W. E. B. DuBois described the trial as "the greatest case against peonage and mob law ever fought in the land." In January 1925, the last of the Elaine defendants were set free.

Finally absolved, the defendants posed for pictures with Jones. Those aging photos show the defendants incongruously dressed in coats and ties, but with worried looks on their faces. Jones stands slightly off to the side, his hat in his hand and a hint of a smile on his lips.

Jones continued to practice law through the Great Depression and until shortly before he died on March 28, 1943. He was buried at Haven of Rest Cemetery in Little Rock. North Little Rock honored Jones in 1928 by naming its black high school after him, and in 2007 the Little Rock Post Office on Main Street was named for him.

FOR MORE INFORMATION:

Dillard, Tom W. "Scipio A. Jones." *Arkansas Historical Quarterly* 31 (Autumn 1972): 201–19.

Stockley, Grif. *Blood in Their Eyes: The Elaine Race Massacres of 1919.* Fayetteville: University of Arkansas Press, 2001.

Whitaker, Robert. *On the Laps of Gods: The Red Summer of 1919 and the Struggle for Justice That Remade a Nation.* New York: Crown Publishers, 2008.

CHAPTER VI

Entrepreneurs

Nathan Warren

Nathan Warren was a remarkable man. He not only survived as a free African American in antebellum Little Rock, he actually prospered. He was a businessman of considerable talent, a religious leader of note, and he had friends among both races in a time when racism ran rampant.

Warren was born a slave in Maryland about 1812, probably the son of a white man. He was brought to Little Rock about 1834 as a slave of Whig political leader Robert Crittenden. Crittenden died unexpectedly not long after Warren arrived on the scene, leaving his widow heavily in debt. It is not clear how Warren obtained his freedom, but by 1840 he was free.

Free blacks were not common in Arkansas, unlike some areas such as New Orleans. The 1850 U.S. Census recorded 608 free blacks in the state, with the largest number, 129, in rural Marion County in the Ozarks near the Missouri border. (The black population in Marion County represented an anomaly, a colony consisting of the extended families of Peter Caulder and David Hall Sr.)

Camden, Van Buren, Fort Smith, and Little Rock were centers of free black population, but none had more than twenty-five such individuals in 1850. Despite their small numbers, white residents complained about the presence of free blacks. In 1843 the legislature enacted a law forbidding the entry of free blacks into the state, and those living here were required to file bonds guaranteeing good behavior.

Apparently the law of 1843 was not widely enforced, but Nathan Warren was one of those who did post bond. He married a slave of Chester Ashley, a "wily [land] speculator and devious politician," as one historian described this namesake for Ashley County. Anne Warren came to the marriage with a son, W. A. Rector, who would later become a leader in Reconstruction Little Rock.

The late Margaret Ross, in a pioneering article on Nathan Warren, described the free man as having worked as a barber, carriage driver, and general handyman—though his great popularity among the white elite of Little Rock was due to his skills as a confectioner. He was not the first black confectioner in Little Rock. Indeed, Henry Jackson, another free black man, had earlier operated a confectionery in Little Rock, but he had invented a popular cook stove that took him to Evansville, Indiana, where the stove was manufactured.

Warren's confectionery shop was a two-story frame building on West Markham Street, where the Capital Hotel now stands. Margaret Ross wrote that Warren never wanted for customers and that he was "always called upon to provide the refreshments at weddings and other social events." His tea cakes were especially popular.

Warren used some of his financial resources to join with his free brother, Henry Warren, in purchasing their slave brother, James, whom they manumitted. When his first wife died, Warren married another slave of the Ashley family, Mary Elizabeth. Warren purchased his new wife and her daughter, Ida May. He did not buy his children by his first wife, although Mrs. Ashley manumitted their sickly daughter, Ella. (Ella got the last laugh as she lived to be eighty-five.)

Despite his popularity with the city's elite, or at least their wives, Nathan Warren chaffed from the many roadblocks thrown in his way. When his store caught on fire in 1852, Warren believed it to be the work of a white arsonist. In 1858 Warren took his family to Xenia, Ohio, where the couple later had three children of their own. Sources differ as to how well the Warren family did in the North, but the family moved back to Little Rock soon after it fell to federal troops during the Civil War.

Warren opened another confectionary shop, but it was not as popular as before the war. The 1870 census recorded him as a grocer, but within two years he had his own bakery. An organizer of Bethel African Methodist Episcopal Church at 9th and Broadway streets in Little Rock, Warren was ordained an elder in 1882. He was also a 32nd Degree member of the black Masonic Lodge.

Nathan Warren died on Sunday, June 3, 1888. His Masonic funeral filled Bethel Church. Interestingly, Warren was buried at Mount Holly Cemetery, one of the few blacks to be interred in what would later be known as the "Westminster Abbey of Arkansas."

FOR MORE INFORMATION:

Ross, Margaret Smith. "Nathan Warren, a Free Negro for the Old South." *Arkansas Historical Quarterly* 15 (Spring 1956): 53–61.

Scott Bond

Scott Bond was one of those remarkable black men of the early twentieth century who rose above the obstacles of segregation to succeed. Bond not only succeeded, he became known as the "black Rockefeller of Arkansas." Bond, who was born a slave in rural Mississippi about 1852, was able through determination and hard work to build a network of farms, cotton gins, a sawmill, and a large mercantile store, before dying in 1933 as a very wealthy man.

Scott's biological father was a white overseer, Wesley Rutledge. Scott's mother, a house slave, married William Bond when her son was about two years old. About 1855, the owner of the Bond family moved from Mississippi to Tennessee. After about five years, the family was relocated to Cross County, Arkansas. Upon obtaining their freedom in April 1865 when the Civil War ended, William and Ann Bond, along with Scott, began a new life by moving to Madison, a small town about four miles east of Forrest City.

Scott's mother died not long after the family moved to Madison, and the boy was raised by his stepfather, a sharecropper. At about the age of twenty-two, young Scott went out on his own and rented twelve acres; the following year he expanded to thirty-five acres. By 1877 he felt secure enough to marry Miss Magnolia Nash, who proved to be a full partner for her enterprising husband.

The plantation owner who rented land to Bond asked him to take over management of the entire 2,200-acre farming operation. Bond took charge of the various sharecroppers working on the plantation, fenced the entire farm, worked his own fields, and turned a profit of $2,500.

Bond would probably have continued with his comfortable life as a plantation manager and farmer had it not been for an unusual opportunity. Normally, Bond never saw the money he generated for the white landowner, since it was handled by a local credit merchant.

One year, however, the landowner was feuding with the merchant, and Bond was asked to deliver the full $1,250 rental income in cash. On his way to the landowner's home, Bond felt compelled to look at the cash in his pocket—an amount of money he had never seen before.

Finding a secluded spot, Bond located a log and "pulled out my money . . . and scattered it up and down the log." He stepped back from the log and said, "This is the product of labor of my own hand. Here is $1,250 which I am giving the landlord to let me cultivate her land." Bond concluded that paying rent "was just like taking that money and casting it into the fire." He went home to his wife and said, "Wife, I am going tomorrow and buy 300 acres of land. I have learned today what it is to own a farm."

Over the years, Bond purchased many more farms, ultimately totaling 12,000 acres of land. He also invested in town lots, and his Madison Mercantile Company sold everything from side meat to coffins. Bond was nothing if not diversified. He built a number of cotton gins, so as to better control costs. Unlike most farmers who cleared their land by burning the trees, Bond built a sawmill and sold the resulting lumber. He also owned a brick-making firm and sold fruit from large orchards. Perhaps Bond's most shrewd investment was in a gravel mining operation. Many of the railroad beds in eastern Arkansas are built of gravel from Bond's land.

As befitted a man of such success, Bond built a nice home he named "The Cedars." He erected large barns to house his fine pure-bred livestock. Bond's success was enhanced by his accomplished wife, who not only bore eleven sons but also worked tirelessly alongside her husband. In 1917 Bond's son Theo, along with a professional writer, published a biography of Bond titled *From Slavery to Wealth: The Life of Scott Bond,* now a rare book that fetches a high price.

Bond's success and growing fame brought him into contact with black leaders in Arkansas and beyond. After 1900 Bond was active in Booker T. Washington's National Negro Business League. Bond delivered an address at the 1902 annual meeting of the league in New York City, and the following year the league held its convention in Little Rock. After the convention, Bond hosted Washington at his home, followed by an address by the "Wizard of Tuskegee" and a barbeque.

In March 1933, at the age of eighty-one, Scott Bond was killed by one of his prized purebred Hereford bulls. He was buried in Madison.*

FOR MORE INFORMATION:

Bond, Theo., and Daniel A. Rudd. *From Slavery to Wealth: The Life of Scott Bond.* Madison: Journal Printing Co., 1917. Reprinted with an introduction by Willard B. Gatewood. Fayetteville: Phoenix Press, 2008.

Chowning, Robert W. *History of St. Francis County, Arkansas.* Forrest City, AR: Times-Herald Publishing Co., 1954.

Gordon, Fon Louise. "Scott Winfield Bond (1852–1933)." *The Encyclopedia of Arkansas History and Culture.* http://encyclopediaofarkansas.net/encyclopedia/entry-detail.aspx?search=1&entryID=1594.

Richardson, Clement, ed. "Scott Bond." *The National Cyclopedia of the Colored Race,* 92–93. Montgomery, AL: National Publishing Co., 1919.

*In about 1974 I traveled to Madison in search of any remnants of the Scott Bond empire. My community contact told me that she was only vaguely aware of the Bond family. Efforts to locate Bond's mercantile store proved fruitless. As I was driving out of town in despair, a white sign appeared on the street announcing the location of Bondol Laboratories. The name "Bondol" was enough to get my attention, so I stopped. Inside I met Dr. Charles Latimer, a well-known chemistry educator who had joined with Scott Bond's son, U. S. Bond, and another businessman in forming Bondol Laboratories in 1939, only six years after Scott Bond's death. Latimer informed me that the business, which still exists, is known for its line of embalming chemicals. Bondol Laboratories provided about one-half of the embalming supplies used by black undertakers nationally in 1954. Theo Bond, another of Scott's sons, worked in the family enterprises, including helping run their large casket manufacturing operation.

Green Thompson

The murder of Green Thompson in 1902 ended the life of an amazing African American Arkansan—a businessman, reformist politician, and social leader. Thompson was in the vanguard of those eager young freedmen who wanted to make a mark in post–Civil War Little Rock.

Born about 1848 to a slave mother on the Robert Elliott farm in Ouachita County, young Green went by the name Elliott until his mother married a man named Thompson, whereupon he assumed the name of his stepfather. Thompson's biological father was undoubtedly white, as indicated by his listing as a mulatto in the 1880 census. At the end of the Civil War in 1865, Thompson, like thousands of other Arkansas freedmen, exercised his new freedom by moving to Little Rock.

In this new urban setting Thompson quickly established himself as a businessman, first going into the grocery business, then opening a saloon and later a feed store. Like many of the emerging black elite, Thompson invested in real estate and eventually owned his own real estate business. One of his major assets was Thompson Hall, a large brick building with a public meeting room that was the scene of many black social and political events in the capital city.

By 1880 Thompson had married Darthulia W. Thompson and fathered two sons, the older being Green Walter Thompson Jr. Apparently this child died an early death, leaving only a son named Wade. Mrs. Thompson was a popular leader herself, being president of the Arkansas Women's Colored Baptist Missionary Association and also active in sorority circles. She chaired the board of the Old Ladies Home, a retirement home for black women endowed by black judge-lawyer-businessman Mifflin W. Gibbs. Mrs. Thompson fell victim to "lung trouble" and died in 1896. Her death was reported in the *Arkansas Gazette,* a rare occasion for an African American.

Like a moth to light, Thompson was drawn inexorably to politics. While still in his mid-twenties, he was elected to the Little Rock City

Council in 1875. For the next eighteen years he served on the council, setting a tenure record for blacks not broken for almost a century.

The quarter-century following the Civil War was a thrilling time for black politicians in Arkansas, especially in eastern and southern Arkansas, where black voters often outnumbered whites. Pulaski County was also a battleground for black politicos, especially Little Rock's Sixth Ward, where Green Thompson lived. The *Arkansas Gazette* described the ward as "the bloody sixth," betraying the newspaper's vehement opposition to Thompson and his fellow black Republicans.

In 1888 Thompson won election to the state House of Representatives, where he served one term. In the 1890 elections he was the unsuccessful Union-Labor Party nominee for state senator. During all this time he retained his seat on the Little Rock City Council.

During the early 1890s the legislature began adopting a series of bills to curtail black voting. A poll tax dramatically reduced voting among poor people of both races. Disfranchisement was completed when the legislature adopted election laws that consolidated the voting process in the hands of the Democratic Party.

While these laws were successful in totally eliminating blacks from the state legislature, Green Thompson retained his city council seat a little longer. In 1893 the city disposed of its ancient system of electing aldermen by ward and implemented citywide at-large elections. Thompson waged a valiant fight to retain his seat, but whites far outnumbered blacks citywide and his campaign was doomed. No other black citizen served on the Little Rock City Council until Charles Bussey was elected in 1969.

On March 20, 1902, Green Thompson was murdered at his home in Little Rock. Up to this point Thompson's life is fairly clearly documented in the historical record. His sudden and tragic death, however, cast his historical record into turmoil and confusion.

Blackberry winter held Little Rock in a tight grip the night Green Thompson was murdered. He had spent the evening at Thompson Hall, his well-known rental facility, where a church social was in progress. It was about midnight before Thompson reached his home at 1006 West 10th Street. The wind rattled the barn doors as he unharnessed the team and fed them. Thompson probably never heard or saw the person who stepped from behind a door and buried an ax deep into his chest. The howling of the wind was punctuated by the snorting and stamping of two agitated horses. The next day all of Little Rock read the lurid headlines in the newspaper, "Green Thompson Dead, Son Is Charged with Murder."

The prosecutors were confident that Thompson's son, Wade, was the murderer. Indeed, the Pulaski county coroner's inquest reported that Thompson died of "wounds received at the hands of Wade Thompson with malice aforethought." A long-time wastrel who had an extensive police record, Wade was reported to be confident of vindication. With the help of the legendary black attorney Scipio A. Jones, Wade was eventually freed for lack of evidence. Then Thompson's second wife, Mary, who was half the age of her fifty-two-year-old husband, was charged along with an itinerant musician who was supposed to be her lover. Mrs. Thompson was charged after an intense investigation by the longtime black Little Rock police detective Sam Speight. Apparently, they too were set free, and we do not yet know who murdered Green Thompson.

It appeared that Mary Thompson would inherit her husband's substantial estate. A woman by the name of Lula Brown, however, had other plans. It was a miserably hot day on July 8, 1902, when Lula Brown and her prominent white attorney, W. H. Pemberton, made their way to the Pulaski County probate clerk's office and filed a petition seeking recognition of Lula as a legitimate heir of Green Thompson.

Lula Brown's petition claimed that she was born of a slave marriage between Green Thompson and a young slave woman in Ouachita County shortly before the end of the Civil War. Over the next several months the widow Mary Thompson and Lula Brown waged a fierce fight for control of the Green Thompson estate, with Wade caught in an uneasy alliance with his stepmother. This legal contest resulted in the creation of a fifty-one-page legal-sized typed transcript of depositions taken from a host of parties who had known Green Thompson both as a young slave in Ouachita County and as a mature politician and businessman in Little Rock. The typescript, which is in Green Thompson's probate file in the Arkansas History Commission, provides fascinating accounts of life during the final years of the slave regime in south

Arkansas, as well as the swirling events that comprised black business and society in the state's capital over the next forty years.

Among those who testified on behalf of Lula Brown was her mother, Dora Hildreath Townsend, who said she and Green Thompson (who then went by the name of Elliot, his owner's family name) were married in 1863, and their daughter, Lula, was born shortly after emancipation, after which Green abandoned the family and moved to Little Rock. She also testified that Green asked for the daughter later, but she refused until the child reached her teenage years. She then accompanied Lula to Little Rock, where Lula lived with her father and his wife.

One revealing moment in the deposition came when the opposing counsel asked Dora why she did not "come up here and live with Green Thompson here?" Dora answered, "I wouldn't come without he would come and get me right; he didn't come after me; he come after the child . . . I didn't run after him."

The court was not swayed by the testimony, and in the end Wade Thompson and his stepmother (who was the same age as her stepson) inherited Green Thompson's entire estate.

Lula Brown at least got her day in court, and historians got a magnificent peek into a nineteenth-century black family saga.

FOR MORE INFORMATION:

Dillard, Tom W. "Green Walter Thompson (1848?-1902)." *The Encyclopedia of Arkansas History and Culture.* http://encyclopediaofarkansas.net/encyclopedia/entry-detail.aspx?search=1&entryID=1783.

"Green Thompson Dead; His Son, Wade, in Jail." *Arkansas Gazette,* March 21, 1902.

Conrad Elsken

Arkansas never received the waves of German immigrants that flocked to such Midwestern states as Ohio and Illinois. Occasionally the state tried to entice Germans to settle in Arkansas. The Reconstruction government created a Bureau of Immigration and State Lands, and in 1874 the state published a German-language pamphlet touting Arkansas as a destination, but it drew few immigrants.

German immigration also received a push when the Roman Catholic bishop of Little Rock, Edward Fitzgerald, made it a priority. In a shrewd strategy, Bishop Fitzgerald teamed up with the newly built Little Rock and Fort Smith Railroad in 1877 to jointly attract Catholic German and Swiss immigrants to the Arkansas River Valley. The Railroad had been given large tracks of land as an incentive to build the tracks, and immigration would not only allow the company to sell land but also to provide customers in the form of passengers and freight. The railroad entered into exclusive contracts with German religious orders, which not only offered cheap land to Catholic immigrants but also guaranteed land and financial support for religious facilities.

Some of these German-speaking immigrants, such as those who settled in the new town of Conway, tended to come in colonies. Others came as individuals or as family groups. A surprisingly large number of these immigrants had settled earlier in the Midwest, especially in Missouri and Illinois. Among the more successful German immigrants to Arkansas was Conrad Elsken, one of the many German Catholic settlers in the rolling hills of Logan County.

Elsken was born in 1850 to a family of Prussian farmers. The family emigrated to Belleville, Illinois, when Conrad was nine. He attended the local schools, learned English, worked on his father's farm, and eventually got a job clerking in a store. In 1873, after the death of his mother, the family moved to the vicinity of Morrison Bluff in Logan County, Arkansas, where they farmed. After a short time, Elsken moved to Paris, Arkansas, where he worked in a store and then became a land agent for the Fort Smith and Little Rock Railroad.

An entrepreneur at heart, Elsken began a transfer business, shipping freight by wagon from Altus to Paris. Before long, he opened a boardinghouse called the Elsken Hotel in Paris, which kept his wife and his daughter, Gusta, busy. He also established successful stores at Paris and Charleston. Like many successful businessmen, Elsken was adept at selecting business partners. He joined with other German immigrants in establishing the Yunker, Schneider, and Anhalt Company, which operated stores in Paris, Spielerville, and Shoal Creek. The company advertised, "We sell goods at low prices and buy all farm products that have a market value." Elsken was also a builder, including being the successful bidder for the construction of the original Logan County jail in 1886. Built at a price of $3,890, it continued in use as a jail until 1971 and was converted into the Logan County Museum in 1972.

Elsken was alert to new business opportunities, and in 1900 he foresaw the possibilities offered by the telephone. Along with a number of partners, Elsken organized the Citizens Telephone Company, which began with only twenty-eight subscribers. Elsken served as president and general manager of the company, posts he held until the system was sold to Western Telephone Company in 1928. He was also an organizer of the Bank of Paris, which he served as vice president.

In 1908 Elsken moved from Paris to the community of Subiaco, where he built a home and, as usual, opened a store. He also served as the new town's first mayor and postmaster. His home survives.

Amazingly, Elsken made time for a busy life outside of business. He was active in public affairs, serving for eight years as treasurer of Logan County. He also worked tirelessly in the good roads movement, and he was particularly proud of his efforts to secure the construction of state highway 22 from Fort Smith to Dardanelle. He also promoted railroad expansion and served as a director of the Fort Smith, Subiaco, and Rock Island Railroad.

A devout Catholic, Elsken became the founding president of the Catholic Union of Arkansas in 1890. Earlier, while living at Morrison Bluff, he was an organizer of the Saints Peter and Paul Church, and the church's first Mass was said in the Elsken home by Father Stephen Stenger, a priest from nearby Subiaco Abbey. Elsken was the father of

Conrad Elsken, a German immigrant and Logan County entrepreneur and political leader. *Photo courtesy of Special Collections, University of Arkansas Libraries.*

fourteen children, seven by his first wife, Elizabeth Besselman Elsken, who died in 1899, and seven by his much younger second wife, Gretchen Margaret Kramer Elsken, a native of Leistadt, Germany.

Conrad Elsken died at the age of eighty-one in May 1931. In a front-page story, the Paris Progress told of Elsken's death and editorialized that "we believe we can truthfully say that there is not a man in the county who had more friends than Mr. Elsken." The papers also reported that "all business in Paris was suspended during the funeral," a fitting tribute to such an entrepreneur as Conrad Elsken.

FOR MORE INFORMATION:

"Conrad Elsken Dies at His Subiaco Home." *Paris Progress,* May 7, 1931.

"Conrad Elsken Announces Candidacy for Logan County Treasurer." *Arkansas Echo,* March 3, 1892." Reprinted in *Wagon Wheels* 26 (Fall/Winter 2006): 12.

Ben Pearson

Arkansas has been the home to a surprising number of very successful and innovative entrepreneurs. One of the most daringly successful Arkansas manufacturers was Ben Pearson, an internationally known pioneering maker of archery equipment and a resident of Pine Bluff.

Ben Pearson was born November 16, 1898, at Paron in Saline County. The family moved about, and Ben received only a few years of education, though he was a gifted child. What he lacked in education, however, was more than compensated for in other natural gifts, including a deep sense of determination.

That drive helped young Pearson land his first real job. In later life, Pearson recalled that he long had "a little hankering for electricity." He studied with single-minded determination, and before long he was employed as an electrical appliance repairman and ultimately with the Little Rock Railway and Electric Company. In 1925 he took a job with Harvey Couch's Arkansas Power & Light Company (AP&L).

In 1932, at the height of the Great Depression, Pearson left AP&L and went into business on his own. He sank his savings of $500 and a great deal of sweat on an experiment to grow plants by starting them in hotbeds heated by electrical cables. Pearson reasoned that the use of electricity allowed him to start plants much earlier than in conventional solar-heated hotbeds. He was also growing dewberries "on a large scale for shipment to Eastern markets."

The *Arkansas Democrat* ran an article with three pictures on Pearson's revolutionary hothouses. The article portrayed a brash young man whose shock of thick wavy hair would come to symbolize his penchant for taking risks. With a straight face, the newspaper reporter told of Pearson's strongly held theories on marketing agricultural products: "He thinks he has a plan by which this can be largely overcome, if not entirely so. However, he is not making public any of his plan until he develops it a little further."

Grand marketing plans and determination were not enough to

save Pearson's foray into farming, and he soon found himself selling Caterpillar tractors in Little Rock. He would have an interest in large farm equipment for the remainder of his life. At night, he made arrows in his garage, for himself and for sale.

Pearson developed an interest in archery as a child. A model he found in a Boy Scout magazine enabled him to make a replica of an English longbow. In 1926 Pearson made his first bow, which had a ninety-pound pull, named "Old Hickory." It was important to be able to make bows and arrows, for they were not readily available for purchase at that time.

Also in 1926, at the age of twenty-eight, Pearson entered the Arkansas State Archery Championship in Little Rock. The results were humbling, but he set about to make better archery equipment and to practice more intensively. The following year he won the state championship. He competed nationally for the next decade, ranking seventh in the 1938 National Archery Association's Nationals.

In March 1938, Pearson incorporated the Ben Pearson Company, issuing its first catalog the same year. The catalog offered only "arrows of distinction" at first. Though he was able to stay in business, profits were limited by a lack of capital, not to mention the continuing Great Depression. About 1937, a wealthy Oklahoma oilman by the name of Carl Haun appeared on the scene asking to buy some of Pearson's arrows. When Haun left for home at the end of the weekend, he was an investor in Ben Pearson, Inc.

With increased capital, the company built a new plant in Pine Bluff that included several machines either designed or modified by Pearson himself. Production soared to thousands of arrows per day. Income soared too, and by 1939 Pearson was the largest manufacturer of bows and arrows in the nation.

For years Pearson's bows tended to be traditional long bows—the kind of bow he had learned to use with incredible accuracy. Pearson, who was a skilled showman, put together a traveling archery extravaganza that played in arenas throughout the nation and Mexico.

At first, Pearson, like hundreds of generations of Native Americans before him, used wood from the native bois d'arc tree (also known as Osage orange) to make his bows. His employees often went home with yellow hands, testifying to the yellow sap of the bois d'arc.

By 1963, average daily production exceeded 3,000 bows and about 3,500 dozen arrows. Prior to 1958, Pearson sold his bows by catalog number. That year the company brought out Bushmaster and Cobra, later joined by Cougar, Javelina, and Safari. The Cougar was a popular bow, being in production from 1959 to 1977.

Pearson sold his company in 1967 to Leisure Group, and the headquarters departed Pine Bluff for Los Angeles. A succession of corporations owned the company until 1996. McPhearson Archery of Alabama bought the company name in 2000, so one can still find Ben Pearson bows for sale. Older Pearson bows show up on Internet auctions daily.

Pearson was among the charter inductees in the National Archery Hall of Fame in 1972. He was also inducted into the National Bow Hunters Hall of Fame, the Arkansas Outdoor Sportsman's Hall of Fame, as well as the Arkansas Bow Hunters Hall of Fame and the Arkansas Sports Hall of Fame.

This sketch is too brief to touch on every aspect of Pearson's productive life. Amazingly enough, he was one of the early manufacturers in America of mechanical cotton pickers. Toward the end of his life, Pearson invested heavily in saving historic buildings in downtown Pine Bluff, and he lived in one himself. He owned a cattle ranch and rental properties, and he shared his resources with many philanthropies.

Pearson died on March 2, 1971, at the age of seventy-two.

FOR MORE INFORMATION:

Chandler, Arline. "Arkansas' Famous Archer, Ben Pearson—His Legacy Lives on at Longbow." *Ozarks Mountaineer* (August/September 1997): 41–45.

"Garden Beds Heated by Electricity Produce Vegetables and Flowers Weeks in Advance of Those Grown Naturally." *Arkansas Democrat,* April 17, 1932.

Pearson, Ben, Jr. "Archer and Father Extraordinaire." *Jefferson County Historical Quarterly* 34 (March 2006): 4–11.

Williams, Fay. "Ben Pearson Built an Early Hobby into an Industry." *Arkansas Democrat Magazine,* October 12, 1952, 6–7, 10.

Williams, Harry Lee. "Ben Pearson: He Helps Preserve an Old, Enduring Art." *Arkansas Gazette,* November 7, 1965. This heavily illustrated feature deals with Pearson's hunting skills as an archer, including his kills of grizzly bears and a giant polar bear.

CHAPTER VII

Artists and Writers

Edward Payson Washbourne

Edward Payson Washbourne was possibly the best-known artist in ante-bellum Arkansas. His painting *Arkansas Traveler*, based on Sanford C. Faulkner's folktale, became a visual icon of Arkansas history soon after it was finished about 1855. Tragically, the young artist died in March 1860, but not before seeing his painting engraved for mass distribution.

The Washburn family, headed by Rev. Cephas Washburn, came to Arkansas in 1820 to minister to the Cherokee Indians at a settlement called Dwight Mission. The last of six children, Edward was born in 1831 after the family relocated from Arkansas to the new Cherokee reserva-tion in what is today northeastern Oklahoma. Though isolated, the New Dwight Mission school was probably among the best in the west, plus the Reverend Washburn was a renowned scholar and educator.

About 1840, after twenty years in charge of the Mission, Washburn retired and moved his family to Benton County in northwestern Arkansas. Edward would have been about nine years of age at the time. He attended Cane Hill College in western Washington County, a Cumberland Presbyterian institution.

The late Margaret Ross, the prominent historian who undertook a study of the Washburn family, said Edward "showed a marked artistic ability at an early age, but his parents neither discouraged nor encour-aged its development." Formal art instruction was not available on the Arkansas frontier, so young Edward Payson Washbourne (who along with his elder brother Woodward insisted on an older spelling of the family name) learned by watching visiting artists. For a brief time he studied under a visiting portraitist in Van Buren, but for the most part he was self-taught.

In 1852 Washbourne announced his availability to paint portraits, a fact the *Arkansas Gazette* commented on: "Mr. Washbourne is a native of our state, and has never been beyond her limits, except in the Indian Country and a few miles into the State of Missouri, and yet, not withstanding the disadvantages under which he has labored[,] he exhibits a talent for the art which he has adopted for a livelihood."

Making a livelihood for this young untutored artist meant the itinerant life of a portrait painter. No town in frontier Arkansas had a population sufficient to support a formal studio, so the painters went to the homes of the affluent. While most early Arkansans labored long hours to make a living from the land, a fortunate few built sizable fortunes. Men of this successful class wanted their likenesses captured in the best medium available, which in the days before photography meant paint on canvas.

The University of Arkansas Mullins Library owns a portrait of Albert Pike painted by Washbourne around 1854. Washbourne captured Pike in the prime of early middle age, his full mane of black hair not yet turned the magisterial gray of so many later renderings of this great man. Patrons like lawyer Albert Pike kept Washbourne financially afloat.

Interestingly, it was not a portrait that gave young Washbourne artistic immortality, but rather a rendering of the already famous folktale "Arkansas Traveler." This tale, which apparently was based on an actual encounter between some traveling political figures and a country fiddler in 1840, was told by politician and planter Sanford C. Faulkner with such gusto and wit that it became a popular form of entertainment in after-dinner speeches. (Faulkner was said to have given the "Traveler" oration even at his daughter's wedding.) Faulkner County is named after this great storyteller.

A fiddle tune arose to accompany the telling of the story, and in 1847 the tune came out in print under the title "The Arkansas Traveler and Rackinsack Waltz." One historian has written that the tune and story became "a vehicle for improvisational humor."

Washbourne finished *Arkansas Traveler* around 1855 and then set about getting it engraved for mass distribution. Some years ago a young scholar named Sarah Brown wrote a penetrating analysis of the Washbourne painting, theorizing that it was a direct representation of what is known as "Southwest humor." Regardless of how one categorizes *Arkansas Traveler*, its national success had an impact on how Americans viewed frontier Arkansas.

In 1859 Washbourne sent the painting to Leopold Grozelier in

Boston, who prepared a good engraving. The following March, Washbourne's father visited him in Little Rock, whereupon the elder Washburn took pneumonia and died. His son apparently contracted the same disease and died nine days later. Both men are buried in historic Mount Holly Cemetery in Little Rock.

Washbourne's death had no negative impact on his success. Ten years after his death, Currier and Ives copyrighted a set of two companion prints, which brought even more fame to Washbourne. In 1875, when a group of journalists visited Arkansas, Washbourne's *Arkansas Traveler* was trotted out as an example of local art.

A painting purported to be Washbourne's *Arkansas Traveler* hangs on the walls of the Arkansas History Commission in Little Rock. There is certainly no agreement among scholars as to whether this is Washbourne's actual painting or a poorly restored version of it. Regardless, the engraved version became an icon of Arkansas history.

FOR MORE INFORMATION:

Brown, Sarah. "The Arkansas Traveller: Southwest Humor on Canvas." *Arkansas Historical Quarterly* 46 (Winter 1987): 348–75.

Lemke, Walter J., ed. *Some Notes on the Washburns—Father and Son: Cephas Washburn, Founder of Dwight Mission, 1820, and Edward Payson Washburn, Painter of "The Arkansas Traveler."* Fayetteville: Washington County Historical Society, 1955.

Ross, Margaret. "Edward Payson Washburn Had Artistic Ability, and Became Well-Known Painter." *Arkansas Gazette,* March 26, 1967.

———. "The Original Arkansas Traveler 'Joins' the Northwestern Editorial Excursion." *Arkansas Gazette,* June 12, 1960.

John Hallum

John Hallum, a prominent Little Rock lawyer and writer, authored the first book-length history of Arkansas. Published in 1887 at 581 pages, *Biographical and Pictorial History of Arkansas* was not a true history of the state, in the sense that most of the book consisted of biographical sketches. But, still, it included a wealth of information not found in other published works on Arkansas.

Despite his success as a lawyer, Hallum is better remembered for his books. Born in 1833 in Middle Tennessee to a hard-working and self-educated farmer-gunsmith, Hallum managed to attend college for two years before beginning to teach school. Later in life, Hallum remembered leaving college as "the mistake of my life," but he was intent on becoming a lawyer. Teaching in a rural school during the day and reading law at night, Hallum lacked the benefit of studying under a practicing attorney. After only two years, during which Hallum "hugged law books to my bosom," he was admitted to the bar at Memphis in May 1854.

Hanging out his shingle in Memphis, Hallum quickly established himself as a first-rate criminal lawyer. Among his clients was Sam Houston of Texas, who needed help in dealing with land claims near Memphis.

In the presidential campaign of 1860, Hallum supported Democrat Stephen A. Douglas. He was firmly opposed to secession, but when hostilities broke out he enlisted in the Confederate army, becoming a lieutenant. He served on the staff of Gen. Gideon J. Pillow of Helena. His opposition to secession continued even during his military service. He wrote from camp near Memphis not long after joining: "I greatly fear the South will not, cannot succeed. Slavery will perish, or be rendered absolutely worthless in the clash of arms." He was discharged after two years of service due to illness.

Reestablishing his law practice in Memphis, Hallum found prominent clients, including former Confederate Gen. Nathan Bedford

Forrest. Hallum got to know Albert Pike after Pike moved to Memphis following the war. Pike, who had long been a prominent legal and political leader in Little Rock, became a close friend and associate.

In 1870 Hallum relocated to St. Louis, where he practiced law; in 1874 he moved to Colorado, where he engaged in some highly contentious litigation dealing with land ownership. Finally, he moved to Little Rock in 1876, and in Arkansas found his final home. His Little Rock practice was extensive and lucrative.

Hallum's professional success allowed him to dabble in a variety of causes and diversions. An early Prohibition leader, he served four terms as president of the Prohibition Alliance of Arkansas. He was an ardent member and officer of the Knights of Pythias, one of the many fraternal organizations with wide followings in nineteenth-century America. But, it was writing, especially history, that was Hallum's passion for the remainder of his life.

Hallum found Arkansas's historical resources in a mess. There was no state archives, and all efforts before the Civil War to create a state historical society had failed. No one had published a history of the state, though several people, including Whig political leader and lawyer Jesse Turner of Van Buren, were interested in the subject. Hallum wrote that his objective became "to rescue this history from threatened oblivion, before it passed beyond the reach of authentic record."

Historians today realize that Hallum's books must be used with considerable discretion. Much of his work was based on participants' memories—what we call oral history today—but, unlike today, Hallum did not have written sources to corroborate the memories of his informants. Still, Hallum's publications—not just his 1887 book— are indispensable sources for modern historians because they are so early and on the whole quite good.

Some of the earliest American settlers in Arkansas were still living when Hallum began his research. Albert Pike was one of his best sources, and Pike even wrote several of the biographical sketches in Hallum's *Pictorial History.* Pike was a wonderful observer of human nature, though he tended to go easy on fellow Whigs. That did not keep him from noting, however, that the great Fayetteville jurist David Walker "was careless of his own personal dress."

Hallum sought out early settlers and asked them to submit written memoirs of their experiences. Judge John T. Jones of Helena recalled his arrival in Arkansas in 1835, fresh out of the University of Virginia. By 1842 Jones was a circuit judge in a huge district spanning northeast Arkansas. During a snowstorm he journeyed to Greene County, where he found the circuit clerk unaware of the scheduled court, and the sheriff "was twenty miles off at 'Uncle Peter's Still,' where he had been drunk the past two weeks." Without a jail, prisoners were tied to a large oak tree.

All of Hallum's books can be read with value. His *Diary of an Old Lawyer* (1895) is a fun read, while his *Reminiscences of the Confederacy* (1903) fills 400 pages with important documentation on Confederate Arkansas.

Hallum died July 11, 1906, after falling from the steps of a hotel in Pine Bluff.

FOR MORE INFORMATION:

Hallum, John. *The Diary of an Old Lawyer: Scenes behind the Curtain.* Nashville: Southwestern Publishing House, 1895.

Alice French

Arkansas has been the home of a remarkable number of writers of national reputation, perhaps none as well published as the stoutly built New England–born woman named Alice French, who wrote under the pen name of "Octave Thanet." At the height of her career, from 1896 to 1900, French published fifty short stories and five books. She was America's most highly paid female writer at that time. Today, however, she is little more than a literary footnote.

Born in Andover, Massachusetts, in 1850, French grew up the only daughter of a prosperous leather merchant. The family moved to the then frontier town of Davenport, Iowa, in 1856. She was well educated, attending Vassar College and later Abbot Academy, though she never took a degree.

She published her first story in 1871, at the age of twenty-one, under the pen name "Francis Essex." Later, she adopted the name Octave Thanet, apparently in deference to a common prejudice against female writers. *Atlantic* magazine published her first major piece in 1881, and before long her stories began appearing in such popular magazines as *Century, Scribner's,* and *Harper's.*

In 1882, just before she established her winter home in Arkansas, French published an unsigned piece in which she told of her decision not to marry. It is not clear whether this decision was due to sexual orientation or a personal philosophy.

The following year she visited Arkansas with Jane Allen Crawford, her lifelong companion who had inherited Clover Bend Plantation in Lawrence County. For the next quarter century the two women maintained their winter residence at Clover Bend. Historian Michael B. Dougan described their lifestyle: "With rare wines from France, ice from Poplar Bluff, Missouri, and groceries from S. S. Pierce in Boston, the two women held sway amid a 5,000 acre feudal domain flanked by cypress swamps."

When the plantation house burned in 1896, a large new one was

Alice French, a popular writer by the pen name Octave Thanet. *Photo courtesy of Special Collections, University of Arkansas Libraries.*

built and named "Thanford," a combination of the names Thanet and Crawford. It was a magnificent place, two and a half stories high, and replete with a carpentry shop where Alice liked to make furniture and a darkroom where she developed her own photographs. The gardens were extensive, including separate rose gardens, dozens of flowers, shrubs, and many rare trees.

William Allen White, the famed Kansas newspaperman, has left a vivid description of Thanford: "because she was passing rich, Octave

Thanet lived in feudal splendor. There, for the first time, we had high class southern cooking—turkeys stuffed with chestnuts, and roast pig stuffed with apricots and almonds, quail fried exquisitely, and all manner of gorgeous pastry. For four days she put on a real gastronomic parade. Miss French, who weighed something over 240 pounds in her six foot stature, enjoyed stuffing us as much as a taxidermist loves his art. We sat after dinner before her great log fire and talked far into the night."

During her years at Thanford, French set many of her stories in Arkansas. Her first Arkansas story, "Ma' Bowlin," which dealt sympathetically with a mentally challenged child and its father, was published in *Harper's Weekly* in 1887. The story "Trusty No. 49," which was set in a store in Powhatan because the new courthouse was not yet finished, dealt with the corrupt and abusive leasing of state convicts to private contractors. "Why Abbylonia Surrendered" was something of a feminist piece, dealing with a preacher's wife who secretly wrote sermons for her incompetent husband.

Despite her penchant for employing heavy and hard-to-read dialect, French provided vivid accounts of northeast Arkansas in the years after the Civil War. "Trusty No. 49" describes the small county seat of Powhatan: "It is an ancient town for Arkansas; in keelboat times it was bustling and prosperous, but the railroads passed by on the other side, and it fell into a gentle decay."

Not all the stories are set in Lawrence County. "Sist' Chaney's Black Silk" is set in Hot Springs and deals with a black woman who is trying to save money to buy a black dress for a dying relative. French's description of late nineteenth-century Hot Springs recorded the unchanging nature of a city built on therapeutic bathing: "the Hot Springs main street is a picturesque scene, a kaleidoscope of shifting figures, all tints of skin, all social rank: uncouth countrymen on cotton wagons; negroes in carts drawn by oxen or skeleton mules with rope harness; pigs lifting their protesting noses out of some carts, fowls squawking in others; a dead deer flung over a horseman's saddle; modish-looking men and women walking; . . . cripples on crutches . . . hugging the sunny side of the street before the bath-houses; pale ghosts of human beings in wheeled chairs—so the endless procession of wealth or poverty or disease or hope oscillates along the winding street between the mountains."

She concludes, "The houses are as different as the people, squalor and roughness of a mining camp flung cheek by jowl against brick facades of the American renaissance, with terra cotta ornaments and low arched windows. Booths innumerable lean out over the mud sidewalk; Hot Springs crystals glitter in jewelers' windows;. . . . Every house that is not a hotel has a sign of 'Rooms to Let.' Visibly the town lives upon the stranger within its gates."

While French could be sympathetic toward African American characters, she was not particularly enlightened on race matters. Professor Dougan described French's racial attitudes thusly: "Her South was neither moonlight and magnolias nor the southern Gothic; her racism was white supremacist without being race baiting."

As time passed and her health and fortunes declined, French spent less time in Arkansas. By 1909 French complained in her diary of the effort and money required to keep Thanford going. The plantation was sold in 1918, and French never returned to Arkansas. The world changed so dramatically that French felt out of place in the modern era. Her writing declined, and she lived in near poverty by the time she died in 1934.

FOR MORE INFORMATION:

Dougan, Michael B., and Carol W. *By the Cypress Swamp: The Arkansas Stories of Octave Thanet.* Little Rock: Rose Publishing Co., 1980.

McMichael, George. *Journey to Obscurity: The Life of Octave Thanet.* Lincoln: University of Nebraska Press, 1965.

Dionicio Rodriguez

When thinking of the Hispanic impact on Arkansas history, most Arkansans probably think of the sixteenth-century explorer Hernando de Soto. As the first European to explore what is now Arkansas, de Soto deserves his historical standing. However, more Arkansans ought to know and appreciate the obscure Dionicio Rodriguez.

While few Arkansans might recognize Rodriguez's name, anyone who has been to the Old Mill in North Little Rock knows the artistic creations of this quiet Mexican immigrant. Rodriguez was an artist who worked in concrete; more specifically, he used concrete to fashion creations that resembled wood. Known as *faux bois* in French, this process involved creating sculptures of reinforced concrete, which are finished with hand-sculpted surfaces often inseparable from real wood.

Rodriguez was born around 1891 in Toluca, about sixty miles from Mexico City. We know little of his youth, except that as a teenager he worked for an artist who produced imitation rocks, ruins, and grottos. Among his early projects was work on the Mexican presidential residence in Mexico City, Chapultepec Castle. As Sybil F. Crawford has noted in an article in the *Pulaski County Historical Review,* Rodriguez's work grew out of a Mexican folk tradition known as *el trabajo rustico* (rustic work)

Around 1920 Rodriguez moved to Laredo, Texas, and then to San Antonio. He was apparently unmarried and came alone to the United States. By 1932, he was in North Little Rock working for legendary real estate developer Justin Matthews, creating sculptural pieces for three parks: Crestwood, Lakewood, and the T. R. Pugh Memorial Park, site of the famed Old Mill. Matthews paid a premium wage to his immigrant artist, as much as seventy-five dollars per week even though the Depression raged.

Modern authorities consider Rodriguez's work at the Old Mill to be among his best. *Faux bois* bridges, benches, and fences abound; the mill's water wheel, which weighed 10,000 pounds, was made entirely of concrete. The Old Mill became an immediate success upon its dedication in 1933, at which Rodriguez spoke through an interpreter, noting that he considered the Old Mill his greatest achievement. By 1939 the Old Mill was well enough known to be chosen as the backdrop for the opening scenes in the film "Gone with the Wind." This special—and maybe a bit eccentric—creation is now an Arkansas icon.

Harvey C. Couch, the prominent utility executive, commissioned Rodriguez to produce a number of pieces for his country retreats in Garland and Hot Spring counties. Rodriguez's work at Couchwood near Hot Springs is considered to be the best collection of his domestic/residential work. Many of the sculptures at Couchwood are practical features, such as steps and flower planters. Others are whimsical, especially a concrete owl peering from a knothole in a "log" retaining wall, its marble eyes seeming to follow passersby. An ice cooler was made to resemble a hollow tree stump, with a plugged "knothole" to serve as a drain.

Crawford, who has written the entry on Rodriguez for the *Encyclopedia of Arkansas History and Culture,* described the work this way: "Helpers built concrete footings for his sculptures, and the underpinnings were made with reinforcing bars, rods, mesh screen wire, and rubble, held together with a rough coat of concrete. Metal materials were bound together with wire, not welded. Working outdoors, the sculptor himself applied the surface coat of smooth concrete or 'neat' cement, a term for pure Portland cement. To imitate nature, varied textures were created using his hands, forks, spoons, or handmade tools."

Rodriguez was secretive about his methods. He did not plan his work through sketches or drawings. He also refused to discuss the ingredients used in tinting the sculptures.

Dionicio Rodriguez died in San Antonio on December 16, 1955. He was buried in San Fernando Archdiocesan Cemetery. Though rumored to have been married as a young man, he left no known survivors.

In recent years Rodriguez's sculptures have been extensively researched, and his North Little Rock work has been included on the National Register of Historic Places.

FOR MORE INFORMATION:

Crawford, Sybil F. "Dionicio Rodriguez (1891–1955)." *The Encyclopedia of Arkansas History and Culture.* http://encyclopediaofarkansas.net/encyclopedia/entry-detail.aspx?search=1&entryID=503.

Crawford, Sybil F. "Dionicio Rodriguez: The *Faux Bois* Sculptor." *Pulaski County Historical Review* 50 (Spring 2002): 13–24.

Light, Patsy Pittman. *Capturing Nature: The Cement Sculpture of Dionicio Rodriguez.* College Station: Texas A & M Press, 2008.

Brewer Family

No family contributed more to the history of Arkansas art than the Brewer clan of Little Rock and elsewhere. That three generations of Brewers could make their livings as artists in Arkansas spoke well for the arts in a relatively small southern capital city.

The earliest of the Brewer artists was Nicholas R. Brewer, who was born in 1857. He became a well-established painter of portraits and landscapes and began exhibiting at the National Academy of Design in New York in 1885. A resident of St. Paul, Minnesota, Brewer traveled widely, exposing his son Adrian to art and artists from around the world.

Adrian developed his own interest in art at an early age. By age twelve Adrian had his own "artistic little studio," with a desk, library, and drawing supplies. He was particularly fond of drawing horses, and he kept a diary of his daily visits to a local blacksmith shop so he could draw horses. His father treated Adrian as a serious student, and he admonished, "When you can draw the human figure as faithfully as you can draw a horse, you'll be all right."

In 1911, Adrian entered the University of Minnesota, where he studied art. At the same time, he began studies at the Art Institute of St. Paul, and later he studied for a short time at the Art Students League in New York. Jolynda Hammock Halinski, author of the entry on Adrian Brewer in the *Encyclopedia of Arkansas History and Culture,* wrote that "he learned more about art from some of his father's associates than from his classes."

After graduation, Adrian returned to St. Paul, where he taught at local art institutes before opening a commercial art studio in Minneapolis. He had major clients, including Pillsbury. His work in commercial art had a substantial impact on his later work as a painter.

During World War I, Adrian enlisted in the army, where he was soon painting patriotic posters, cartoons, and other works. After his military service, Adrian joined his father as business manager and assistant, a role he played on and off for years. He also continued his own painting, and he won many awards in St. Paul competitions.

Adrian and his father came to Arkansas in 1919, when the Art Association of Little Rock sponsored an exhibit of Nicholas's work. While in Little Rock, Nicholas received several commissions, and he took his son with him to Hot Springs, where they set up a studio in the Eastman Hotel. While in Hot Springs, Adrian met Miss Edwina Cook, whom he married in 1921.

After his marriage, Adrian made another foray into the commercial art business, before tiring of it and resolving to be a professional artist. Again, he worked for his father, using the time to hone his own skills at landscape painting. In 1928 Adrian made a splash in the art world by winning the huge $2,500 Edgar B. Davis Prize for his painting of Texas bluebonnet landscapes. The painting is in the holdings of the Witte Museum in San Antonio. An example of this "bluebonnet period" is a large painting held by the Butler Center for Arkansas Studies at the Central Arkansas Library System in downtown Little Rock. The Davis Prize resulted in numerous commissions and financial gain, but Adrian was fearful of becoming known as a "flower painter," so he traveled to New Mexico, where he produced 126 landscape paintings.

Fortunately, Adrian Brewer spent a great deal of time painting Arkansas scenes. He often painted from mountaintops, such as Petit Jean Mountain. He also found a steady stream of clients wanting portraits, including U.S. Sen. Joseph T. Robinson. The Robinson portrait was later hung in the state capitol. He painted portraits of more than three hundred Arkansans during his long life. Commissions in Washington and New York also helped the Brewer family survive the Great Depression.

Brewer painted many Arkansas landscapes during the 1920s and 1930s, often from atop Petit Jean Mountain in Conway County. Biographer Halinski wrote that Brewer's Arkansas paintings went beyond his usual "quasi-impressionist" style, "the light and colors changed less, and the natural detail is almost photographic; dabs of strong color indicate a more romantic approach to nature."

It was a painting of the U.S. flag just before the outbreak of World War II, however, that became Adrian's most famous work. Depicting an American flag hanging loosely from a pole, the painting is a majestic and inspiring interpretation that caught on immediately. Reproductions of this painting hung in countless classrooms and movie theaters during the war. It can still be found in antique stores and online auctions. The original painting became the property of the U.S. Naval Academy.

Like his father before him, Adrian Brewer passed on his artistic abilities to his son, Edwin, who was a painter of note in Arkansas and later in California. Several of Edwin's works are in the collections of the Butler Center in Little Rock, especially noteworthy being a series of large watercolors depicting historic sites in Arkansas.

While Adrian was primarily known as an artist, some in Little Rock later recalled him as an art educator and patron of other artists. With the help of another gifted artist, Powell Scott, Brewer opened the Adrian Brewer School of Art in downtown Little Rock. While students learned lessons in painting, they also heard poet John Gould Fletcher read poems, architect Max Mayer lecture on great buildings, and the beloved Josef Rosenberg play the piano.

While the first school failed due to the Depression, Adrian and his sons started the Cedar Street Studio after World War II. For years this studio was a haven for Arkansans who craved an artistic presence in their lives.

FOR MORE INFORMATION:

Brett, Mary Margaret. "Adrian Brewer: Joint Exhibits Honor One of State's and Nation's Outstanding Artists." *Arkansas Gazette,* February 5, 1961.

Davis, Charles T. "Adrian Brewer, Arkansas Artist, Builds a Studio." *Arkansas Gazette,* December 6, 1951.

Halinski, Jolynda. *Adrian Brewer, Arkansas Artist.* Exhibit Catalog. Little Rock: University of Arkansas at Little Rock Department of Art, 1996.

———. "Adrian Louis Brewer (1891–1956)." *The Encyclopedia of Arkansas History and Culture.* http://encyclopediaofarkansas.net/encyclopedia/entry-detail.aspx?search=1&entryID=451.

Vance Randolph

Until his death in 1980, Vance Randolph was the dean of Ozark folk-lorists. Although he was not actually of academia, he operated around the edges of the University of Arkansas and his reputation in academia has continued to grow.

Randolph spent most of his long life tramping around in the Arkansas and Missouri Ozarks, in the process becoming the nation's foremost authority on the people and ways of this mid-continent mountain range. He wrote more than twenty books and hundreds of articles.

Born in Kansas in 1892, Randolph came to folklore after an unfo-cused career as a journalist (mostly for socialist newspapers) and a high school teacher. After stateside service in World War I, he pur-chased a small cabin in the Missouri Ozarks. For the next sixty years he devoted his life to documenting Ozark life. To make a living, Randolph wrote for a variety of popular magazines. Often under a pseudonym, he authored a number of "Little Blue Books" for a social-ist publisher in Kansas.

While Randolph was well read and held a graduate degree in psy-chology from the University of Massachusetts, he was not an academic. Indeed, he called himself a "collector," meaning what he did best was get out among the hill folk and collect information based on close and personal observation. One journalist described Randolph's tech-niques: "For more than 60 years Randolph lived among the Ozark hill people, traveling in mule-drawn wagons, dancing the 'Chicken Reel' at hoedowns, witnessing cussings and baptizings and joining the men-folk in drinking 'mountain dew' around campfires at fox hunts."

Randolph published his first two books in the early 1930s, *The Ozarks* and *Ozark Mountain Folks*. From 1946 to 1958 he published eleven volumes, including his four-volume *Ozark Folksongs*. In 1951 came the first of his impressive folktale collections, beginning with *We Always Lie to Strangers*, which was followed by four more folktale

Vance Randolph, a famed folklorist and curmudgeon. *Photo courtesy of Special Collections, University of Arkansas Libraries.*

books. In 1965 Randolph brought out *Hot Springs and Hell,* which one reviewer called "America's first fully annotated jokebook." Finally, in Randolph's waning years, society was ready for his long-suppressed bawdy tales and songs. *Pissing in the Snow,* published in 1976, became his best selling book.

Among Randolph's books can be found two classic reference works, the massive *Ozark Folklore: A Bibliography* (1972) and *Down in the Holler: A Gallery of Ozark Folk Speech* (1953). The bibliography is a trove for Arkansas history researchers, replete with over 2,500 annotated references on every aspect of Ozarkiana. Randolph was not a gentle or easy man, and his folklore bibliography contained stark evaluations. He said Guy Howard's Ozarks novel *Give Me Thy Vineyard* (1949) was "a very poor novel containing some of the worst dialect I have ever seen in print."

Down in the Holler, on the other hand, had an appeal far beyond academia. Every Arkansan with a sense of humor could enjoy and learn from this book. In the chapter on "Sayings and Wisecracks," Randolph wrote of the hillman's "habitual use of picturesque comparisons, outlandish metaphors and similes, ... and bucolic wisecracks generally." He noted, "The Ozarker is not content to observe that any object is cold; he likes to say it's cold as a banker's heart." Attractive girls and women were referred to as "pretty as a speckled pup" or "cute as a bug's ear."

Randolph's sense of humor pervaded *Down in the Holler.* The chapter on wisecracks included many references to bootlegging. "One of our neighbors," Randolph wrote, "always spoke of a special kind of moonshine as 'Bottled in the Barn,' doubtless an imitation of 'Bottled in Bond.' They tell me that a fellow near the Missouri-Arkansas line used regular printed labels bearing the words 'Bottled in the Barn,' but I never saw one of these."

The final seventy-five pages of this book contain a detailed Ozark word list with definitions. Readers always learn something from a dip into this chapter, though sometimes it can be painful. For example, the word "arkansaw" was sometimes used to mean to cheat or take advantage of: "When a hunter shoots a quail on the ground, the bird is said to be *arkansawed.*"

If Randolph were still living, he might be amazed to learn that some of his books are now rare and fetch (or *fotch*) hundreds of dollars. Regardless of their prices, books by Vance Randolph read as well today as they did decades ago when the author was making his way through the most distant Ozark hollers and hills.

In his later years, Randolph married Mary Celestia Parler, who was a noted folklorist and professor of English at the University of Arkansas. He died at age eighty-eight in 1980.

FOR MORE INFORMATION:

Cochran, Robert. *Vance Randolph: An Ozark Life.* Urbana: University of Illinois Press, 1985.

———. "Vance Randolph." *Arkansas Libraries* 38 (March 1981): 15–18.

Cochran, Robert, and Michael Luster. *For Love and for Money: The Writings of Vance Randolph: An Annotated Bibliography.* Batesville: Arkansas College Folklore Archive Publications, 1979.

"Noted Folklorist Dies at Age 88: Vance Randolph, Expert on Ozarks." *Arkansas Gazette,* November 2, 1980.

Randolph, Vance. *Ozark Folklore: A Bibliography.* Bloomington: Indiana University Research Center for the Language Sciences, 1972.

Randolph, Vance, with George P. Wilson. *Down in the Holler: A Gallery of Ozark Folk Speech.* Norman: University of Oklahoma Press, 1953.

Miss Lily Peter

Miss Lily Peter of Phillips County was among a select group of renaissance women in Arkansas. Before her death in 1991, at the age of 100, Miss Lily, as she was called by everyone who knew her, was known far and wide as a pioneering woman farmer, an environmentalist before it became popular to be one, a supporter of the arts, and a poet of no mean ability.

A few years ago former Arkansas Tech University English professor AnnieLaura M. Jaggers wrote a book-length biography of Miss Lily, the story of a remarkable woman of the Delta who carried on life in a way that would be considered adventurous even by modern standards. Miss Lily herself said she had lived three separate lives, or "incarnations," as she called it. "My first incarnation, I was a schoolteacher. In my second, I was a farmer. I began my third incarnation in 1978 when I began trying to be a full-time writer."

Miss Lily was not inclined to discuss her precise age, so many were surprised to learn from her obituary that she was 100 years old. She was born in Phillips County on June 2, 1891, one of five children of William O. and Florence M. Peter. Her father, descended from German Moravian missionaries, moved to Arkansas from Ohio. Miss Lily grew up deep in the rich lowlands of Phillips County, at the confluence of Big Creek and Big Cypress Bayou.

Educated at home until the age of ten, Miss Lily was sent to Ohio for better schooling. During her first year in Ohio, Miss Lily faced the tragedy of her father's early death. At her mother's urging, she stayed in school and upon returning to Phillips County a few years later became a teacher. She taught for forty years, a career that would satisfy most normal folks.

But, all the time she was teaching, Miss Lily was helping her brother Jesse run the family farm. Eventually, the siblings accumulated over four thousand acres of land in Phillips and Monroe counties. Miss Lily graduated from a cotton grading school in Memphis with skills that allowed her to deal directly with cotton buyers. When her brother died in 1956, Miss Lily went into heavy debt in order to acquire total ownership of the farms. She lived in a modest home near the small town of Marvell. Her banker, J. J. White of Helena National Bank, said her handling of farm affairs was excellent, adding, "Lily Peter is by far the most brilliant, far-sighted farmer I have ever dealt with."

Miss Lily was a natural farmer. She had always loved the land itself, and she viewed the farm as part of the larger landscape. The busy little woman studied soils, the weather, and the cycles of nature. Her award-winning photographs often featured the majestic cypress swamps she had come to love as a child.

In the early 1970s, Miss Lily read Rachel Carson's *Silent Spring,* a book that created conservationists across the nation and around the world—including Lily Peter. It was Miss Lily's 1977 decision to forgo most chemical insecticides that caused her to become an icon to the environmental community.

Miss Lily's third incarnation, as a writer, continued for the remainder of her long life. She had always read widely, and her academic life included study at Columbia and Vanderbilt, where she took a master's degree in English. She wrote poetry from her youth, and as the years passed she delved deeply into the craft. In 1964, Miss Lily published her first book of poetry, and two years later she brought out what many believe to be a classic epic on the great Spanish explorer Hernando de Soto, *The Great Riding.* Gov. Dale Bumpers named Miss Lily poet laureate of Arkansas in 1971.

Miss Lily, who enjoyed the limelight, came to the attention of every Arkansan in 1969 when she brought the Philadelphia Symphony to perform free of charge in Little Rock. It was a gift to the state in honor of the 150th anniversary of Arkansas becoming a territory in 1819. The *Arkansas Gazette* ran a long front-page story on the arrival of conductor Eugene Ormandy and the plan to perform a composition by Pulitzer prize–winning composer Dello Joio, "Homage to Haydn," which Miss Lily commissioned. Newspapers around the world hailed the achievement of this cotton farmer from a place called Marvell.

Miss Lily Peter, poet, farmer, ecologist, and patron of the arts. *Photo courtesy of Special Collections, University of Arkansas Libraries.*

FOR MORE INFORMATION:

Dillion, Kathy. "Lily Peter (1891–1991)." *The Encyclopedia of Arkansas History and Culture.* http://encyclopediaofarkansas.net/encyclopedia/entry-detail.aspx?search=1&entryID=1736.

Jaggers, AnnieLaura M. *A Nude Singularity: Lily Peter of Arkansas.* Conway: University of Central Arkansas Press, 1993.

"Lily Peter Obituary." *Arkansas Democrat,* July 27, 1991.

Patterson, Carrick. "A New Experience, Ormandy Declares As He Meets 'Angel.'" *Arkansas Gazette,* June 3, 1969.

Shiras, Ginger. "Organic Farming Brings Big Savings." *Arkansas Gazette,* November 6, 1977.

CHAPTER VIII

Education, Science, and Medicine

Dr. Charles McDermott

Dr. Charles McDermott was one of those amazing Americans of the nineteenth century who could do just about anything. A prominent physician, founder of the town of Dermott, plantation owner, inventor, and tinkerer extraordinaire, McDermott was above all a visionary and dreamer. Had McDermott lived to witness the flight of the Wright brothers in 1903, most likely he would have cheered loudly—and then, perhaps, muttered to himself, "I could have done that."

McDermott was born in southeastern Louisiana in 1808, a mere five years after the area became part of the United States through the Louisiana Purchase. He was born into the wealthy landowning family of Patrick and Emily Ozan McDermott, his mother a member of the local French-speaking population.

As was the case with most male offspring of the local aristocracy, young "Charlie" was sent to private boarding schools, and he eventually took a degree in what we would call mechanical engineering from Yale. While at Yale he converted to Presbyterianism under the tutelage of famed theologian Lyman Beecher.

The twenty-year-old Charles decided to study medicine under Dr. Henry Baines, his brother-in-law and a distinguished graduate of a London medical school. After four years of this study (and practicing on the family's slaves), Charles "made a place for himself as a successfully practicing physician," to quote McDermott's biographer, Robert Diffee.

For unclear reasons, perhaps involving family jealousies and intrigue, about 1835 Dr. McDermott and his brother Edward relocated to southeastern Arkansas, establishing a flourishing farm on Bayou Bartholomew in what is now extreme northwestern Chicot County. McDermott was fascinated by the wildlife, boasting of one bear hunt in which three bears were killed—along with wolves, deer, turkey, and foxes. The brothers bought as much land as they could get, gradually building vast holdings along Bayou Bartholomew. Until 1844

McDermott apparently lived mostly in Louisiana near his mother while his brother managed the Arkansas farms. "It was a poor log house I moved into," McDermott wrote years later in a brief memoir, "but within a few years I had paid off my debts and increased my properties."

McDermott's wife, Miss Hettie Smith, was reputed to have been a relative of the future president of the Confederacy, Jefferson Davis. When the Civil War drew near, McDermott became an ardent secessionist. He especially opposed granting citizenship and other rights to African Americans. After the war, an embittered McDermott promoted unsuccessful attempts to establish colonies of ex-Confederates in Central America.

Ultimately, McDermott returned to his large home, and the settlement that grew up around it was named Dermott in his honor. As the years passed, the doctor spent a goodly amount of his time inventing. He patented a cotton-picking machine (nothing ever came of it) as well as a more successful iron wedge. But, it was his flying machine that earned him a footnote in American aviation history.

On November 12, 1872, the U.S. Patent Office granted patent 133,046 for McDermott's flying machine, which is believed to be the first American patent for a heavier-than-air flying machine. Its inventor called it an "Improvement in Apparatus for Navigating the Air." Apparently McDermott had experimented with flight since he was a child. He had studied aerodynamics, the lifting capacity of wind, and wing design, but the available steam power of the day did not allow for motive power, or "horizontal propulsion," as the Doctor called it.

Dr. McDermott's flying machine was unveiled at the 1874 Southeast Arkansas Fair in Monticello. From there it was well received at the state fair, and then it was included in the Arkansas exhibition at the U.S. Centennial Exposition in Philadelphia in 1876.

The McDermott machine was an odd-looking creation, with eleven fixed wings, all mounted one atop the other, the large propeller powered by the pilot's peddling. I could locate no evidence that the model ever flew, although there are references to repeated attempts. As late as 1882, only two years before his death, McDermott was quoted as hoping "to give a flying chariot to every poor woman, far better than Queen Victoria ever rode in."

A replica of McDermott's machine, based on the drawings filed with the patent application, can be seen at the Arkansas Aviation Education Center on East Roosevelt Road, near the Little Rock National Airport, Adams Field.

FOR MORE INFORMATION:

Atkinson, James H., ed. "A Memoir of Charles McDermott: A Pioneer of South-eastern Arkansas." *Arkansas Historical Quarterly* 12 (Autumn 1953): 253–61.

Diffee, Robert A. "Arkansas's Early Aviation Heritage." *Pulaski County Historical Review* 43 (Fall 1995): 50–64.

J. C. Corbin

Joseph Carter Corbin of Pine Bluff was apparently the only black Arkansan to hold statewide public office. From 1872 to 1874 he was the state superintendent of public instruction. Corbin's long career as the head of Branch Normal College in Pine Bluff, however, is what has earned him a place in Arkansas history.

Born to free parents in 1833 in Chillicothe, Ohio, young Joseph was educated in "tuition schools" because the public schools were reserved for white children. At age sixteen, he enrolled himself in a private academy in Louisville in order to study Latin. In 1850 Corbin enrolled at Ohio University in Athens, at age seventeen. He earned a bachelors degree in three years, followed by a master's degree in 1856. Though records are scarce, we know he joined the Philomathean Society, which afforded him the opportunity to hone his debating skills.

After several years as a teacher, Corbin edited and published a newspaper in Cincinnati during the Civil War. It was while in Cincinnati that he met his wife, Mary Jane Ward. The long marriage produced six children.

Corbin moved to Little Rock in 1872, during Reconstruction. He took a job with Republican U.S. Sen. Powell Clayton's *Daily Republican* newspaper, and in his free time he served as a loyal Clayton ally in the growing fight for control of the state Republican organization. When the Clayton faction decided to dump incumbent superintendent of public instruction Dr. Thomas Smith, Corbin received the nomination— while a competing reform faction put Smith on its ticket. Corbin stumped across Arkansas in support of the entire regular Republican ticket.

With Clayton still in control of the election machinery, Corbin won election to state office, only a few months after arriving in the state. Corbin served two years as superintendent of public instruction, a post in which he worked to meet the huge challenge of creating the state's first public school system. However, Arkansans were far more interested in the raging fire that was destroying the Republican Party from within and at the same time paving the way for the end of Reconstruction.

As Powell Clayton, who now struggled to control the Arkansas political scene from Washington, D.C., while serving as a U.S. senator, fought with opponents led by Rev. Joseph Brooks and other reformers, Corbin worked to create educational opportunities. Among other duties, he served as ex-officio president of the board of trustees of the newly created Arkansas Industrial University, and as such he signed the contract for the construction of Old Main in Fayetteville.

Not long after assuming office, Corbin helped prepare legislation to create a college for black Arkansans. The legislation, which was adopted in 1873, authorized the creation of "a branch Normal college, which location—owing to the principal college being located in the northwest portion of the state—shall be made southeast or east or south of the county of Pulaski." The legislation provided that the new branch was "in all things [to] be governed by the same rules and regulations" as the university itself.

Corbin and his Reconstruction allies did not have time to get Branch Normal College into operation before Reconstruction was overthrown in the Brooks-Baxter War of 1874. Corbin, along with all state officials, lost his position with the adoption of the constitution of 1874, the document that still governs Arkansas.

It fell to "Redeemer Democrat" Gov. Augustus Hill Garland to actually implement the legislation authorizing Branch Normal. Garland was a racial moderate for his time, and he not only implemented Corbin's legislation but also hired Corbin to create the college. Branch Normal College opened its doors on September 27, 1875, when seven black students, four from Drew County and three from Jefferson, arrived for registration.

For many years Branch Normal was little more than a public grade school, though it soon offered courses in the higher grades. Students during the first year of operation ranged in age from eight to twenty-eight. Equally amazing, for several years Corbin performed not only as principal but also as teacher, custodian, and administrator as a staff of one.

In 1882 Corbin celebrated the erection of a building specifically for the college on land west of Pine Bluff. The following year he finally received funding for an assistant to help with the teaching load. A few years later came a dormitory. By 1893 Corbin's teaching staff consisted of five, including himself. He was active in the community, including serving as grand master of the Arkansas chapter of Prince Hall Masons. Since the state fair did not normally allow black participation, Corbin was one of the organizers of the Colored Industrial Fair, which usually mounted a large exhibit in Pine Bluff. Perhaps Corbin's major contribution to black education in Arkansas was his work in training black teachers. He conducted summer teacher institutes at black schools throughout Arkansas and much of Texas.

Racism grew more rampant in Arkansas and much of the South during the 1890s, and this brought an end to the career of the remarkable J. C. Corbin. In 1893 the legislature sent a committee to investigate Branch Normal, which resulted in a recommendation that Corbin be fired, but that the school should be continued—as an experiment "in educating the colored race."

Though the university board of trustees kept Corbin as principal, they placed a white faculty member in charge of most administrative tasks. William H. Langford, a white member of the university board of trustees and a Pine Bluff lawyer and banker, became the virtual boss of the college. In June 1902, Langford persuaded the board of trustees to dump Corbin and replace him with a young graduate of Tuskegee Institute, Isaac Fisher.

Corbin did not quietly fade away, but rather mounted a counterattack and asked for reinstatement. Losing this appeal, Corbin became principal of Merrill High School, a large black public school in Pine Bluff. He died in 1911, survived by a son and daughter who took his body to Chicago for burial.

FOR MORE INFORMATION:

Preston, Izola. "Joseph Carter Corbin (1833–1911)." *The Encyclopedia of Arkansas History and Culture.* http://encyclopediaofarkansas.net/encyclopedia/entry-detail.aspx?search=1&entryID=1624.

Rothrock, Thomas. "Joseph Carter Corbin and Negro Education in the University of Arkansas." *Arkansas Historical Quarterly* 30 (Winter 1971): 277–314.

Ida Joe Brooks

In the summer of 1903, a very determined woman was packing her bags to leave Arkansas. Dr. Ida Joe Brooks of Little Rock had left Arkansas once already in order to get a medical degree, and in 1903 she had to leave once again to gain a specialty in psychiatry. By that point in her life, Dr. Brooks had already set many records and was on her way to becoming a renowned leader in Arkansas medical, social, and political circles.

Born in 1853 in Muscatine, Iowa, Brooks was given a masculine middle name in recognition of her father, Joseph Brooks, of Brooks-Baxter War fame. The family moved to Arkansas after the Civil War, and her father became a leader of the badly splintered Reconstruction Republican Party. With the end of Reconstruction in 1874, Brooks lost all his political power, but unlike many Republican leaders he remained in Arkansas, serving as postmaster of Little Rock.

Years later Ida Joe Brooks ran for public office, but from her early years education occupied most of her considerable energies. Little is known of her early education, but she apparently attended local schools and earned a degree from Little Rock University, a private college. In 1873 she became a teacher in the Little Rock public schools. After only four years in the classroom, Brooks was elected the first female president of the Arkansas State Teachers Association.

In 1887 Brooks applied for admission to the University of Arkansas Medical Department, then an all-male institution. Though she protested loudly when denied entry because of her sex, the school refused to bend and Brooks ultimately took her medical degree in 1891 from Boston University School of Medicine.

Amazingly enough, Brooks maintained her loyalty to Arkansas even after being shunned by the state's medical school. With her new diploma in hand, she set up a pediatrics practice in Little Rock, commenting, "I am proud of Arkansas, proud of the advanced ground she has taken on many issues, eager that she shall maintain her position and grow to better things." In 1906 she became the first woman in Arkansas to open a practice in psychiatry.

As noted by the major historian of Arkansas psychiatry, the late Dr. Fred O. Henker, Brooks "was not accepted warmly by the medical establishment." Indeed, she was rejected for membership in the Arkansas Medical Society, so in her characteristically defiant manner she formed her own society, the Women's Medical Club of Arkansas.

Gradually the medical community warmed to Brooks, and in 1914 she joined the staff of the University of Arkansas Medical School as a professor in the Department of Nervous and Mental Diseases, becoming the first female faculty member. In 1916 she was hired as the medical inspector for the Little Rock Public Schools.

Practically every child in the Little Rock schools received an injection at the hands of the tall, brusque doctor wearing a billowing white uniform. The late Booker Worthen of Little Rock once described how intimidating Dr. Brooks could be to a sixth grader. He told of leaving his home on a streetcar one Saturday morning, headed across town to spend the day with a playmate. Suddenly, the streetcar door opened and in stepped Dr. Brooks. Young Booker was too frightened to leave his seat upon reaching his destination, and he continued the ride until Dr. Brooks departed.

Though the students found Brooks more than a little scary, in reality she was a caring and highly competent medical professional. She conducted vision and hearing tests for students, and the school district eventually adopted her recommendation to provide eyeglasses to indigent students. She administered Binet-Simon and Yearkes intelligence tests for those students she thought might need attention. She was instrumental in establishing the Exceptional School for "mentally deficient" students in 1911, the first of its kind in Arkansas. For several years she also served as the psychiatrist for the Little Rock Juvenile Court. University of Central Arkansas history student Gina Bowie has published an interesting article in the *Pulaski County Historical Review* in which Dr. Brooks is placed squarely in the reform tradition of what historians call the progressive movement.

As one might expect given her father and namesake, Brooks had an interest in political affairs. She worked for Prohibition and for decades campaigned to extend the vote to women. In 1920 she became the first woman in the state to file for statewide office, running as a Republican for state superintendent of public instruction. The state attorney general, Democrat John D. Arbuckle, ruled her off the ballot, holding that the newly adopted Nineteenth Amendment did indeed allow women to vote, though it said nothing about them running for office.

Brooks died on March 13, 1939, at St. Vincent Infirmary in Little Rock from complications associated with a broken hip. She was buried at Bellefontaine Cemetery in St. Louis.

FOR MORE INFORMATION:

Bowie, Gina Staggs. "The Progressive Movement in Little Rock Schools." *Pulaski County Historical Review* 45 (Summer 1997): 24–26. This article is illustrated with two fine photographs of Dr. Brooks, among others.

Henker, Fred O., and Edwina Walls Mann. "Ida Josephine Brooks (1853–1939)." *The Encyclopedia of Arkansas History and Culture.* http://encyclopediaofarkansas. net/encyclopedia/entry-detail.aspx?search=1&entryID=6.

Anna P. Strong

Mrs. Anna P. Strong of Marianna, Lee County, was one of those black teachers who accomplished amazing feats in educating the masses of black children during the era of Jim Crow segregation. Working with only a fraction of the resources available to the segregated white schools, Strong and her colleagues managed to keep the school doors open and brought literacy to the children of former slaves.

Born Anna M. Pascal in 1884 in Phillips County, she received a good education at a school operated by Quakers near Lexa in her home county. Originally begun by the Society of Friends at the request of the Union army commander in Helena, at first the school was a home for orphaned black children. After operating several years as an elementary and secondary school, it added college level instruction and became known as Southland College. The major focus of Southland became teacher training, an important quest given the need to educate more than 100,000 suddenly freed former slaves. Anna received her diploma from Southland in 1903. The school functioned until 1925.

Strong was destined for the classroom. She took her first teaching job at Trenton, near Marvell, at the age of fourteen, an early age even for the nineteenth century, when children often entered the workforce at a tender age. Fortunately, she continued to study at Southland during these early teaching stints. Later, she furthered her education at Tuskegee Institute and Columbia University. For many years she was principal of Robert F. Moton High School in Marianna. She received honorary degrees from Arkansas Agricultural, Mechanical and Normal College in Pine Bluff and Bishop College in Texas.

Strong was known as a strict disciplinarian and a strong leader. Two teachers who taught at Moton High School while Strong was principal recalled that "she emphasized the need for self-esteem and self-control and through this she gained the respect and confidence of those whom she led." These teachers also recalled that "the rapid clap of her hands meant that something was in disorder" and must be corrected.

During her long tenure as a school principal, Strong brought many black leaders and professionals to speak to the student body, including Oscar DePriest of Chicago, the first black congressman of the twentieth century, and the famed Olympic gold medal runner Jesse Owens.

Strong's leadership at Moton High School helped propel her to the presidency of the Arkansas Teachers Association in 1929, the second female to hold that post. In her inaugural address, Strong urged black teachers to become active in the National Congress of Colored Parents and Teachers—a group she helped establish in 1926. She also urged teachers to give more attention to the health of each child in the classroom. Stressing the need to make more educational progress, she urged teachers to take college extension courses.

Later Strong served as vice president of the American Teachers Association, the black equivalent of the National Education Association. She also served as president of the National Congress of Colored Parents and Teachers in 1942–45.

Strong was a generally optimistic, forward-looking leader who usually put a positive face on most situations. However, her tenure as president of the 60,000 member National Congress of Colored Parents and Teachers occurred during World War II, when many black leaders were complaining about being expected to fight for a country that did not recognize their rights.

In one address, Strong acknowledged that young black men were presenting some "challenging articulations." Strong proposed, "We must tell them that liberty and justice and equal opportunity are still worth fighting for. We must show them that ignorance, prejudice, and greed are problems of our democracy and the tool of a destructive minority. We must call on all that we have of strength. We must unite all our forces of faith and hope and love to help our youth save itself in this greatest of world crises."

Anna P. Strong was the first president of the National Congress of Parents and Teachers to address the National Parent-Teacher Association. In 1942 she shared the platform with Mrs. Franklin D. Roosevelt.

After twenty-five years at Moton High School, Strong won a scholarship to Columbia University in New York City. She then joined the staff of the Arkansas State Department of Education, where her specialty was improving rural black schools. After eight years, she returned to Marianna and resumed her work as a principal. Moton High School was renamed in honor of Strong, and today a Marianna middle school is named in recognition of this remarkable woman. Anna P. Strong retired in 1957 and lived to witness the beginning of school integration. She died in 1966.

FOR MORE INFORMATION:

Lee County Sesquicentennial Committee. *History of Lee County, Arkansas.* Marianna, AR: Lee County Sesquicentennial Committee, 1987.

"Mrs. Anna M. Strong: Teacher Dies; Two Schools Bear Name." *Arkansas Gazette,* March 17, 1966.

Patterson, Thomas E. *History of the Arkansas Teachers Association.* Washington, DC: National Education Association, 1981.

Dr. William Baerg

The late Dr. William J. Baerg, the founding professor in the entomology department at the University of Arkansas in Fayetteville, was well known for his work with spiders and tarantulas by the time he died in 1980. "Spider man," as he was known to generations of students was adept at using live specimens to help students overcome their irrational insect phobias, especially about spiders and tarantulas.

Baerg came from unusual immigrant stock, German Mennonites who had settled in the Ukraine, then a part of the Russian empire. His parents left Russia in 1874, bringing tools and a wagon made by Baerg's father, a skilled blacksmith and woodworker. The family settled with others of their strict Protestant faith in Kansas, where young William was born in a rude sod house in 1885 to parents who spoke only what was known as "Low German."

Dr. Baerg's youth was full of hard work and strict parental discipline that involved periodic beatings, preceded by fervent prayer. However, the presence of a small schoolhouse near the Baerg home offered some escape from the drudgery of the farm. The young Baerg and his siblings attended innumerable religious meetings, but late in life he recalled, "we would go to all of them because of the need for social life and to take the girls home."

In 1908, at the age of twenty-three, Baerg enrolled in the first class at Tabor College in Hillsboro, Kansas. He also studied at the University of Kansas, where he took a job with the entomology department to study grasshoppers and their damage to crops. He quickly found a field of study that challenged his intellect and one in which much original research was needed.

In the fall of 1915, Baerg began work toward a doctoral degree at Cornell University in Ithaca, New York. Later he got distracted by medical studies, but he abandoned that path to accept a job at the University of Arkansas as an assistant professor of entomology and acting head of the department. Much to his chagrin, he discovered that "there was no one else in the department, not even a stenographer. I and my rolltop desk ran the department."

While at Cornell, Baerg developed an interest in tarantulas. One particularly notable occasion occurred when Baerg gave a lecture to the Entomology Club while carrying a live one in the palm of his hand. He maintained a special interest in tarantulas for the remainder of his long life, and several specimens could usually be found living as pets in the Baerg home. He later published the first full-length academic book on the gentle giants of the spider world.

A few days before departing for Arkansas, Baerg decided at the urging of a Cornell professor to continue his study of spiders and to do some systematic research on the black widow species in particular. As an old man, Baerg recalled how he collected several black widow specimens "where the stadium is now." At first, he used white rats in his research, but the results were unclear, so, as he recalled many years later, "after a couple of failures, I succeeded in getting a widow to get a good hold on me, and expecting the bite to be harmless, I let the spider give me a good dose."

In his memoir, Baerg admits that "the pain was excruciatingly severe unlike anything I had ever experienced." Though young and perhaps foolhardy, Baerg did have the common sense to conduct his research under the supervision of his personal physician, Dr. E. F. Ellis of Fayetteville. He also made arrangements to have a hospital bed ready, another wise decision considering how his experiment turned out.

According to Dr. Baerg's 1923 article in the *Journal of Parasitology*, the experience was severe. At 8:25 A.M., July 10, 1922, Baerg placed a black widow spider on a finger of his left hand, which resulted in a "very faint" pain that increased rapidly. Within twenty minutes the pain had reached his armpit, and the bite area was very red and swelling. Two hours later, Baerg suffered "rather severe" pain while sweating profusely, and an ominous ache grew in his chest. By noon, Baerg was in serious shape, and Dr. Ellis ordered him to bed, where he recorded that his pain was severe, particularly in the hips, and that his "breathing and speech are spasmodic." By 5:15 P.M. he was admitted to the hospital. Sleep eluded the patient, and when he did doze off he dreamed of "frantically and in an utterly aimless fashion working with spiders." Hot baths seemed to provide relief, and he gradually got bet-

Dr. William Baerg and his daughter, Gretchen, with a tarantula. *Photo courtesy of Gretchen Baerg Gearhart.*

ter. By the end of the fifth day, Baerg was feeling "practically normal," but his body temperature fluctuated for about a month more.

As the years passed, Baerg became a popular and memorable classroom instructor. His habit of bringing live tarantulas to class and passing them around to all the students earned him the nickname of "Spider Man." While Baerg's fame rests on his entomological work, his contributions to ornithology are also vast. He retired in 1958 but continued his work on spiders and scorpions. His periodic insect bites did nothing to shorten his life, for he was ninety-four when he died in 1980.

FOR MORE INFORMATION:

Baerg, W. J. "The Effects of the Bite of *Latrodectus mactans* fabr." *Journal of Parasitology* (March 1923): 165–69.

———. "Dr. William J. Baerg: Entomologist Extraordinary." *Flashback* 34 (May 1984): 1–18. This publication is a portion of a memoir written in 1963 for Baerg's grandchildren.

Dozier, Ed. "Spider Man Teaches Creepy Course at UA." *Arkansas Democrat,* September 25, 1958.

Dry, Eddie. "William J. Baerg (1885–1980)." *The Encyclopedia of Arkansas History and Culture.* http://encyclopediaofarkansas.net/encyclopedia/entry-detail. aspx?search=1&entryID=1582.

Keller and Marian Breland

Hot Springs has always been a major tourist attraction—whether for the curative powers of the naturally hot water, the widely accepted gambling and vice, or the beautiful scenery. "Visibly the town lives upon the stranger within its gates," wrote Alice French, a popular writer who had a home in Lawrence County and who set an 1889 short story in the spa city.

The I. Q. Zoo was among the most popular tourist attractions in Hot Springs during the latter half of the twentieth century. The I. Q. Zoo was the work of Keller B. Breland and his wife, Marian, who were pioneering scientists in the field of scientifically validated animal training—what became known as "operant conditioning." Established in 1955, the zoo quickly became a popular tourist destination. Visitors were amazed to see chickens walk tightropes or dance to jukebox music, rabbits ride miniature fire trucks or spin roulette wheels, or raccoons play basketball. The especially venturesome could play "Bird Brain," a tic-tac-toe game against a chicken (which the fowl always won or tied).

While the zoo animals were noteworthy, the people who trained them were much more so. Marian and Keller Breland took applied animal psychology to new heights of both public and professional interest and acceptance.

The Brelands met while both were students at the University of Minnesota. Both studied under B. F. Skinner, the famous behavioral psychologist. During World War II the Brelands worked with Skinner on his "Project Pigeon," an effort to train pigeons to guide missiles for the U.S. Navy. Gradually the Brelands came to the conclusion that animal training of this nature offered commercial possibilities.

In 1947 the Brelands opened their new business, Animal Behavior Enterprises (ABE). Within three years the company was making a profit, which must have validated their decision to leave school without completing their Ph.D. degrees. In the early 1950s the Brelands moved from Minnesota to a large farm at Lonsdale near Hot Springs, where they opened the I. Q. Zoo.

The Brelands' business soon had customers all over the world. They trained animals for Knott's Berry Farm, Opryland, and various Six Flags facilities. Marian was the first person to train animals to star in television commercials. At its height, the business employed forty people. The Brelands, along with a cast of animals, were popular guests on many television programs, including the Ed Sullivan Show, as well as shows hosted by Dave Garroway, Jack Paar, and Steve Allen.

J. Arthur Gillaspy Jr. and Elson M. Bihm, both of the University of Central Arkansas and author of the entry on Keller Breland in the *Encyclopedia of Arkansas History and Culture,* wrote, "Today, the animal training programs at most major theme parks and oceanariums, such as Sea World and Busch Gardens, can be traced back to Keller and Marian Breland."

The Brelands were very different individually, but they made an effective team. Gillaspy and Bihm described their different work roles: "He was the idea man; she made it all work." *Animal Behavior,* their 1966 textbook, was published to great acclaim.

In 1965 Keller Breland died of a heart attack, and his widow became president of ABE. In 1976 she married Bob Bailey, a zoologist and chemist whom the Brelands met when he was in charge of marine mammal training for the U.S. Navy. (The Brelands had trained dolphins to rescue lost sailors, among many other tasks.)

In 1978, over three decades after leaving graduate school, Marian completed her doctorate at the University of Arkansas in experimental psychology. Returning to academia in 1981, she became professor of psychology at Henderson State University in Arkadelphia, though she remained president of ABE. She was a popular professor, and she did not retire until 1998 at the age of seventy-eight. She died in 2001. Her widower, Bob Bailey, continued the family's work. Henderson State University established a scholarship honoring Marian Breland in 2003.

The I. Q. Zoo closed in 1990, and periodic attempts to open new ones have failed. But, the professional reputations of Keller and Marian Breland, as well as Bob Bailey, have been enhanced greatly due to the enthusiastic work of Art Gillaspy and Elson Bihm. They have collected the papers of the Brelands and created an exhibit at the Archives of the History of American Psychology in Akron, Ohio, and they have published widely on the Brelands.

FOR MORE INFORMATION:

Breland, K., and M. Breland. *Animal Behavior.* New York: Macmillan, 1966.

Gillaspy, J. A., and E. Bihm. "Obituary: M. Breland Bailey (1920–2001)." *American Psychologist* 57 (April 2002): 292–93.

———. "Keller Bramwell Breland (1915–1965)." *The Encyclopedia of Arkansas History and Culture.* http://encyclopediaofarkansas.net/encyclopedia/entry-detail.aspx?search=1&entryID=2530.

Samuel Lee Kountz

An African American physician from Arkansas who pioneered kidney transplant work in America, Dr. Samuel Lee Kountz died a lamentably early death. However, he packed a great deal of accomplishment into his short career. Born the son of a preacher and farmer in Lexa, Phillips County, in 1930, Kountz was introduced to medicine by his mother, an occasional midwife. After attending segregated schools in Lexa, Kountz took a bachelor degree from Arkansas Agricultural, Mechanical and Normal College in Pine Bluff. He then further prepared for medical school by earning a master's degree in chemistry at the University of Arkansas, followed in 1958 with a medical degree from the University of Arkansas School of Medicine.

Kountz was a surgery resident at San Francisco County Hospital and then studied at the Stanford Medical Center in California and at Hammersmith Hospital in London. While at Stanford, Kountz began a serious study of kidney transplants. After joining the University of California at San Francisco he became chief of the kidney transplant service.

While at the university he helped develop a process for preserving kidneys for later transplanting. Most of his research focused on ways to prevent the body from rejecting transplanted kidneys. Kountz is credited with the discovery that prednisolone is effective in minimizing transplant rejection. He also became a strong advocate for transplanting a second kidney at the first sign of rejection, commenting that it was "better to save the patient and sacrifice the graft." He transplanted more than five hundred kidneys, with a very high success rate.

Some say Kountz's major contribution to medicine was his work to make the public aware of the need for organ donation. He even performed a kidney transplant on the "Today Show" on national television. He had high standards for himself, once commenting: "From a scientific point of view, I do not consider a kidney transplant operation successful until the patient lives another twenty years."

In 1972 Kountz became professor and chair of the department of surgery at the State University of New York Downstate Medical Center in Brooklyn and surgeon-in-chief at King's County Hospital. This relocation to a poor inner-city area was an attempt to contribute more to black health care. Referring to his efforts to strengthen the center's education programs, he said his goal was "to train people who have to be reckoned with."

Kountz was a diligent researcher as well as educator and hospital administrator. He published dozens of articles in leading medical journals, including the *New England Journal of Medicine*. In 1974 he became the first black president of the Society of University Surgeons.

After a 1977 trip as a visiting professor in South Africa, Kountz developed an illness that defied diagnosis. He suffered brain damage that robbed him of speech and left him bedridden. He died at the age of fifty-one in 1981 and was buried in All Saints Church Cemetery in Great Neck, New York.

The Kountz-Kyle Building at the University of Arkansas at Pine Bluff and the Kountz Pavilion at Harlem Hospital in New York City are named in his honor. Howard University in Washington, D.C., named its international transplant symposium series after Kountz. Before his death he was awarded an honorary degree by the University of Arkansas in 1974.

FOR MORE INFORMATION:

Organ, Claude H., Jr., and Margaret M. Kosiba. *A Century of Black Surgeons: The U.S.A. Experience.* Norman, OK: Transcript Press, 1987.

Harold Alexander

No man has played a more significant role in preserving the natural heritage of Arkansas than the late Harold Alexander of Conway. Harold was the moving force for stream preservation in the state, but he was much more than that. He was a warrior for the environment, a man who realized early on that words without action were meaningless. As an employee of the state Game and Fish Commission, Harold had to keep a low profile. But, behind the scenes he was a torrent of energy and determination.

It would have been easy to underestimate his role in the preservation of Arkansas's natural environment. But, any such thoughts were erased only a short time after his death in 1993 when Harold's widow, Virginia Alexander, donated his papers to the archives at the University of Central Arkansas in Conway. A review of his papers showed that Harold Alexander played such an important role that he has been called "the father of Arkansas conservation."

Alexander was born in Lawrence, Kansas, in 1909. He took a zoology degree from the University of Kansas and then a master's degree at Texas A & M University. Alexander was a talented artist. His master's thesis, a guide to the ducks and geese of the Texas gulf coast, was illustrated with Harold's beautiful color drawings—which still survive in the University of Central Arkansas archives. He soon found a job with the fledgling Arkansas Game and Fish Commission. Drafted into the U.S. Army in 1942, Harold spent most of his time at Wright Field in Ohio, doing scientific drawings. He later returned to his work at the Game and Fish Commission.

Harold could write as well as draw, which were talents that helped him rise through the ranks at the Game and Fish Commission. He worked on a number of projects, including efforts to restore the deer and quail populations in Arkansas.

Harold, who sometimes pushed the envelope as a public employee, was dogged in his determination to awaken Arkansans to the threats to the state's natural legacy. He was one of the earlier voices in opposition to the stream management practices of the U.S. Army Corps of Engineers. Alexander had the ability to digest complicated scientific information and then translate it to the general population. In meetings and private conversations, Alexander urged public land managers and planners to "save our open spaces, wild lands and natural streams and rivers before they are all sacrificed on the altar of our technology."

Dr. Neil Compton of Bentonville, the foremost leader of the effort to save the Buffalo River, credited Harold Alexander with awakening him to the threats posed by dams and streamside development. In his book *Battle for the Buffalo,* Compton wrote of Harold's role: "Harold Alexander is . . . a sort of Aldo Leopold for Arkansas." Alexander was, Compton wrote, "a rumpled but straightforward, clear-headed fellow who laid it on the line."

Harold Alexander could be a lonely figure as he shuffled through the marble halls of the state capitol, casting about with his slightly downcast eyes, looking for a legislator who might listen to another hurried appeal on behalf of yet another environmental cause.

Despite the onset of Parkinson's disease, Harold pushed on with his environmental work till the end. He died on September 14, 1993, a few weeks before being inducted into the Arkansas Outdoor Hall of Fame. After his death, the Arkansas Wildlife Federation renamed its Conservationist of the Year Award in honor of Alexander. Perhaps Harold Alexander's vision is best expressed on a plaque at the Tyler Bend Visitor Center on the Buffalo National River: "A stream is a living thing. It moves, dances, and shimmers in the sun. It furnishes opportunities for enjoyment and its beauty moves men's souls."

FOR MORE INFORMATION:

Alexander, Harold. Papers. Torreyson Library Archives and Special Collections, University of Central Arkansas, Conway.

Compton, Neil. *The Battle for the Buffalo River: A Twentieth-Century Conservation Crisis in the Ozarks.* Fayetteville: University of Arkansas Press, 1992.

"Nationally-Renowned Arkansas Conservationist Alexander Dies." *Benton Courier,* September 16, 1993.

Rogers, Suzanne. "Harold Edward Alexander (1909–1993)." *The Encyclopedia of Arkansas History and Culture.* http://encyclopediaofarkansas.net/encyclopedia/entry-detail.aspx?search=1&entryID=2199.

CHAPTER IX

Entertainers and Performers

Scott Joplin

Arkansas and Texas both claim Scott Joplin, the renowned composer of that distinctive American popular musical form known as ragtime. Solid historical data on Joplin are scarce, but the consensus today places his birth on a northeast Texas farm sometime between June 1867 and January 1868. While he might have been born in Texas, Joplin lived in Arkansas on occasion, had relatives in the state, married a Little Rock woman, and set his grand opera on an Arkansas plantation.

Joplin's father, Giles, was born a slave, but his mother, Florence, was a free woman from Kentucky. The family moved to Texarkana when Scott was young, and he grew up in this new railroad town that straddled the Texas-Arkansas border. He attended Orr School, on the Arkansas side of Texarkana.

Joplin apparently had a natural knack for the piano, and tradition held that he taught himself the rudiments of music. Stephen Husarik of the University of Arkansas at Fort Smith, author of the Joplin biography in the *Encyclopedia of Arkansas History and Culture,* reports the boy's parents provided music lessons. Among his teachers was German immigrant Julius Weiss.

A native of Saxony, Weiss had university training, including music. In the late 1870s Weiss was hired by the prominent Texarkana sawmill tycoon Col. Robert W. Rogers to tutor his numerous children (he had seventeen children by two wives, but seven did not survive childhood). Weiss taught a wide variety of subjects, including German and mathematics, but every child was expected to study music. The boys all took violin, while the girls studied piano.

We do not know how Weiss came across the musically gifted young black boy, but he did and the result was magical for Joplin. Giles Joplin, despite his meager wages, acquired a piano for his son, and Weiss taught him lessons "in piano, sight reading, and the principles to extend and confirm his natural instinct for harmony." Weiss also regaled his young pupil with stories of "great composers and, especially, of the famous operas."

Tradition contends that Joplin left Texarkana after the death of his mother, when his father insisted that his son acquire a practical trade. Joplin left Texarkana at about age seventeen and traveled about the nation, settling for a time in Sedalia, Missouri, where he continued his education at Lincoln High School. Later, while in St. Louis in 1885, Joplin entered the all-night ragtime piano competitions at the Silver Dollar Saloon.

In the summer of 1891, Joplin was back in Texarkana as a part of a minstrel troupe. During the 1893 World's Fair in Chicago, Joplin organized his own band, in which he played cornet. Returning to Sedalia after the fair, Joplin played in local clubs and toured with his Texas Medley Quartette vocal group. It was while on tour in Syracuse that Joplin published his first two compositions. He also took time out in 1896 to study music at the George R. Smith College in Sedalia, a black Methodist institution. He taught music, and he later collaborated with two of his students.

Joplin worked hard at both performance and composition, and he developed an intense interest in the new ragtime music. In late 1898 Joplin published his first ragtime composition, "Original Rags." The following year, with the assistance of a lawyer, Joplin entered into a long-term business arrangement with Sedalia music store owner and publisher John Stark. In the years before recorded music, composers sold their work as sheet music—which found a ready home in Victorian parlors throughout the nation.

The first composition published by Stark turned out to be the iconic rag of all time: "The Maple Leaf Rag." Joplin often played at the Maple Leaf Club in Sedalia, and the piece was named for this black-owned nightclub. The Maple Leaf Rag sold modestly at first, but it grew quickly in popularity and sales. Joplin had insisted on a royalty of one cent per sale, which turned out to be wise, for the music sold well at Woolworth stores, eventually reaching the one million mark. This small but steady income enabled Joplin to concentrate more on composition and teaching.

In 1901 Joplin moved to St. Louis. While there he met the conductor of the St. Louis Choral Symphony, Alfred Ernst. This European-born and trained conductor found Joplin "an unusually intelligent young man and fairly well educated." Ernst believed Joplin's work "so original, so distinctly individual, and so melodious withal, that I am led to believe he can do something fine in compositions of a higher class."

Undoubtedly, Joplin desired to contribute beyond ragtime, in the world of classical music. In early 1903 Joplin filed a copyright application for an opera, "A Guest of Honor," which he formed an opera company of thirty to perform. After rehearsal, Joplin took the show on the road, but it failed when the box office receipts were stolen. The music for this opera was lost. However, his opera "Treemonisha," which Joplin self-published in 1911, survives.

Set on a plantation near the Red River in southwest Arkansas, the opera tells the uplifting story of an educated young black woman named Treemonisha who leads her community away from superstition and voodoo. Tragically, Joplin never succeeded in getting the opera performed. He died April 1, 1917, and was buried in New York.

The recognition that Joplin sought in life came years after his death. In 1973 a popular film titled "The Sting" featured Joplin's rag "The Entertainer." Suddenly, Joplin's compositions reached the top of both the popular and classical charts. In 1976 Joplin received a posthumous Pulitzer prize for his contributions to American music.

FOR MORE INFORMATION:

Belt, Byron. "A National Critic Appraises 'Treemonisha.'" *Arkansas Gazette,* September 10, 1972.

Berlin, Edward A. *King of Ragtime: Scott Joplin and His Era.* New York: Oxford University Press, 1994.

Blesh, Rudi, and Harriet Janis. *They All Played Ragtime.* New York: Oak Publications, 1971.

Hudgins, Mary D. "Scott Joplin's Black Opera." *Arkansas Gazette,* September 10, 1972.

Husarik, Stephen. "Scott Joplin (1868?–1917)." *The Encyclopedia of Arkansas History and Culture.* http://encyclopediaofarkansas.net/encyclopedia/entry-detail.aspx?search=1&entryID=527.

Norm McLeod

Arkansas has always been a land of eccentrics. Many of these eccentrics were also among the state's most valued contributors to business, politics, and culture. Would not most people who knew the late Paul Klipsch, the great sound engineer and businessman of Hope, agree that he was a wee odd? How about Dr. Charles McDermott, the man after whom Dermott in Desha County was named? The good doctor was successful in many fields, not including his persistent efforts to invent a pedal-powered airplane. Then there was the one-eyed sheriff and boss of Conway County, the late Marlin Hawkins.

Among the most widely known Arkansas eccentrics was Norm McLeod, proprietor of the Happy Hollow Amusement Park in Hot Springs. I have been fascinated by McLeod for decades, ever since I saw one of his commercial photographs made at Happy Hollow. To say that McLeod was a photographer is absurdly simplistic. He was a wild man with a camera. His photographs, often 8 x 10 inches and mounted on stiff cardboard with advertising printed on the back, can be located on Internet auctions.

Each McLeod photograph is instantly recognizable. In almost every picture, tourists are placed in outlandish, highly theatrical poses. Most of McLeod's scenes involve animals, such as donkeys, oxen, goats—even a black bear. But, it was the poses that were so outrageous. "Many of his poses are grotesque, but all are artistic," a 1904 biographer said of McLeod's work.

McLeod might be as much to blame as any individual for Arkansas's long association with the backwoods and the emerging hillbilly stereotype. Throughout the 1890s and well into the twentieth century, McLeod made thousands of pictures of well-off tourists posed in the most incongruous hillbilly scenes imaginable. These pictures then traveled across the United States and around the world. Occasionally, a McLeod picture will turn up in Australia.

Norman E. McLeod was born on a farm in Sumter County,

Norman McLeod, a Hot Springs photographer and huckster. *Photo courtesy of Special Collections, University of Arkansas Libraries.*

Georgia, in 1853. At nineteen, he moved to Florida and learned the jeweler and photography trades. Unlike few young men of the time, McLeod won a scholarship and attended college in his native Georgia for two years. At that point, like many young men before and long after him, McLeod became a wanderer. "During the 12 years after leaving college, he was showman, photographer, orange grower, fisherman, and trader in general, and during this time he had many wild and exciting experiences on both land and sea," one source says.

In 1888 he landed in Hot Springs, a village with more than its share of eccentrics already. McLeod started out in Hot Springs as a photographer with a regular studio, but he soon added a shooting gallery, an extensive souvenir shop, and a large petting zoo. Small horses, donkeys, and goats wandered around the grounds. McLeod also rented carriages and carts, as well as the animals to pull them. Happy Hollow was an early tourist trap.

Tourists could choose from a variety of backdrops, one of the most popular being the Wild West theme. In early pictures a live bear was often chained to the stage or the roof of a crude log cabin, but when the bear died McLeod had it stuffed, and it continued as a prop even after its fur became thin and moth eaten.

A born promoter, McLeod mounted his pictures on cardboard frames that prominently carried his name on the front, with a picture of himself in his typically exaggerated pose along with florid advertising copy on the back. McLeod also distributed lyrics to a song he wrote about himself and Happy Hollow. McLeod always had an American Indian in residence. Or, at least, he claimed that the man in the photos wearing the pathetic Indian headdress and laconic look was a red man of the West.

One might suspect Norm McLeod was part huckster. Certainly, he had the scent of patent medicine about him. Happy Hollow was McLeod's own little carnival, except he did not have to pack it up and move every few days. It also gave him the excuse to dress flamboyantly every day of his life and strike the most theatrical poses for his self-portraits. Plus, he made a good living at it.

McLeod was far more than huckster. He was a man fulfilling a dream. Happy Hollow was open free of charge to the public, a service McLeod proudly proclaimed as unique in the spa city. He seems to have been a man of incredible generosity, constantly forgiving rents, giving jobs to the down-and-out, and helping pay for medical care for indigent children.

In 1908 McLeod was forced to sell his attraction. Hot Springs was growing more sophisticated, and a menagerie of animals and stables no longer fit just up the street from the elegant Arlington Hotel.

Norman Evans McLeod died of an apparent heart attack on October 5, 1915, and was buried in Greenwood Cemetery in Hot

Springs. For many years a small tourist court, Happy Hollow Motel, has occupied part of the old park grounds on Fountain Street. It has preserved the name of an attraction that, although popular, helped perpetuate the image of Arkansas as backward and crude.

FOR MORE INFORMATION:

Goodspeed, Weston Arthur, ed. "Norman E. McLeod." In *The Province and the States,* 351–53. Vol. 7, *Arkansas.* Madison, WI: Western Historical Association, 1904.

Hudgins, Mary D. "Norman McLeod and His Happy Hollow." *Record* 10 (1969): 27–31.

"Norman McLeod Obituary." *Arkansas Democrat,* October 6, 1915.

"Norman McLeod Obituary." *Arkansas Gazette,* October 7, 1915.

Broncho Billy Anderson

Arkansas's contributions to the arts and entertainment are remarkably large and surprisingly well known. Everyone knows Arkansas native Glen Campbell, who has had a long and successful musical career. Early twentieth-century African American composer William Grant Still has been rediscovered, and his compositions are performed regularly. Bookstores have shelves full of titles written by many of the fine writers who call Arkansas home. Few Arkansans, however, have an awareness of Gilbert M. Anderson—perhaps America's first cowboy movie star.

The Great Train Robbery, filmed in 1903, introduced the Western genre to films, and Anderson was among the lead actors in that pioneering film. That ten-minute, one-reel film established the Western movie as an American film genre that captivated filmgoers around the world for much of the twentieth century.

Born March 21, 1880, in Little Rock, Anderson's real name was Max Aronson. His parents, Henry and Esther Aronson, were part of the small but vibrant Jewish community in Little Rock. Aronson grew up in Little Rock and later lived for a time in Pine Bluff before the family moved to St. Louis. About 1900, Aronson began a career that would take him to the top of the new movie business. Like many early film stars, Aronson started out in vaudeville, a venue that was fading.

In 1903 Aronson visited the studios of inventor Thomas A. Edison in New Jersey, where he was hired as an actor and immediately appeared in a one-reel film called *The Messenger Boy's Mistake*. Director Edwin S. Porter cast him to play three roles in *The Great Train Robbery* despite his inability to ride a horse. Aronson told Porter, "I was born on a horse. I was raised in Missouri and can ride like a Texas Ranger." Other than having lived briefly in St. Louis, the whole story was pure fabrication. *The Great Train Robbery* is considered a classic today, in part because it was the first movie to tell a story. It was also the first film in which editing techniques were used to speed up the action. Aronson learned a great deal from that film, and six months later he changed his name to Gilbert M. Anderson and left Edison to join its chief competitor, Vitagraph. Starting as a production assistant, he quickly worked his way up to directing and acting.

In 1905 one of Anderson's films, *Raffles, the Amateur Cracksman*, became a hit. He immediately left Vitagraph to work as a director for Col. William H. Selig, leaving after a short time to form a new partnership with George K. Spoor. Their company, named Essanay, was first headquartered in Chicago, but later moved to the San Francisco Bay area.

Essanay signed many of the prominent actors of the day, including Francis X. Bushman, Lewis Stone, and Gloria Swanson. Anderson even lured the young British actor Charlie Chaplin away from a competing studio by offering the astounding salary of $1,000 per week. Anderson's major success, however, came from Westerns in which he starred as Broncho Billy.

A shrewd student of films, Anderson realized that Westerns needed a sympathetic central character and a great deal of action. Between 1910 and 1915, he made almost four hundred two-reel Broncho Billy films, becoming known worldwide as the first great American movie star. He accumulated a tidy fortune, and Charlie Chaplin recalled Anderson's indulgences as "owning flamboyantly colored cars, promoting prizefights, owning a theater and producing musical shows."

In his later years Anderson remembered the Broncho Billy films as "the first westerns, in the first series." He also admitted, "I made 'em like popcorn. I'd write 'em in the morning and make 'em in the afternoon. Sometimes I had the scenario written on my cuff." Regardless of their thrown-together nature, the Broncho Billy films introduced the "movie idol."

Broncho Billy might have been an idol, but Anderson himself certainly was not. Anderson was a stubborn and difficult man. He and partner George Spoor dissolved Essanay in 1916, one source claiming that an argument between the two men caused an immediate closure while a film was in mid-production. After a brief stint as a producer in New York, Anderson retired in 1920 and gradually lost his fortune.

By 1948, when an interest in movie history arose, Anderson was almost totally forgotten. A local reporter found Broncho Billy living in a tiny house near the Los Angeles airport.

In 1958 he was awarded an honorary Academy Award for his early achievements. Though he was married and the father of a daughter, he spent his final days alone in obscurity in Los Angeles, a pauper in the motion picture country home where he died in 1971.

FOR MORE INFORMATION:

Corneau, Ernest N. *The Hall of Fame of Western Film Stars.* North Quincy, MA: Christopher Publishing Co., 1969.

Franklin, Joe. *Classics of the Silent Screen.* New York: Citadel Press, 1959.

Leslie, Jim. "The Late Bronco [*sic*] Billy: First Cowboy Star, Ex-Pine Bluffian, Was Rich Eccentric." *Pine Bluff Commercial,* February 14, 1971.

Schiffman, Marsha. "G. M. Anderson, nee Max Aronson, Reel Cowboy." *Jewish Review (Portland, OR),* April 1, 2003, 20, 27.

Lum and Abner

In 1931 two Arkansans burst onto the national entertainment scene when the *Lum and Abner Show* radio program began broadcasting nationally. The show was set in the mythical town of Pine Ridge, Arkansas, but it was modeled on the settlement of Waters in the western part of Montgomery County. Broadcast from 1931 to 1954, the *Lum and Abner Show* was a national smash, with millions of Americans gathering around their radios several times weekly to listen to the fifteen-minute serials.

The success of the *Lum and Abner* phenomenon was due in large measure to the brilliance of the men who created the show, wrote the scripts, and played the leading roles. Chester "Chet" Lauck played the role of Lum, while Norris "Tuffy" Goff was Abner. Both men were from Mena in Polk County in west-central Arkansas near the Oklahoma border.

Lauck, born in Little River County in 1902, and Goff, born four years later at Cove in Polk County, were naturally gifted comedians. While still in elementary school they were known as class clowns. Both boys came from prosperous families. Chet's father was a banker with lumber interests, and Goff's father had a wholesale general merchandise business.

Lauck and Goff both attended the University of Arkansas, with Lauck receiving a degree in art and business. Goff later took his business degree from the University of Oklahoma. Both returned to Mena after college, joining their family businesses. Photos of Lauck and Goff show handsome young men with full hair and Goff sporting a mustache. At more than six feet, Lauck was both tall and thin, while Goff was short and stocky.

A common story holds that young Goff came to know of Dick Huddleston's general store in the tiny town of Waters as he made deliveries for the family wholesale company. Other stories say the Goff and Lauck families hunted in the Waters area.

Goff and Lauck were active in the Mena Lions Club, and they engaged in various amateur theatricals. Their specialty was blackface, in which they performed racist parodies of black characters—which was popular across the nation at the time. In 1931 the two men went to Hot Springs to participate in a talent program sponsored by the prominent KTHS radio station. Upon discovering, as one journalist later wrote, "the program already filled with burnt cork," they switched to a routine involving two country merchants: Lum Edwards, played by Lauck and pronounced "Eddards," and Abner Peabody, portrayed by Goff.

The routine was an immediate success, and KTHS kept them on the air for a few months—time they used to develop the story and hone their portrayals. After an audition in Chicago, the show was picked up by NBC radio. For almost twenty-five years, Lauck and Goff entertained Americans by the millions.

The *Lum and Abner Show* was simple but classic radio acting. The story line involved two older men running the Jot 'Em Down General Store in Pine Ridge. Kathryn Moore Stucker, owner of the store building and manager of a small museum in it, described the characters this way: "Lum was a bachelor with an eye for women, and his ego usually got in the way of common sense. Abner was a hen-pecked married man, and his gullibility was enormous. They were civic-minded merchants who never seemed to have any money in the cash register. Their schemes for grandeur always brought them to the brink of tragedy."

As the plot developed, a whole cast of new characters evolved. Lauck played the appealing but dimwitted Cedric Wehunt and patriarch Grandpappy Spears, while Goff portrayed such characters as the scheming Squire Skimp, the town barber Mose Moots, and the unsavory Snake Hogan. Goff also played Dick Huddleston, a character who was in real life the owner of the store in Waters.

Historian Randal L. Hall, who published a book on the *Lum and Abner Show*, believes Lauck and Goff should get credit for "defying the widespread stereotypes of hillbillies." The shows tended to feature gentle humor, perhaps in the mode of the later *Andy Griffith Show* on television.

Until 1940, Goff and Lauck wrote the scripts and performed them. Lauck would sit at a typewriter while Goff would pace the room brainstorming aloud. Sometimes the team would complete scripts only minutes before live broadcast from the NBC studios in Chicago.

Between 1940 and 1946, Lauck and Goff made six Hollywood films while continuing to perform on the radio. The *Lum and Abner Show* ceased broadcasting in 1955 as the growing popularity of television wreaked havoc on radio programming.

In Arkansas, the *Lum and Abner Show* was immensely popular. The residents of Waters changed the name of the town to Pine Ridge in 1936 during the state centennial celebration. Both the radio programs and movies are available today, and the National Lum and Abner Association has a nationwide membership.

Goff died in 1978 and is buried in Palm Desert, California. Lauck moved back to Arkansas in 1963 and died in Hot Springs in 1980.

FOR MORE INFORMATION:

Hall, Randal L. "Lum and Abner: An Early Episode." *Arkansas Historical Quarterly* 66 (Winter 2007): 444–51.

Hall, Randal L. *Lum and Abner: Rural America and the Golden Age of Radio.* Lexington: University Press of Kentucky, 2007.

Spiro, J. D. "Arkansas's Hollywood Hillbillies." *Arkansas Gazette,* January 30, 1938.

Louis Jordan

Louis Thomas Jordan, one of the most amazing Arkansans in the field of music, was born July 8, 1908, in Brinkley, Monroe County. Jordan was not only a popular and successful black entertainer but also an innovator whose work impacted more than one genre of modern American music.

Jordan's father, James Aaron Jordan, was leader of the Brinkley Brass Band and an agent for the Rabbit Foot Minstrels. At the beginning of the last century, most towns of any size had some sort of town band, and cities like Brinkley, with its large black population, might have had more than one black band.

Adell Jordan, Louis's mother and a native of Mississippi, died when he was young. In addition to attending public school, Jordan studied music under his father and was gifted with both the clarinet and saxophone. Later he played professionally in his father's band, including summer tours out of state.

Jordan studied music at Arkansas Baptist College in Little Rock for a short time, but he mostly played in his father's band or with Little Rock groups, including Jimmy Pryor's Imperial Serenaders. The oil boom put Union County on the touring map, and Jordan played with Bob Alexander's Harmony Kings in El Dorado and Smackover. He later relocated to Hot Springs, where he played at the Eastman Hotel among other places. By 1932, Jordan moved to Philadelphia, where he played saxophone with the band of Clarence Williams and clarinet in the Charlie Gaines band.

Jordan received a break in 1936 when Chick Webb asked him to join the Savoy Ballroom Orchestra in New York City. This prestigious band, which was broadcast on radio, gave Jordan the opportunity to work with a wide variety of talented entertainers, including a young Ella Fitzgerald, who was then gaining prominence as Webb's lead female vocalist. It was apparently during this time that Jordan developed his own distinctive style, which included sophisticated saxophone playing and talented singing, all performed with a certain unselfconscious comedic flair. His performance of "Rusty Hinge" was recorded in March 1937.

Jordan and Webb worked together closely for two years before Webb discovered that Jordan was trying to woo Ella Fitzgerald and others to his new band. Thus was born Jordan's longtime band, the Tympany Five. Stephen Koch, a keen student of Arkansas music and leader of an effort to reestablish Jordan's prominence, noted that this band, "which changed American popular music, was always called the Tympany Five, regardless of the number of pieces."

Landing a residency at the Elks Rendezvous Club on Lenox Avenue in Harlem gave Jordan a base from which to work, and his fame spread. He had his first recording date for Decca Records in December 1938. Three months later, Jordan and his band made more recordings, including "Keep a-Knockin'," which Little Richard made famous. In January 1940, Decca recorded two more Jordan classics, "You're My Meat" and "You Run Your Mouth and I'll Run My Business."

Interestingly, in 1941, Decca created a new line of records featuring artists with "crossover potential," meaning performers who could appeal to both white and black audiences. Jordan and his band, as well as the Nat King Cole Trio, disappeared from Decca's "race label," though certainly his appeal remained strong on the "race charts."

Jordan's first record to reach the top of the Harlem Hit Parade came in December 1942 with "What's the Use of Gettin' Sober (When You're Gonna Get Drunk Again)." Jordan's 1943 release "Five Guys Named Moe," which has been described as "a comical call-and-response number," was a hit both in America and with its soldiers fighting overseas.

Altogether, Jordan and his Tympany Five had fifty-four singles on the Rhythm and Blues charts during the 1940s. Eighteen songs reached number one status. "Choo Choo Ch'Boogie" topped the charts for eighteen weeks, while "Ain't Nobody Here But Us Chickens" stayed on top for seventeen weeks. "Caledonia," which featured Jordan's falsetto voice, reigned for nearly two months at number one.

As the titles suggest, Jordan enjoyed having fun with his music. He wore outlandish clothes, used exaggerated moves on stage, and had a certain cartoonish aspect. Old black and white film footage—he was the subject of and appeared in several films—shows an energetic performer who obviously enjoyed his work. Music historians note that Jordan's "swinging shuffle rhythms" have been coined the "jump blues," a forerunner to rhythm and blues and rock and roll.

Stephen Koch, in his sketch of Jordan in the *Encyclopedia of Arkansas History and Culture,* wrote that Jordan's "endless rehearsals, matching suits, dance moves, and routines built around songs made the band." Koch also noted that Jordan's "humorous, over-the-beat monologs and depictions of black life are a prototype of rap."

Jordan's last hit came in 1951, and he was dropped by Decca in 1954. He continued to perform to large audiences, especially in Europe, but his records did not sell well. He made his last recording in 1972 and died three years later.

Like Scott Joplin, another black entertainer from Arkansas, Louis Jordan was rediscovered long after his death when in 1992 the musical "Five Guys Named Moe," based on Jordan's life and music, became a successful Broadway play.

FOR MORE INFORMATION:

Chilton, John. *Let the Good Times Roll: The Story of Louis Jordan and His Music.* Ann Arbor: University of Michigan Press, 1994.

Koch, Stephen. "Louis Thomas Jordan (1908–1975)." *The Encyclopedia of Arkansas History and Culture.* http://encyclopediaofarkansas.net/encyclopedia/entry-detail.aspx?search=1&entryID=1685.

Emma Dusenbury

Polk County has had a major impact on American entertainment history. Everyone knows about Lum and Abner, the famed radio and movie comedy team from Mena, but only a few specialists know of a Polk Countian by the name of Emma Dusenbury. Vance Randolph, the premier student of Arkansas folklore, once called Emma "the greatest ballad singer I ever knew." Yet, she died in poverty and obscurity.

Emma Hayes was born in Georgia in 1862. The family moved to Arkansas when she was ten, settling near Gassville in Baxter County. Later she moved to Marion County, near Yellville, where she worked as a nurse and eventually married Ernest Dusenbury, an itinerant worker from Illinois. After having her only child, a daughter named Ora, Emma was struck by a mysterious malady that left her blind.

For the next fifteen years the family "went to ramblin'," all three of them working odd jobs. In late summer they picked cotton, with Emma picking about fifty pounds daily despite her blindness. In the evenings the family turned to music and dance to forget their poverty, with Emma remembering, "I wasn't blind in my heels, nohow."

About 1907 the family finally got enough money to buy a small farm near Mena, in the Ouachita Mountains near the Oklahoma border. Just when things began to look better, Emma's husband was thrown from a buggy when his horse panicked, leaving him unable to work for the remaining fifteen years of his life. When he died in 1933, the local newspaper noted that the death was especially distressing, "in that a blind wife and an invalid daughter are the only survivors."

It was about this time that Emma's repertoire of songs came to the attention of folklorists and music scholars. F. M. Goodhue, a New England scholar who taught at Commonwealth College, the labor school near Mena, first brought Emma to the attention of researchers. Laurence Powell of Little Rock, conductor of the Arkansas Symphony at the time, wrote of his visit with Emma: "Hidden away in the Arkansas wilderness, near Mena, in a tiny shack with a leaky roof, lives

Emma Dusenbury, a gifted but tragic singer of ballads. *Photo courtesy of Special Collections, University of Arkansas Libraries.*

a 74-year-old woman with an amazing memory, a clear unwavering voice—and sightless eyes."

John Gould Fletcher, the Little Rock writer and recipient of the 1938 Pulitzer prize for poetry, visited Emma and wrote about her. John A. Lomax, the leading collector of American folksongs, recorded Emma at her home. In his autobiography, Lomax recalled her having "the serene face one finds in the pictures of saints and martyrs." During their two-day meeting, Emma sang "almost continuously," with Lomax recording eighty-two songs for the Library of Congress.

The year 1936 was the high point of Emma's musical recognition. In October of that year she was brought to Little Rock to perform as a part of the state's centennial celebration, which resulted in a front-page article in the *Arkansas Gazette*. The symphony's Powell went to Polk County to visit Dusenbury and later included an interpretation of a selection of Dusenbury songs in his "Second Symphony" composition.

Professor Robert Cochran notes that after her Little Rock performance Emma "lived on in the same bone grinding poverty." A photograph of Dusenbury in the University of Arkansas Libraries Special Collections Department provides simple yet stark evidence of her living conditions. Standing beside her teenage daughter, Emma stares into an unseen world, her clothing coarse and threadbare. Her daughter, perhaps showing off her only possession, holds a young kitten aloft.

A few years before she died, Emma and her daughter lost their farm but continued to live there. When the new owners arrived to occupy the home late one January night, Emma refused them entry, crying, "You are trying to put us out in the cold under a tree." The new owners allowed the Dusenburys to live with them until new arrangements could be made.

Emma died in May 1941 and was buried beside her husband in Rocky Cemetery, west of Mena. A pauper, her burial expense of $33.10 was paid by the county. Shortly after Emma's death, her middle-aged daughter married a man in neighboring Montgomery County. Emma still has descendants living in Arkansas.

Professor Cochran summarized Emma's life: "It has its triumphs, certainly, since the tapes are safe in Washington and Emma Dusenbury has a larger lock on immortality than most of us. But it's also a sad story—how do you put from mind the picture of a frightened old woman crying in a January night for fear of being forced 'out in the cold under a tree'?"

FOR MORE INFORMATION:

Cochran, Robert. "'All the Songs in the World': The Story of Emma Dusenbury." *Arkansas Historical Quarterly* 44 (Spring 1985): 3–15.

Cochran, Robert. "Emma Hays Dusenbury (1862–1941)." *The Encyclopedia of Arkansas History and Culture.* http://encyclopediaofarkansas.net/encyclopedia/entry-detail.aspx?search=1&entryID=1634.

"Singin' in the Wilderness." *Arkansas Gazette Magazine,* October 18, 1936.

Hazel Walker

A reasonable person could argue that Hazel Walker might just be the single greatest athlete in Arkansas history. And that is a high accolade given the wide range of nationally recognized athletes from this state. She was one of those amazing women of Arkansas history who has not received the public recognition she deserves—not yet at least.

Born August 8, 1914, on the family farm near Oak Hill in Little River County, Hazel was the second of three children born to Herbert S. and Minnie L. Walker, both Arkansas natives believed to have been of Cherokee ancestry. Historians know almost nothing about Walker's youth, since, unlike many prominent athletes, she did not write an autobiography. We do know that by 1928, her freshman year, Hazel was playing basketball as a member of the Ashdown High School Pantherettes.

Gary Newton, a Little Rock resident who has written extensively on Walker, noted that "by the end of her senior season, [Walker] had been named All-Conference three times, All-District twice, and had grown to a muscular five foot, nine inches." Hazel's rise to athletic prominence was rapid. During her senior year, the Pantherettes traveled to the state capital to compete in the first state basketball tournament for girls. While Ashdown lost in the finals, Hazel was a real hit. She was named to the all-state team and also selected "Most Beautiful Girl in the Tournament."

Many years later, while living in retirement in Little Rock, Walker recalled that graduation from high school did not quench her thirst for basketball. "I didn't want to teach or go to college, so I went to Tulsa to get a business degree [and] because they had a pretty good amateur team and I still wanted to play basketball." Tulsa Business College gave Walker a partial scholarship, and she was a star Stenographer, as the team was named. During her second season, Walker took the Stenos to the 1934 Amateur Athletic Union (AAU) national championship, and for the first time she was named to the All-American Team.

With her degree in hand, Walker took a bookkeeping job at Lion

Oil Company in El Dorado. She took the job, however, because Lion sponsored a women's basketball team, the "Oilers." Once again, Walker was an immediate star. It might seem surprising that an oil company would sponsor an amateur athletic team; however, before the advent of television, a time when Americans were eager to go out after work and cheer for a variety of local amateur teams, it was not unusual for businesses to underwrite basketball teams.

It was while Walker worked at Lion Oil that she married Everett Eugene Crutcher, a railroad brakeman from McGehee. Lion Oil Company had a policy against hiring married women, so the newlyweds kept their marriage secret. When word leaked out, company chairman T. H. Barton granted an exception to his star player.

At the conclusion of the 1936 season, the Crutchers moved to Little Rock, so Hazel could play on the new Lewis and Norwood Flyers, which was sponsored by an insurance agency. Over the next five years, Hazel led the Flyers to three national championships, losing only eight games.

In 1940, when Hazel was twenty-six, her husband was killed in a railroad switching accident in California. Without children, Hazel threw herself even more into basketball. World War II interrupted amateur athletics, even for female teams, as many American women took jobs in the war effort. Hazel, however, was able to continue playing by being a manager-player for such small teams as the Little Rock Dr. Pepper Girls.

Looking back on those fourteen years as an amateur, Hazel could count four national championships, being named All-American by the AAU on eleven occasions, and winning six national free-throw championships. She hit forty-nine of fifty shots in one competition.

In 1946, with America still celebrating its victory in World War II, Hazel turned pro. She signed on with Olson's All-American Red Heads. Hazel was a star Red Head (though her hair was black). She excelled at the entertaining style of the Red Heads, something akin to the modern Harlem Globetrotters.

By 1949, Hazel was ready to go out on her own. She established her own professional team, the Arkansas Travelers. The team played only against male teams, and they played a grueling schedule. They played an amazing 220 games each year, often two games in one evening. In sixteen seasons on the road, the Travelers lost only nineteen games. A major part of each game came during halftime when Hazel put on a free-throw demonstration and often challenged anyone in the audience to a competition. She never lost.

After almost four decades in basketball, Hazel Walker retired in 1965 at the age of fifty. She was already a legend, having been inducted into the Arkansas Sports Hall of Fame in 1959. She was posthumously inducted into the national Women's Basketball Hall of Fame in Knoxville in 2001.

After a series of strokes, Hazel Walker died on December 18, 1990, at the age of seventy-six. She was buried in Ashdown Cemetery.

FOR MORE INFORMATION:

Bailey, Jim. "Walker Dominated Amateur Ranks." *Arkansas Gazette,* December 19, 1990.

Ikard, Robert. *Just for Fun: The Story of AAU Women's Basketball.* Fayetteville: University of Arkansas Press, 2005.

Newton, Gary. "Hazel Leona Walker (1914–1990)." *The Encyclopedia of Arkansas History and Culture.* http://encyclopediaofarkansas.net/encyclopedia/entry-detail.aspx?search=1&entryID=669.

CHAPTER X

Religious Leaders

Rev. Cephas Washburn

The Reverend Cephas Washburn came to Arkansas in 1820 to minister to the Cherokee Indians who had been awarded a large reservation in northwest Arkansas. He established Dwight Mission near modern Russellville, which provided educational and religious instruction to tribal children before the Cherokees were moved into modern Oklahoma. Washburn then moved the mission to the Cherokee Nation, where he continued to provide pioneering educational opportunities for Indian children.

A native of Vermont, Washburn managed to get a university education and in 1818 was licensed to preach by the Congregational Church (though he later became a Presbyterian). Later that same year he married Abigail Woodard, also of Vermont, and they eventually had four sons and two daughters.

After a brief stint as a missionary in Savannah, Georgia, Washburn was sent in 1820 by the American Board of Commissioners for Foreign Missions to establish a mission among the Cherokees at their new reservation along the Arkansas River. These Cherokees were removed voluntarily from their traditional homelands in Georgia, Tennessee, and other southeastern states to a large reservation in northwest Arkansas. Known as the "Old Settlers," they were despised by the Cherokees who refused to surrender their homelands in the southeast. This schism caused intense stress between the factions, sometimes involving murder.

Washburn and his party, which included his brother-in-law, Rev. Alfred Finney, a third cleric, and two hired men, had to lay over in Little Rock due to "the ague," an early term for malaria. On July 4, 1820, Washburn preached what is believed to be the first sermon in Little Rock. Arriving at the reservation, Washburn discovered that chief Tolontuskee, who had invited the mission board to establish the school, had died and John Jolly was the new chief. Within a month Washburn concluded an agreement with Jolly and was able to start construction on his mission. The first house was raised on September 29, 1820. The mission was named after Rev. Timothy Dwight, president of Yale College.

The site chosen for the mission was a beautiful one. It was four miles north of the Arkansas River on the west side of Illinois Bayou. Today the site is under Lake Dardanelle. Within a year Washburn could report that twenty acres had been cleared and fenced, not a small task for a handful of men and animals. He could also brag about building "four cabins of hewed logs for dwelling houses, two of which are 20 feet square, with piazzas on two sides, and two are 18 feet by 22, with piazzas on one side." A gristmill was constructed, as well as a sawmill, possibly the first in Arkansas.

The mission school was conducted in a building twenty-four by thirty-six feet in size, suitable Washburn said for the one hundred students who were to be taught using the Lancasterian plan. Devised by English educator Joseph Lancaster, the Lancasterian system involved using older students as mentors, and it was at the height of its popularity when Dwight Mission was established. The very first school in Arkansas was caught up in the educational reform controversies of the day, a process that continues to the present.

Whatever the theory of the moment, it is clear that Washburn intended his school to bring change to the reservation. By today's standards, Washburn was culturally unenlightened, his methods archaic. Intensely devout, Washburn intended his school to promote the "habits of industry, temperance, and sobriety." He wrote, "the plan requires that all the children taken into the school be received also into our family, that they may be constantly under our care and direction." Washburn concluded that "by taking them before their habits are formed, placing them in a Christian family, and teaching them . . . there will be a foundation laid . . . that the condition of our aborigines will be essentially improved."

Washburn did not speak Cherokee, and Sequoyah's tribal alphabet was not yet finished, so the missionaries used translators to deliver sermons. A contemporary of Washburn's and a fellow cleric told how the congregation "composed of both sexes and all ages, took their seats with unusual stillness, the very smallest children keeping their seats without noise" when Washburn took the pulpit. On at least one occasion, however, Washburn found his Cherokee translator putting his own theological spin on the reverend's remarks.

No sooner did Washburn get Dwight Mission up and running than the federal government negotiated a new treaty with the Cherokees in 1828 that dissolved the reservation in Arkansas and moved the Indians into what is now northeastern Oklahoma. Washburn followed the tribe, and a new Dwight Mission arose along Sallisaw Creek in modern Sequoyah County, Oklahoma. By 1838 the mission school had an enrollment of 138 children, much to Washburn's delight. Without a doubt, these children, though deprived of tribal connections, were offered educational opportunities hardly found on the frontier outside the homes of the rich.

In 1840, after almost two decades in service to the Cherokees, Washburn left the mission and moved his family to Benton County in northwest Arkansas, where he organized a Presbyterian church. He later lived and preached in Fort Smith and Norristown, Pope County. While in Pope County, he helped organize new churches at Dardanelle and near Galley Rock. He died suddenly on March 17, 1860, in Little Rock, where he had stopped on his way to establish a new church. He was buried in historic Mount Holly Cemetery in Little Rock. In 1937 the Presbyterian Church erected a monument at his grave.

Unfortunately, Washburn's son, Edward Payson Washbourne (who used an older spelling of the family name), died in the same month as his father. He has his own place in Arkansas history as the painter of the *Arkansas Traveler*.

FOR MORE INFORMATION:

Ross, Margaret. "Rev. Cephas Washburn was an Expert on the Cherokee Indians of Arkansas." *Arkansas Gazette*, August 16, 1959.

———. "Pope County's Famous Dwight Mission Opens." *Arkansas Gazette*, June 17, 1959.

Washburn, Cephas. *Reminiscences of the Indians*. Richmond: Presbyterian Committee of Publication, 1869.

Bishop Edward Fitzgerald

While Arkansas has never had a large Catholic population nor held much sway within the Catholic Church, a nineteenth-century bishop of Little Rock gained international note for opposing the pope on a major theological issue. In 1870 Pope Pius IX convened the first General Ecumenical Council of the Catholic Church in Rome, with 689 prelates gathering from around the world. Representing the Diocese of Little Rock was Bishop Edward Fitzgerald. The pope and the bishop did not agree on the proposal for papal infallibility.

Born in Limerick, Ireland, in 1833, Fitzgerald came to the United States when his parents emigrated in 1849 during the great potato famine. He was educated at Mt. St. Mary Seminary in Ohio and Mt. St. Mary's College and Seminary in Maryland. Ordained in 1857 in Cincinnati, Ohio, Fitzgerald served for a decade as pastor of St. Patrick's in Columbus, Ohio, where he gained a reputation for competency and peacekeeping.

The diocese of Little Rock was organized in 1843, and it included Indian Territory until 1891. The entire diocese included only about 1,600 Catholics, served by a handful of priests. The most blatant example of neglect of this frontier diocese was the failure to name a bishop for almost five years before February 1867 when Fitzgerald was consecrated.

Interestingly, the thirty-two-year-old parish priest turned down the pope's initial offer of appointment as the second bishop of Little Rock. Pope Pius IX then sent Fitzgerald a mandamus ordering him to accept the appointment. He was the youngest bishop in the nation.

Immediately upon his appointment, Bishop Fitzgerald undertook a vigorous journey across the diocese, speaking to ecumenical audiences, meeting with the few faithful he could find, and generally assessing the challenge before him. He said mass at a Presbyterian church in Washington, Hempstead County, but could identify only five Catholics in the whole town outside of occupying Union soldiers. Catholic schools functioned only at Little Rock and Fort Smith.

Edward Fitzgerald, Roman Catholic Bishop of Little Rock, stood up to the pope.
Photo courtesy of Special Collections, University of Arkansas Libraries.

Bishop Fitzgerald was a vigorous administrator. He eagerly sought new priests for new congregations, such as at Pocahontas. Under a blazing August sun in 1869, Fitzgerald dedicated the first Catholic church in Hot Springs, and soon he had an additional priest ministering in Little Rock.

Such was the situation a few days before Christmas in 1869 when Fitzgerald, various other bishops, archbishops, and others met in the first council in about three hundred years. Within a few days it became clear that the major topic for discussion was the doctrine of papal infallibility. Professor James M. Woods, the author of a fine history of the diocese of Little Rock, has written that Fitzgerald's consistent opposition to the pope on the infallibility issue had earned "a place in American Catholic history by demonstrating immense courage as a man and loyalty as a bishop."

From Rome the bishop wrote of the difficulty he encountered at the Vatican, noting, "There is no danger that the Holy Father will take me from Arkansas, except to put me in the prisons of the Inquisition, perhaps. I have not been in his good book since coming to Rome. There are others here who wish to put an end to my banishment, but I will not leave Arkansas."

Fitzgerald caught the attention of one reporter who described him as a "stalwart, manly man, a typical missionary bishop who had served his apprenticeship in rough and lonely country missions."

A fierce debate raged between supporters of the proposed doctrine, mostly from countries with large Catholic populations and vocal opponents who mostly represented non-Catholic areas. Soon it became clear that the proposed doctrine would be accepted by the council members. On the first vote, 451 prelates voted for the proposed doctrine, while 88 voted against and 62 said they could support it if modified. A large group of 70 bishops simply failed to show up for the vote. The pope ordered a new vote.

In the four days between the two elections a great deal of soul searching took place—along with some considerable arm twisting. The second ballot was a runaway in favor of infallibility, although some opponents again boycotted the vote. Only a very young bishop from the wilds of Arkansas actually attended the vote and stood up to vote no, although an Italian bishop later dissented too. A reporter recalled the scene a half century later: "Four hundred and ninety-one bishops recorded their votes consecutively in favor of the definition when the name Eduardus Fitzgerald was called out. . . . The Bishop of Little Rock rose to his feet, and said 'non placet,' breaking the solidarity of the vote, inviting the curiosity of all, and the indignation of a few."

The final vote was 533 in favor of fallibility and 2 opposed. As James Woods has written, "From the back of the hall, in his big booming Irish brogue, Fitzgerald became a footnote in the history of the universal Catholic Church." Later, Fitzgerald acknowledged the supremacy of the new doctrine.

While Fitzgerald did not relish his assignment on the western frontier, he made the most of it. He gets credit for evangelizing the African American community, including establishing the first black parish in Arkansas, at Pine Bluff. Fitzgerald also sought to increase Catholic immigration to Arkansas, even making a deal with a local railroad to set aside land to be sold to Catholics.

During his four decades as bishop, the number of Catholic priests increased from six to forty-three. Only nine Catholic churches existed in Arkansas when Fitzgerald arrived, but the total stood at fifty-one parishes in 1900. Fitzgerald encouraged the creation of hospitals, and he opened four facilities during his tenure, including St. Vincent Infirmary in Little Rock, Arkansas's first real hospital, which opened in 1888.

Bishop Fitzgerald died on February 3, 1907, having celebrated his fortieth anniversary as bishop only a few days earlier. He was widely mourned as a popular and successful bishop and was buried under the Cathedral of St. Andrew in Little Rock.

Fitzgerald's audacity in opposing the pope on infallibility was remembered in the diocese of Little Rock for generations, with some teaching nuns in northeast Arkansas, noting that the contest pitted "the Little Rock against St. Peter's Rock."

FOR MORE INFORMATION:

Petersen, Svend. "The Little Rock against the Big Rock." *Arkansas Historical Quarterly* 2 (June 1943): 164–70.

Woods, James M. "Edward Mary Fitzgerald (1833–1907)." *The Encyclopedia of Arkansas History and Culture.* http://encyclopediaofarkansas.net/encyclopedia/entry-detail.aspx?search=1&entryID=1644.

Woods, James M. *Mission and Memory: A History of the Catholic Church in Arkansas.* Little Rock: August House, 1993.

Rev. Hay Watson Smith

The battle between theological conservatives and liberals has deep roots in Arkansas religious history. While it is undoubtedly true that most Arkansas religious leaders lean to the conservative side, exceptions have dotted the historical landscape from the beginning. One of the most liberal ministers of the gospel in Arkansas between the world wars was Rev. Hay Watson Smith, pastor at Second Presbyterian Church in Little Rock from 1911 until ill health forced his retirement in 1939. Smith's ardent support for Darwinian evolution especially angered the denomination's conservatives and Smith had to defend himself against charges of heresy.

Born the son of a Presbyterian cleric in Greensboro, North Carolina, in 1868, Smith graduated from Davidson College and then took graduate degrees in religion from Union Theological Seminary in New York and Oglethorpe University in Georgia. Because he disagreed with some doctrines of Southern Presbyterianism, Smith chose to be ordained in 1901 as a Congregationalist minister. He served Congregational churches in Brooklyn and Port Chester, New York, prior to becoming president of Selma Military Institute in Alabama. After a year in Selma, he accepted a call to become minister of Second Presbyterian Church of Little Rock, a congregation he had served briefly in 1900 as a supply minister.

His coming to Little Rock was undoubtedly influenced by the fact that his wife, Jessie Rose Smith, was a native of Little Rock and the daughter of U. M. Rose, a prominent attorney and founder of the Rose Law Firm.

As historian Gene Vinzant has noted, Smith made no secret of his liberal persuasion: "Upon applying for ministry within the Arkansas Presbytery, Smith clearly stated his acceptance of evolution, his rejection of biblical inerrancy, along with his disagreement with some aspects of the Confession of Faith." The presbytery accepted his credentials anyway.

Dr. Smith was a dynamic, if highly opinionated, leader, and Second Presbyterian prospered during his pastorate. Growing from a membership of 200 to 965 during his tenure, it became the largest Presbyterian church in Arkansas.

Despite his success as a minister, Smith was a lightning rod within the conservative religious culture in Arkansas. During the 1920s the Presbyterian Church was caught up in a tug of war between traditionalists who believed in a literal interpretation of the Bible and modernists who followed a more nuanced interpretative approach. Nowhere was this division more pronounced than on the issue of evolution.

Charles Darwin published his treatise *On the Origin of Species* in 1859, but America was on the verge of the Civil War and evolution failed to catch on then as a major topic of public interest. The fundamentalist movement emerged as a major social and political force by 1920, and several states adopted laws to prohibit the teaching of evolution in the schools. The most famous confrontation came in 1925 when John T. Scopes, a teacher in Dayton, Tennessee, challenged that state's law. The resulting trial, which featured famed lawyers William Jennings Bryan and Clarence Darrow, brought the issue to the forefront.

In January 1927, two antievolution bills were introduced in the Arkansas legislature; the one sponsored by Rep. A. L. Rotenberry of Pulaski County was supported by the Rev. Ben Bogard, the popular pastor of Antioch Missionary Baptist Church in Little Rock.

On the Sunday after the Rotenberry bill was introduced, Rev. Hay Watson Smith told his congregation: "I say that people who oppose teaching evolution do so through ignorance." On January 28, the reverends Bogard and Smith confronted each other before the House Education Committee. The committee held its meeting on the floor of the House, with the chamber and balcony packed. Eleven people, about equally divided between supporters and opponents, were scheduled to testify on the bill.

Julia Burnelle "Bernie" Babcock, a prominent Little Rock writer, said she preferred to be "modern and right," declaring that the Bible is a wonderfully inspiring book but solely a book of symbolism. Rev. J. William Smith, a Sheridan minister and educator, refuted Babcock by saying he would rather be "old-fashioned and right, than modern and wrong."

The Reverend Bogard took the floor to say, "I do not want any single feature of Christianity taught in the public schools, but I ask in the name of God, don't teach my boy or my girl anything contrary to the Christian religion and make me pay for it."

Finally, Smith arose and proclaimed, "I believe evolution is the most beautiful truth I know. It has given me an insight into the human spirit and the wonderful things of nature. It has brought me closer to God than anything but Christ's own truths as exemplified by His own life."

Legislators surprised observers by barely passing the bill in the House and by tabling it in the Senate. Bogard then organized a petition campaign to refer the matter to voters as an amendment to the state constitution. Smith waged a strong campaign against the proposed amendment. He printed and distributed a fifteen-page booklet titled *Evolution and Intellectual Freedom: A Compilation of Opinion,* which contained quotes defending evolution by a host of prominent scientists, as well as former presidents Theodore Roosevelt and Woodrow Wilson. All this effort was to no avail, and in October 1928 Arkansans adopted the amendment by a vote of 108,991 to 63,406.

In the aftermath of the evolution debate, fundamentalists in the Presbyterian Church attempted to defrock Smith. Rev. William McPheters of South Carolina branded Smith a "heretic." The combative Smith struck back, calling McPheters an unreasoning traditionalist and "the outstanding heresy hunter in the Southern church." The presbytery of Arkansas investigated Smith's orthodoxy and accepted his explanation of his beliefs, and ultimately the denomination's general assembly sustained that verdict.

Contrary to popular belief, Smith was never actually tried for heresy. Rev. Marion A. Boggs, who succeeded Smith at Second Presbyterian, was chairman of the investigating commission. Shortly before his death in 1983, Boggs recalled in a letter that "Dr. Smith was never placed on trial. It was only an investigation from start to finish. The proceeding lasted four full years, and it was a demanding and sometimes discouraging undertaking. I look back upon the record of it as one of the deeply satisfying experiences of my life. Our decision, in my opinion, saved the Second Church for the Presbyterian Church of the United States. If we had placed Dr. Smith on trial, I feel sure that he would have taken the church into the Congregational fellowship."

Ecclesiastical confrontations take a long time to die, and even today Presbyterian conservatives cite Smith as the pioneer who took the church away from fundamentalism. Smith died in January 1940, only a few months after resigning as pastor of Second Presbyterian Church.

FOR MORE INFORMATION:

Boggs, Marion A., to Miss Sara Draper, Little Rock, February 11, 1980. Typed letter signed by Dr. Boggs. Copy in possession of the author.

"Dr. Hay Watson Smith, Liberal Leader, Passes . . . Had Been Pastor Here 29 Years." *Arkansas Gazette,* January 21, 1940.

"Ministers Clash on Evolution Bill." *Arkansas Gazette,* January 29, 1927.

Smith, Hay Watson. *Evolution and Intellectual Freedom: A Compilation of Opinions.* N.p.: Privately printed by the author, 1927.

Vinzant, Gene. "The Case of Hay Watson Smith: Evolution and Heresy in the Presbyterian Church." *Ozark Historical Review* 30 (Spring 2001): 57–70.

Rabbi Ira E. Sanders

One of the most amazing religious leaders in Arkansas history is Reform Jewish Rabbi Ira E. Sanders of Little Rock's Temple B'nai Israel. Over a tenure of thirty-seven years, and another twenty-two years as rabbi emeritus, Sanders was a mighty presence on both the religious and secular fronts. His pioneering work for social welfare brought about a more humane society, and he mentored others to carry on the work. He took a firm stand against racial segregation long before most other white religious leaders found the courage to stand up.

Ira Eugene Sanders was born on May 6, 1894, in Rich Hill, Missouri, the son of Pauline and Daniel Sanders. His father was a wholesale meat packer. The family moved to Kansas City, Missouri, when Ira was six, and he attended local public schools there. He graduated from the University of Cincinnati in 1918 and then entered Hebrew Union College, a leading seminary for followers of the reform movement. He later received a graduate degree in sociology from Columbia University. On March 21, 1922, Sanders married Selma Loeb, a fellow Rich Hill, Missouri, native and a Wellesley graduate. They had one child, Flora Louise.

After ordination in 1919, Sanders served a congregation in Allentown, Pennsylvania, and in 1924 he became an associate rabbi at Temple Israel in New York City. One spring day in 1926, Rabbi Sanders gave a sermon on "Why the North and the South Should Meet Together." Among the audience members stirred by the heartfelt message of reconciliation and healing of old Civil War wounds was the "Pulpit Committee" from Temple B'nai Israel of Little Rock. They immediately asked Sanders to accept the leadership of their synagogue.

Sanders arrived at the Little Rock train station on September 1, 1926, and was not pleased with what he found. Compared to New York, Little Rock seemed provincial and isolated, but he agreed to give it a try.

Little Rock was probably not as unwelcoming to a new Jewish rabbi as one might assume. The city had a long tradition of religious toleration, with Jews holding political and social positions of note. Historian Carolyn Gray LeMaster of Little Rock noted in her encyclopedic history of Judaism in Arkansas, *A Corner of the Tapestry* (1994), that of thirty-six social and fraternal clubs in Little Rock in 1900, twenty-five had Jewish members. Sanders's predecessor at Temple B'nai Israel, Rabbi Emanuel Jack, a World War I veteran, was a Veteran of Foreign Wars commander and chairman of the American Legion's Americanization Committee. (It is true that some candidates endorsed by the revived Ku Klux Klan won election in Pulaski County in 1922, but the hooded bigots saw their power wane quickly.)

Sanders threw himself into his new community. He immediately noticed the need for improved social services for the poor. Within a year of arriving, he began the Little Rock School of Social Work, which soon became a part of the University of Arkansas extension program. Within two years, the school had sixty tuition-paying students.

The School of Social Work was the source of a bitter lesson in racial segregation for the newly arrived Sanders. When three black students applied to the school, Sanders accepted them. He overrode the objections of white students, but he could not convince university officials to disregard state laws mandating segregation in the classroom.

Sanders managed to keep the School of Social Work going during the Great Depression, and many of his students took jobs with the federal relief programs created during the New Deal. Sanders was the founding president of the Pulaski County Public Welfare Commission and helped create the Arkansas Human Betterment League, the Urban League of Greater Little Rock, and the Lighthouse for the Blind. He served on the board of the Little Rock Public Library for forty-one years.

The new rabbi also made a splash in the local press when he invited the great defense lawyer and religious skeptic Clarence Darrow to come to Little Rock for a debate. Sanders came up with the idea as a way to raise money for the new Temple Men's Club. On November 3, 1930, more than two thousand people filled the auditorium at the new Central High School to hear Sanders debate Darrow on the question "Is man immortal?"

The rabbi made his case without ever mentioning God, Judaism, Christianity, or religion in general. He took a scientific approach, which might have surprised the opposition. Sanders stressed that the concept of immortality was universal and that humans possessed the power of moral aspiration and spirituality. The rabbi admitted he did not know the form immortality would take, but that the very complexity of evolution, for example, pointed toward a creator and immortality. After a scrappy debate, Sanders heaped praise on his opponent, saying "his good deeds will win for him life immortal, and in the Choir Invisible, no illustrious name will be sung more fervently than the name of Clarence Darrow."

During the Little Rock school integration crisis of 1957, Sanders joined fourteen other religious leaders in calling upon the governor and legislature to comply with the Federal court orders for integration.

Sanders died on April 8, 1985, and was interred at Oakland Jewish Cemetery in Little Rock, the only rabbi buried there.

FOR MORE INFORMATION:

LeMaster, Carolyn Gray. *A Corner of the Tapestry: A History of the Jewish Experience in Arkansas, 1820s–1990s*. Fayetteville: University of Arkansas Press, 1994.

———. "Ira Eugene Sanders (1894–1985)." *The Encyclopedia of Arkansas History and Culture.* http://encyclopediaofarkansas.net/encyclopedia/entry-detail. aspx?search=1&entryID=1755.

Perry, Elizabeth C., and F. Hampton Roy. "The Rabbi and Clarence Darrow." *Pulaski County Historical Review* 28 (Summer 1980): 2–3.

"Rabbi I. E. Sanders, 90, Rabbi Emeritus at B'nai Israel, Dies." *Arkansas Democrat,* April 9, 1985.

"Rabbi Ira E. Sanders Dies; Long-Time Leader." *Arkansas Gazette,* April 9, 1985.

"Rabbi Will End 37 Years at B'nai Israel August 31." *Arkansas Gazette,* June 8, 1963.

Sanders, Ira E. *The Centennial History of Congregation B'nai Israel, Little Rock, Arkansas, 1866–1966.* Little Rock: Congregation, 1966.

CHAPTER XI

Seers, Spiritualists, and Skeptics

Caroline Dye

One of the paradoxes of the Jim Crow era of segregation was the allowance made for black female fortune tellers. "Aunt" Caroline Dye of Newport, Arkansas, was perhaps the most famous of these black clairvoyants.

During 1890–1965, Arkansas and the rest of the American South was a land of strict segregation. Black children studied in all-black schools, black travelers were denied lodging in hotels, almost all churches were segregated, and when black folks cast off their mortal coil, they were buried in black cemeteries. Still, large numbers of white people not only sought out Mrs. Dye but also paid her well for her services.

Born a slave in South Carolina around 1850, she was brought to Arkansas by her owners when they moved to Independence County. After the Civil War, she married Martin Dye of Sulphur Rock, and about 1900 the couple settled into a home on Remmel Avenue in Newport.

Dye's reputation as a seer started when she was a child. After moving to Newport, her fame spread rapidly. She was reputed to be especially successful in locating lost articles such as jewelry. One man remembered Dye as having a devoted clientele: "there were scores of both negroes and white people who regarded her as lawyer, doctor, preacher, confessor, and adviser."

First-time visitors were surprised by Dye's understated style. She dressed simply, and she made no use of crystal balls or other traditional fortuneteller props. Sometimes she used a deck of cards, though she said they merely served to focus her concentration and had no psychic powers. She usually received clients while sitting in a rocking chair on her large back porch.

Dye's fame spread as many of her predictions proved accurate, or at least almost nearly accurate. Famed bluesman W. C. Handy made Caroline Dye a central figure in two songs, "St. Louis Blues" and

"Sundown Blues." The latter song, about a woman's "two-timing papa," contains the lines "I'm goin' to Newport ... I mean Newport, Arkansaw! / I'm goin' there to see Aunt Car'line Dye."

By 1909 Dye's powers landed her on the front page of the *Arkansas Democrat*, where she was reported to have been visited "by a deputation of citizens in an endeavor to ascertain whether a cowering wretch being guarded by a mob was the right man to hang, following an assault upon a young woman."

Sometimes predictions were attributed to Dye that she denied. For example, the same 1909 newspaper account cited above mentions that Dye had disclaimed any predictions of impending disaster for the town of Newport, "and as a result many uneasy feelings have been calmed."

Clients paid handsome fees for Dye's services, usually in cash. She owned a large home, which provided housing not only for Dye and her husband, but also for a retinue of staff and friends. Being totally illiterate, she maintained a fulltime secretary. At one time she owned eight farms. Without offspring of her own, she raised a number of foster children.

When Dye died in 1918, her executor called authorities to her home, where a search reportedly yielded $12,000 in cash, about one-third in silver dollars. For years before her death rumors had circulated that Dye distrusted banks and had buried her wealth in various locations.

About twenty years after her death, newspapers reported that a Newport man had supposedly located Dye's buried money. This rumor brought scores of spade-wielding searchers into Newport's back allies and lanes. "Men and women are digging feverishly in old fence corners and under gnarled trees," reported one journalist.

Regardless of her wealth, Caroline Dye will be remembered as a black woman who rose above the constraints of slavery and segregation to build an independent life.

FOR MORE INFORMATION:

"Caroline Dye: Date of Birth." *Stream of History* 5 (October 1967): 41.

Morgan, James L. "She Put Newport on the Map: A Biography of Aunt Caroline Dye." *Stream of History* 5 (January 1967): 17–18, 28–32.

Wolf, John Quincy. "Aunt Caroline Dye: The Gypsy in the 'St. Louis Blues.'" *Southern Folklore Quarterly* 33 (1969): 339–46.

Lessie Stringfellow

When Stephen Chism published his book *The Afterlife of Leslie Stringfellow: A Nineteenth-Century Southern Family's Experiences with Spiritualism,* he shed light on a subject that has received little attention in Arkansas history.

Spiritualism is usually traced back to the Swedish mining engineer and physician Emanuel Swedenborg, who at the age of fifty-six in 1744 began writing about his ability to communicate with spirits. During the remaining twenty-eight years of his life, Swedenborg wrote thirty books in which he portrayed a spiritual world that parallels our physical one. The movement grew in the United States with the publication in 1848 of *The Great Harmonia,* by the American mystic Andrew Jackson Davis.

Although Davis's book was published in 1848, it apparently had nothing to do with developments of that same year when a "haunted house" in Hydesville, New York, captured the popular imagination. John and Margaret Fox, along with their two young daughters, started noticing strange sounds after moving into the simple two-story house. The parents became exasperated with all the banging and knocking, but fifteen-year-old Margaret Fox and her twelve-year-old sister, Kate, came to believe the sounds were made by a spirit—and they worked out a means of communicating with it. The news media learned of the Fox sisters, and soon their stories were publicized around the world.

Spiritualism grew rapidly in both the United States and Britain. No less than the president of the Royal Society of Science in England, Sir William Crookes, was a believer, as was the writer Lewis Carroll. Perhaps the best known spiritualist in England was the creator of the Sherlock Holmes series, Sir Arthur Conan Doyle. In America, leading proponents of spiritualism were writers Harriet Beecher Stowe and James Fenimore Cooper. Most spiritualists considered themselves Christians.

The arrival of spiritualism in Arkansas is not documented, but we do know that psychics were advertising their services in the *Arkansas Gazette* by 1872. Five years later the *Gazette* reported that 150 members of a "Spiritualist sect" were living in Little Rock. Among the well-known spiritualists in Arkansas was Julia Burnelle "Bernie" Babcock, a novelist and founder of the Arkansas Museum of Science and Natural History in Little Rock.

On the surface, the Stringfellow family might not seem destined to become spiritualists. Alice Johnston was only sixteen when she fell in love with a young Confederate officer named Henry Martyn Stringfellow. In December 1863, they were married in Houston, Texas. The young couple settled on Galveston Island, where Henry made a fortune establishing the citrus industry along the Texas coast.

In March 1866, the Stringfellows had their only natural child, a son named Leslie. A precocious child, Leslie was talented in music and the darling of both parents. In September 1886, Leslie died unexpectedly after an illness of only three days. While dying, the twenty-one-year-old Leslie vowed to his mother that he would contact her after death.

The bereaved parents traveled to Boston, then a spiritualism center, where they sought a medium who could connect them to their son's spirit. After participating in several séances, the Stringfellows returned home dissatisfied. Despite early disappointment, the persistent pair located a medium in Galveston who directed Mrs. Stringfellow to purchase a planchette. This instrument, which later played a role in creating the Ouija board, held a pencil above a piece of paper. At first Mrs. Stringfellow could coax nothing from the planchette, but when she asked her husband to place his hands on hers, the instrument began writing.

Beginning in 1886, the Stringfellows held séances nightly at 7 P.M. For the remainder of the century, the family received more than four thousand messages from their dear Leslie. At first the family talked publicly of their successes, but they stopped after friends and neighbors reacted badly.

In 1911, the aging Stringfellows moved to Fayetteville, apparently because of Henry's failing health. They brought along a daughter, Lessie, whom they adopted after the death of their son, and Lessie's husband, pharmacist James Read. Henry Stringfellow spent his time in Fayetteville experimenting with grafting English walnuts onto native black walnut rootstocks. The great horticulturist Luther Burbank lived with the Stringfellows for a short time while he collaborated with Henry in his experiments. Henry Stringfellow died after living in Fayetteville only a short time.

When Lessie's husband abandoned her, she went to work as a reporter for the *Fayetteville Democrat* newspaper, which was published by Roberta Fulbright. She eventually became editor, serving twenty-eight years in the position. She was also an active clubwoman, and she was a founding member of the Arkansas Historical Association in 1942.

As time passed, Alice Stringfellow became interested in publishing a selection of her communications with her deceased son. In 1919 she sent a copy of her manuscript to the best-known spiritualist of the day, Sir Arthur Conan Doyle, who urged her to publish it. In 1926, *Leslie's Letters to His Mother* was published in a print run of one hundred copies. Only a tiny fraction of Leslie's thousands of spirit letters are included in Alice's edition. Chism reproduces these letters in his book, so readers can see how a young man's spirit communicated with his family.

Alice and Lessie lived together for many years. In 1942 Alice died at the age of ninety-seven. Lessie continued to live in the family home, where she held meetings of Rosicrucians, a spiritualist group to which both she and her adopted father belonged. She died in 1971.

FOR MORE INFORMATION:

Chism, Stephen J. *The Afterlife of Leslie Stringfellow: A Nineteenth-Century Southern Family's Experiences with Spiritualism.* Fayetteville: University of Arkansas Press, 2006.

———. "'The very happiest tiding': Sir Arthur Conan Doyle's Correspondence with Arkansas Spiritualists." *Arkansas Historical Quarterly* 59 (Autumn 2000): 299–310.

Bernie Babcock

Julia Burnelle "Bernie" Babcock lived a very long and productive life. A writer, museum founder, and all-round character, Babcock left a large imprint on the history of Little Rock and Arkansas.

Many people who knew only her name were surprised to meet Bernie and discover she was a woman. She was born Julia Burnelle Smade on April 28, 1868, in Unionville, Ohio, the daughter of educated parents. Her family moved to Russellville when Bernie was ten, and she grew up there and in Little Rock.

She studied at Little Rock University, a Masonic institution, but left school at eighteen to marry William Babcock, an express company agent. In 1897, after eleven years of marriage, William died, leaving behind five children, a twenty-nine-year-old widow, and many medical bills. There were no safety nets or social programs for impoverished families at that time, and the widow Babcock turned to writing to support her family. Having written poetry since childhood, she threw herself into her new career and success came remarkably quickly.

She shared her mother's fierce opposition to liquor, and temperance themes appeared frequently in her work. In 1900, she published her first novel. Titled *The Daughter of a Republican,* this biting attack on saloons sold 100,000 copies in six months.

As soon as her children began school, Babcock took a job at the *Arkansas Democrat.* For $12.50 per week she edited both the society and book pages. She is also believed to have been the first female to edit stories received by telegraph, the equivalent of the modern wire editor.

When her workday at the newspaper ended, she went home and continued to write, producing hundreds of poems, short stories, and novels. Her best-known work is *The Soul of Ann Rutledge* (1919), the first of five novels Babcock wrote about President Abraham Lincoln. This novel, written in the stilted prose of the late Victorian era, was an account of a supposed relationship between young Lincoln and Ann

Bernie Babcock, a successful novelist and museum founder. *Photo courtesy of Special Collections, University of Arkansas Libraries.*

Rutledge, the daughter of an innkeeper in Salem, Illinois, where the future president lived for six years. *The Soul of Ann Rutledge* went through fourteen printings as well as several foreign language editions. The book is still easily located in the used book trade.

Many of her books were thinly disguised political or personal statements. Her initial books were temperance novels, full of vivid detail of the suffering caused by liquor consumption. *Justice to the Woman* (1901) and *A Political Fool* (1902) were political novels but with temperance overtones. One of her books touched on human evolution, a subject that fascinated Babcock. Darwin's *Origin of Species* and the Bible were the first two books Babcock acquired after marrying. A fascination with evolution led Babcock to vigorously speak out against a 1928 constitutional amendment outlawing the teaching of evolution in Arkansas schools.

After leaving her job with the *Arkansas Democrat,* Babcock edited and published her own quarterly magazine, *The Arkansas Sketch Book,* which folded after three years. This first major attempt at a state literary magazine was well done with fine photography and original poems and stories. In 1908 she published the first anthology of Arkansas poetry, *Pictures and Poems of Arkansas,* which included one hundred poems as well as seventy original photographs.

As time passed, Miss Bernie, as she was often called, became interested in establishing a museum for Arkansas, believing it would help build state pride. She was highly offended when H. L. Mencken and others criticized the state, and she wrote a blistering indictment of Thomas W. Jackson's joke book *On a Slow Train through Arkansas.*

Eventually a museum was opened on the third floor of Little Rock city hall, but it closed during the Great Depression. During that time she found work with the Federal Writers' Project, where she helped produce several books and guides to Arkansas topics and organized oral history interviews with former slaves.

In the 1940s, though over seventy years of age, Babcock prodded the city of Little Rock into reestablishing a museum, this time in the old Arsenal Building in what is today MacArthur Park. Hired as the museum director, she worked hard to build the Little Rock Museum of Science and Natural History into a real institution, but support was scanty and it never reached its potential. The museum was the forerunner of today's Museum of Discovery.

Babcock was a follower of the popular early twentieth-century Spiritualism movement. She reportedly held séances at the museum, though none were known to produce historical discoveries.

Babcock retired in 1953 and moved to a home on Petit Jean Mountain, where she continued to write and resumed her earlier interest in landscape painting. On June 14, 1962, at the age of ninety-four, she died at her desk, a manuscript in her lap.

FOR MORE INFORMATION:

"Bernie Babcock made Notable Contributions to Literature—and History." *Arkansas Gazette,* July 22, 1962.

Camp, Marcia. "Bernie Babcock (1868–1962)." *The Encyclopedia of Arkansas History and Culture.* http://encyclopediaofarkansas.net/encyclopedia/entry-detail. aspx?search=1&entryID=1097.

Camp, Marcia. "The Soul of Bernie Babcock." *Pulaski County Historical Review* 36 (Fall 1988): 50–62.

"Nationally Noted Author, History Museum Leader Dies at Petit Jean Home." *Arkansas Gazette,* June 15, 1962.

Harold M. Sherman

One of the most remarkable men of Arkansas history was Harold Sherman, a writer, a playwright, an authority on extrasensory perception and the paranormal in general, a community activist and promoter, and a man with vast energy and personal appeal. Working in a small backroom study in their rustic home about ten miles south of Mountain View in Stone County, Sherman made a living as a freelance writer. It is possible he is the most widely published author in Arkansas history.

Born in 1898 in Traverse City, Michigan, Harold Morrow Sherman began writing at an early age. His first publication was a history of Traverse City, which won a state essay contest while Sherman was still in high school.

In 1920 Sherman married Martha Bain, a woman he loved passionately for the remainder of his long life. They had two daughters, Mary and Marcia. His first job was in journalism, writing for an Indiana newspaper. Later he moved to New York City, where he worked as an editor and in advertising—and where he developed an interest in writing sports literature for boys. He published about forty books for boys with titles such as *Touchdown!* (1927) and *Block That Kick* (1928). In 1933 he brought out *Tahara: Boy Mystic of India,* a book that not only sold widely but also hinted at Sherman's growing fascination with what he called "the field of psychic phenomena."

Sherman's first public foray in the realm of psychic phenomena turned out to be a resounding success, in part because of Sherman's promotional skills. In 1938 he and Arctic explorer Sir Hubert Wilkins undertook an experiment in mental telepathy, which was published in 1942 under the title of *Thoughts through Space.* Over the next forty years Sherman published dozens of books dealing with psychic phenomena; he also regularly turned out self-help books. His book titled *Your Key to Happiness* went through multiple editions, and Sherman helped market an LP album based on the book. He also published a series of sex education books for young people.

In 1947 Sherman moved his whole family to a rustic mountain farm in southern Stone County. This must have been a shocking experience for the city-bred and -born Sherman family to move into a mere shack without electricity or running water. (The first time the family inspected their new home, it was occupied by squatters, and baby chicks were wandering around the floor. When asked why the chickens were in the house, the squatter said his wife was ill in bed and he could not attend to both at the same time, so he brought the chicks inside.)

As was traditional in rural mountain areas, the Sherman family was looked upon with some suspicion when they first arrived. Certainly, Harold Sherman's penchant for wearing white shirts on weekdays raised eyebrows. But, Sherman was a friendly man, and he soon settled into his adopted home. Before long he was promoting a wide array of community activities. Harold was supported by his brother Thomas, who relocated his family to Stone County, where he lived across the highway from Harold and Martha.

Sherman organized automobile caravans of Stone County residents to the state capital to lobby Gov. Sid McMath and the legislature to pave roads in the area. Sherman knew how to make the effort into a media event, and it raised his profile in his adopted county. Before long he was president of the local Lions Club in Mountain View.

Sherman organized an effort to convince Arkansas Power & Light Company (AP&L) to extend electrical service to the rural areas south of Mountain View. Among the Sherman archives were aging black-and-white pictures of a grateful Stone County farmer presenting a piglet to smiling AP&L president C. Hamilton Moses. Later, Sherman was a moving force in securing development of Blanchard Springs Caverns by the U.S. Forest Service and the creation of the Ozark Folk Center as an agency of the Arkansas Department of Parks and Tourism.

Not all his efforts yielded results. An effort to promote Stone County as a haven for crossbow archery fell flat. Perhaps his most notable failure was an effort in the late 1950s to film a television show on location in Stone County. The story, which Sherman wrote with his close friend Al Pollard of Little Rock, was about a white dog named Sheppy who rescued a lost girl from a threatening bobcat. Neither Sherman nor Pollard seemed to understand that bobcats were not threats to humans. (Amazingly, nine bobcats were killed in making the pilot—all having been trapped by the Arkansas Game and Fish Commission through the intercession of Gov. Orval Faubus.) Set in Stone County and replete with a cameo performance by local folksinger Jimmy Driftwood, the pilot debuted in Batesville's Melba Theater in July 1958. That was its first and only public showing until recent years.

Setbacks never slowed Harold Sherman. He lectured around the world, especially in Japan, where his work in the paranormal was popular. His books were translated into many languages, including Icelandic. He continued to write books until he died in 1987.

FOR MORE INFORMATION:

Sherman, Harold M. Papers. University of Central Arkansas Archives, Torreyson Library, Conway. A detailed guide to the collection can be found at http://archives.uca.edu/special_collection/m87–08.htm.

———. *How to Make ESP Work for You.* New York: Devorss and Co., 1964.

———. *You Live after Death.* New York: C. & R. Anthony, 1949.

Sherman, Harold M., and Sir Hubert Wilkins. *Thoughts through Space: A Remarkable Adventure in the Realm of Mind.* New York: Creative Age Press, 1942.

CHAPTER XII

Eccentrics, Frauds, and the Inexplicable

William Hope "Coin" Harvey

While Bill Clinton was the first Arkansan elected president, he was certainly not the only resident of the state nominated for the highest office in the land. In August 1931 William Hope "Coin" Harvey of Benton County was selected as the Liberty Party nominee for president. While his quixotic campaign barely made a blip on the political radar, it was merely one chapter in the life of an amazing individual.

Born in 1851 near Buffalo, in what is now West Virginia, Harvey attended local country schools as well as Buffalo Academy. After a brief stint teaching elementary school, he spent a summer at Marshall College in Cabell County, West Virginia, thus ending his formal education. He commenced the study of law by reading in the law office of his older brother, Thomas, and in 1870, at the age of nineteen, he was admitted to the bar in his home state.

Harvey practiced law in a number of states, including Ohio, where he met and married Anna Halliday in 1876. A few years later Harvey moved his growing family to southwestern Colorado, where he operated the highly successful Silver Bell silver mine. When silver ore prices declined, he moved his family to Pueblo, Colorado, where he helped develop the Mineral Palace, a large exhibition hall that promoted the state's mining resources. Later he moved the family to Chicago, then to Ogden, Utah.

As was typical of the energetic Harvey, no sooner had he settled in Ogden than he began promoting the town. Given Ogden's large Mormon population, we have no idea why Harvey spent a great deal of his own money organizing a Mardi Gras celebration, which, of course, was a dismal failure.

In 1893 Harvey relocated again to Chicago, where he established the Coin Publishing Company. Since his days in Colorado, Harvey had been studying the national economy, and he came to believe that the nation's economic ills—especially the contraction of the national money supply—could be cured by backing paper currency on the relatively abundant silver rather than the much scarcer gold.

A gifted writer and promoter, Harvey soon became a national spokesman for "bi-metalism," which was the name given to the theory that the U.S. currency should be based on both silver and gold. The great silver versus gold debate of the late 1800s was the primary domestic issue of the day. In 1894 Harvey published his first book, *Coin's Financial School,* a great financial and popular success that featured a fictional young financier named Coin. He pioneered in the use of cheap paperback books to influence public opinion. Soon thereafter, Harvey became known everywhere by the nickname "Coin."

Harvey's political influence peaked in the mid-1890s when his theories were adopted by the wildly popular Democratic politician William Jennings Bryan of Nebraska. Bryan won the Democratic presidential nomination in 1896, after giving his famous "Cross of Gold" speech, in which he stated that America's economy was being crucified on a cross of gold. Republican William McKinley defeated Bryan in a campaign that saw the rise of the professional manager and the use of huge campaign treasuries.

During the 1896 campaign, Harvey worked for Bryan in northwest Arkansas, and he was attracted to the area in part due to its lack of large cities or a wealthy class. In 1900 he settled in the area on a large acreage south of Rogers. He created a luxurious summer resort named Monte Ne. He claimed the name was a mixture of Spanish and American Indian words for "mountain" and "water." Not long afterward the Harvey home burned, and Anna moved back to Chicago, ending an unhappy marriage.

Monte Ne was an amazing undertaking. Developed around a large lagoon that featured an Italian gondola rowed by "gay gondoliers," Monte Ne was probably Arkansas's first large tourist attraction. By 1902, the Hotel Monte Ne was complete, and it was later joined by two more hotels, tennis courts, and an indoor swimming pool, said to be the first in Arkansas. Nevertheless, Harvey had overreached once again, and Monte Ne faced growing financial peril.

In an attempt to save Monte Ne—as well as promote northwest Arkansas—Harvey organized the Ozark Trails Association in 1913. The association embarked on an effort to improve Benton County roads, mark routes, and erect mile markers. Despite all his efforts, the coming of the automobile signaled the end of Monte Ne and most such large resorts across the nation.

By 1920 Harvey concluded that America and the world was headed for ruin, and he set about to create a great monument filled with artifacts and books that would await discovery by future generations. Termed a "pyramid" by most, the planned structure was actually a series of buildings topped by a tall obelisk. The obelisk was never completed, though an amphitheater and other structures were.

Harvey's monetary theories came into vogue again after the onset of the Great Depression in 1929. In 1931 he organized the Liberty Party at a convention at Monte Ne. Meeting under a huge circus tent, the 786 delegates from twenty-five states nominated Harvey for president and Andrae Nardskog of Los Angeles for vice president. The team campaigned for government ownership of utilities and industries, limits on landholdings, and free silver.

Democratic nominee Franklin D. Roosevelt swamped all his opponents in the 1932 general election, with Harvey and Nardskog receiving a mere 53,000 votes—over half coming from the state of Washington.

Harvey lived only four more years, dying in February 1936. He was buried in a tomb at the base of his planned pyramid. Survivors included his second wife, May, and three children.

Harvey's tomb was relocated in 1962 when the new Beaver Lake flooded the area. Occasionally, during severe droughts, Harvey's wondrous amphitheater arises from the dark waters to remind us of the eccentric visionary who built it. Harvey's death mask, as well as other information on him and Monte Ne, can be seen at the Rogers Historical Museum.

FOR MORE INFORMATION:

Bland, Gaye. "'Coin' Harvey (1851–1936)." *The Encyclopedia of Arkansas History and Culture.* http://encyclopediaofarkansas.net/encyclopedia/entry-detail.aspx?search=1&entryID=1666.

Nichols, Jeanette P. "Bryan's Benefactor: Coin Harvey and His World." *Ohio Historical Quarterly* 67 (October 1958): 299–325.

Stokes, Harry A. "William Hope Harvey: Promoter and Agitator." Master's thesis, Northern Illinois University, 1965.

King Crowley

Archeological fakery is probably as old as archeology itself. In Italy, one can even tour a museum dedicated to faked artwork, and the Piltdown Man artifacts of England were not exposed for forty years after their much-heralded discovery in 1912. The best-known archeological fake in Arkansas history was "King Crowley," a reputed prehistoric stone carving of a human head supposedly found near Jonesboro on Crowley's Ridge. Although authorities at the time said it was a fake, the foot-high bust with glaring eyes has retained much of its mystique and appeal.

The statue first came to light in the early 1920s, when a Jonesboro jeweler and gunsmith named Dentler Rowland claimed to have found a cache of ancient stone carvings in a gravel bar south of Jonesboro. Rowland, nicknamed "Deef" because of his deafness, was a native of Indiana and had lived in Jonesboro since about 1913. According to a 1945 article in the *Arkansas Democrat,* Rowland was walking across a gravel bed and poking at stones with his cane when he "unearthed a small black foot. Thinking it was the foot of a petrified baby, he instituted a search for the body. . . . This curious find was followed by digging which resulted in the discovery of King Crowley and 60 other valuable specimens."

Dentler found a ready buyer in Julia Burnelle "Bernie" Babcock, the founding curator of the Museum of Science and Natural History in Little Rock, who reportedly paid the substantial sum of $600 for the collection. Rowland sold artifacts to Babcock and others for more than a decade. Approximately eighty pieces have been identified. They were carved from sandstone and stained to appear old.

Babcock, a popular writer and history buff with no training in archeology or anthropology, was mesmerized by the stone carvings and soon began referring to the bust as "King Crowley." A 1945 article in the *Arkansas Democrat* reported that Babcock "calls King Crowley

King Crowley, a fake archeological find from Crowley's Ridge. *Photo courtesy of Special Collections, University of Arkansas Libraries.*

her 'boyfriend,'" saying that he was given to "staying put" and "never engaging in silly talk."

Like many boyfriends, however, King Crowley was not all that he seemed. And, like some admiring older women, Babcock knew more than she was willing to state publicly. In a 1942 letter to the Smithsonian Institution in Washington, D.C., Babcock admitted, "Before I bought the stones I was warned they were fakes. All down the line I have been told the same thing."

Dan Morse, retired archeologist at Arkansas State University in Jonesboro and author of the entry on King Crowley in the *Encyclopedia of Arkansas History and Culture,* described the artifact as "a stern-looking young male with hair swept back, metal eyes, metal ear ornaments, and a metal heart set into the chest. The statue is about twelve to fourteen inches tall and weighs about forty pounds, based on observations made before it disappeared."

In addition to King Crowley, Babcock purchased a variety of other artifacts from Rowland, including a stone phallus. Archeologist Morse said it was rumored that Babcock kept the phallus in her desk and would show it to trusted friends only.

Morse believes Rowland might have been motivated by the international excitement surrounding Egyptian archeological discoveries. A hippopotamus and camel are included in the Rowland collection, though neither animal was native to North America.

Babcock was not the only person who defended King Crowley's authenticity. Fred Allsopp, the Little Rock newspaperman and poet, included a large picture of the bust in his popular two-volume *Folklore of Romantic Arkansas,* published in 1931. Allsopp described the carvings as "a mystery," but he went on to state, "The charge that these strange stone pieces have been recently faked, aged, and buried is disproved by the fact that in the bottom of the hole from which they were taken, roots from an oak tree growing on a nearby hill, wound around a mortar of conglomerate, binding it into the earth."

A close examination of King Crowley should have convinced Babcock and Allsopp of the carvings recent origin. The statue's copper eyes were the same size and composition as harness studs. Inlaid on the chest was a metal rendering of a valentine-shaped heart—a motif that was unknown to prehistoric American Indians. Some of the other carvings included eyes made from metals that were unavailable prior to the arrival of Europeans. Many of the carvings had eyes made from furniture tacks.

Babcock eventually came to realize that King Crowley and the other Rowland discoveries were fakes. The carvings were removed from the museum, and King Crowley and related correspondence were sold to a collector in California. Other Rowland pieces do exist, however, including a large collection held by the Arkansas State University Museum in Jonesboro. While the objects are poor examples of archeological fakes, they are generally considered as fine specimens of folk art. Dan Morse, and his archeologist wife, Phyllis, eventually tracked down the current owner of King Crowley—but he wishes to remain anonymous.

FOR MORE INFORMATION:

McCracken, Lloyd, Dan Morse, and Phyllis Morse. "Dentler Rowland and King Crowley and Those Mysterious Stone Images." *Craighead County Historical Quarterly* 42 (July 2004): 3–14.

———. "Dentler Rowland and King Crowley and Those Mysterious Stone Images—Part II." *Craighead County Historical Quarterly* 42 (October 2004): 21–27.

———. "Dentler Rowland and King Crowley and Those Mysterious Stone Images—Conclusion." *Craighead County Historical Quarterly* 43 (January 2005): 22–27.

———. "Dentler Rowland and His Workshop." *Craighead County Historical Quarterly* 43 (April 2005): 21–25.

Morse, Dan. "King Crowley." *The Encyclopedia of Arkansas History and Culture.* http://encyclopediaofarkansas.net/encyclopedia/entry-detail.aspx?search= 1&entryID=568.

Old Mike

One of the more macabre episodes in Arkansas history took place in the small town of Prescott, the county seat of Nevada County. On the morning of August 21, 1911, an unidentified man was found dead in Prescott City Park. For the next sixty-four years the body lay unclaimed in a local mortuary, all the while on public display.

The *Prescott Daily News,* a long extinct newspaper, described the dead man as "about 5 feet and 4 inches high, brown eyes, brown hair, partly bald on top of head, brown mustache, tattoo on right arm . . . left leg a little shorter than right, stiff ankle . . . old scar on top of head and two gold teeth." The news report concluded by noting that "the remains were embalmed by Undertaker [John D.] Cornish and will be held here for a few days with the hopes that something may be learned of the deceased's relatives." The author of the entry on Old Mike in the *Encyclopedia of Arkansas History and Culture* speculated that he died of a heart attack or stroke.

When no one came forward to claim the body, despite widespread press coverage, the Nevada County sheriff distributed flyers throughout the country seeking relatives. Several people viewed the body in hopes he was a lost relative, but as the weeks turned to months and then to years no one claimed the corpse. As the years passed, the embalmed body became a fixture at Cornish Mortuary. In 1921, after a decade at the mortuary, the body was photographed while posed in front of a new Studebaker hearse.

The picture depicts a dark-skinned man, despite the fact that he was white. Some speculated that the deceased was of foreign birth, noting that he had sophisticated dental work that was typical of European dental practices. The body shrank considerably in height and weight, standing four feet six inches in height and weighing fifty pounds. When the cadaver's eyes dried out, wax replicas were inserted. The embalming process, along with the natural dehydration of the body, left a mummified cadaver that was sometimes described as "petrified."

Old Mike with a new Studebaker hearse. *Photo courtesy of Special Collections, University of Arkansas Libraries.*

The Cornish Mortuary staff gave the corpse the name of "Old Mike" in order to distinguish it from another unclaimed and unidentified body nicknamed "Pat," which was eventually claimed. While the mortuary staff treated Old Mike with a certain respect (such as cleaning and redressing the corpse yearly), as time passed storing the cadaver took on the trappings of a sideshow. A glass case was made in which the corpse was displayed, standing upright on contorted feet. Wide-eyed school children came to see the body, as did tourists. On Saturday nights teenage boys brought their dates by to peek at Old Mike through the mortuary windows. Offers were made to purchase the body, including one from a circus. A museum in Kansas also sought to buy Mike.

Finally, on May 12, 1975, Old Mike was buried at the insistence of the state. Cornish Mortuary purchased a plot in De Ann Cemetery in Prescott and provided a casket as well as a wreath of red carnations. Rev. Jerry Westmoreland, pastor of the First Christian Church in Prescott, conducted the graveside funeral. The mortuary also provided a tombstone, which reads simply "Old Mike, Died August 21, 1911."

In 2003 Prescott novelist Penny Richards and local history buff Karen Ward wrote and produced a play on Old Mike, which was described as a "Corpus Opus" by a journalist in the *Texarkana Gazette*.

FOR MORE INFORMATION:

Nichols, Mike. "The Mystery of Prescott's Ol' Mike." *Old Time Chronicle*, February–March 1996, 10–12, 42.

Sesser, David. "Old Mike." *The Encyclopedia of Arkansas History and Culture*. http://encyclopediaofarkansas.net/encyclopedia/entry-detail.aspx?search=1&entryID=4924#.

Dr. John R. Brinkley

Located a few miles south of Little Rock on Arch Street Pike stands a majestic building that has had a remarkably diverse history. The large stone structure was built in the 1920s by the Shriners as a country club, but it failed and later became a Roman Catholic Carmelite Monastery. Between the Shriners and the Catholics, however, the building was owned by one of America's most famed medical quacks, Dr. John R. Brinkley.

Born into a North Carolina family of modest means in 1885, young John worked at a variety of jobs, all the time consuming a strange combination of books on home medical treatment and theology. In 1907 he married and began practicing medicine as a "Quaker doctor," whatever that was. He then relocated to Chicago, where he studied at Bennett Medical College, a school for "eclectic" physicians.

After giving birth to four children in less than six years, the hapless Mrs. Brinkley got a divorce in 1913. Immediately remarrying, Brinkley began practicing in South Carolina as an "Electro Medic Doctor." After spending a while in jail for failure to pay his bills, Brinkley relocated to Judsonia, White County, Arkansas, where he had a successful practice. But, he had much grander dreams.

In 1915 Brinkley graduated from the Eclectic Medical University in Kansas City, Missouri, a diploma mill recognized by only eight state medical boards, including that of Arkansas. After being licensed in Arkansas, he soon left the state for Kansas, arriving in the little village of Milford with thirty dollars in his pocket, a medical bag, a Saxon automobile, and his new wife, Minnie Telitha Brinkley. And then his life really got interesting.

Whatever Brinkley lacked in medical skill, he made up for in innovation and bravado. Realizing that impotent men would pay any price to have their sexual vigor restored, the new Kansas doctor developed a surgical procedure he called the goat-gland operation, by which he transplanted goat gonads into "tired men." Many of his customers were quite satisfied with the procedure, and soon Brinkley built his own hospital and a string of drugstores. And for good measure, he acquired a radio station.

Brinkley used his radio station to sell a mixture of fundamentalist religion and sexual rejuvenation, prompting one historian to quip that the doctor transformed the three R's into radio, rejuvenation, and religion. As many evangelists have discovered, the radio proved to be an easy way to riches.

In 1930 Brinkley's world came crashing down when the Federal Communications Commission (FCC) closed his radio station and the Kansas medical authorities revoked his license. He immediately began a campaign for governor as a write-in candidate. One biographer noted Brinkley's penchant for political showmanship, including "such innovations as a private plane and sashaying around in the most expensive car ever seen in Kansas, lavish use of the radio, a sound truck, cheer leaders to drill the write-in vote, hillbilly music and an astrologer." In 1932 he again ran for governor, and he so split the vote that Republican Alf Landon was elected, the only Republican gubernatorial candidate to survive Franklin D. Roosevelt's landslide.

Brinkley was anything but a quitter, so he convinced Mexican authorities to allow him to build a radio station in Villa Acuna, Mexico, just across the Rio Grande from Del Rio, Texas. Having escaped the regulation of the FCC, Brinkley fitted his station, XER, with a huge 50,000-watt transmitter. The station could be heard across North America, drawing thousands of patients to Brinkley's new hospital in Del Rio.

Though Brinkley discontinued his goat gland operation while in Del Rio, he developed a prostate operation that was popular even though it was nothing more than a dressed-up vasectomy. He reportedly earned $8 million during his Del Rio days. The arrival of a competitor, who performed the same operation at a discount, drove Brinkley from Texas to Arkansas, though he kept his residence in Del Rio and his Mexican radio station.

He established a hospital in the old St. Luke's Hospital at 1924 Schiller, adding a Romulus Drug Store nearby. Though he operated in the Schiller Street hospital, he established a convalescence facility at the old Shriners Country Club, christening it the Brinkley Country Club Hospital.

Things went smoothly for a while, but Brinkley's luck ended when Dr. Morris Fishbein of the American Medical Association included him among a list of modern medical charlatans. Brinkley sued for libel, and at the trial in Del Rio, Fishbein turned the tables on his accuser by maintaining that he could not be convicted of libel since his charges were true. The courts agreed, and soon Brinkley faced a string of civil suits. In 1941 he declared bankruptcy. This was followed by federal indictments for mail fraud.

Brinkley never came to trial because he died in his sleep in May 1942. Neither he nor the goats died in vain, however, for all the scandals surrounding Brinkley forced the Arkansas legislature to adopt laws regulating the practice of medicine.

FOR MORE INFORMATION:

Brock, Pope. *Charlatan: America's Most Dangerous Huckster, the Man Who Pursued Him, and the Age of Flimflam*. New York: Crown Publishers, 2008.

Carson, Gerald. *The Roguish World of Doctor Brinkley*. New York: Rinehart & Co., 1960.

Hull, Clifton E. "History of Carmelite Monastery Varied and Interesting." *Arkansas Gazette*, December 8, 1974.

Juhnke, Eric S. *Quacks and Crusaders: The Fabulous Careers of John Brinkley, Norman Baker, and Harry Hoxsey*. Lawrence: University Press of Kansas, 2002.

Lee, R. Alton. *The Bizarre Careers of John R. Brinkley*. Lexington: University Press of Kentucky, 2002.

Schneider, Albert J. "'That Troublesome Old Cocklebur': John R. Brinkley and the Medical Profession of Arkansas, 1937–1942." *Arkansas Historical Quarterly* 35 (Spring 1976): 27–46.

Ted Richmond

Throughout its history, Arkansas has been a land in which eccentrics and characters are amazingly common. Ted Richmond, of rural Newton County, would have to be considered among the elite of community oddballs. In Richmond's case, Arkansas had a man with a mission to provide books for his isolated Ozark neighbors, an eccentricity that was long remembered in the hills and hollers of Newton County.

James Theodore Richmond was born in Nebraska but grew up in Iowa. After serving as a soldier in France during World War I, Richmond set about wandering, an urge that resurfaced throughout his life. He studied for a time in Chicago, where he also worked as a reporter. He also attended a teachers college in Missouri, followed by a stint in an Illinois business college. Settling in Evening Shade, Missouri, Richmond worked as a magazine editor and postmaster.

In addition to his editorial and postmaster stint, the *Christian Science Monitor* claimed in a 1947 feature article that Richmond had worked as a "school teacher and Sunday school teacher, lay preacher, farmer, janitor, railroad section hand, mill worker, amateur photographer, cement plant straw boss, salesman, and operator of a mission for down-and-outers." However, it was Richmond's Wilderness Library that was his passion.

In 1930 Richmond homesteaded "the roughest 160-acres I could find in fair Newton county, seven and a half miles northwest of Jasper." On this rugged farm atop Mount Sherman, Richmond raised dairy goats and hogs. While goats and hogs paid the bills, Richmond's passion lay in books. Not long after building a small log house on his homestead, Richmond conceived the idea of creating a library to bring books to the isolated homes in the Ozarks. He recalled later in life how he went into a cave near his home, "opened the Bible and prayed through the night that God would help me bring good books to bright mountaineers."

Like many writers on a mission, Richmond was something of a promoter. He was able to get substantial publicity through the years, and after World War II he periodically undertook publicity tours. Books were donated from across the nation, and before long Richmond's small cabin was packed. He then abandoned the cabin, leaving it filled with books while he built a larger house nearby.

Ultimately, Richmond filled two houses with books, and a neighbor, Jeff Raney, voluntarily built a branch near the post office. Books were distributed from these libraries in a variety of means, mostly by hand. Sometimes neighbors would come to the unstaffed library and choose titles, leaving a list of books taken. Often Richmond delivered the books from a gunnysack slung across his shoulder, walking miles to reach the houses tucked in among the hills and hollows. In addition, he milked more than fifty goats twice daily.

As a general rule, "Twilight Ted," as Richmond was affectionately known, was warmly received by his neighbors. He partook in local activities, knew his neighbors, was always ready to help out in times of need, and seemed to be free of condescension.

Richmond might have lived in rural isolation, but he certainly did not hesitate to travel nationally on behalf of his library. He gave lectures and made public appeals for books and money, which were often publicized in the news media. On one occasion, however, Richmond caused considerable discord in Newton County. In 1952 the *Saturday Evening Post* sent a reporter to visit the Wilderness Library, and the resulting feature article portrayed Newton County as backward, a land "where the hand-hewn log cabin is still every man's dwelling and the timber wolves howl by night." Within a few days, 200 local citizens met and created the Newton County Betterment Group with the intention of disproving the "unmerited black eye" resulting from the *Post* feature. Richmond received a special invitation to attend the meeting, and he joined in the protests.

Harriet Jansma, who has written about Twilight Ted, reported that the Wilderness Library was doomed even before the *Post* article appeared. In 1937 the Arkansas General Assembly created a state library commission with the task of organizing county libraries. In 1944 the North Arkansas Regional Library was organized to serve Boone, Carroll, Marion, and Newton counties. Indeed, Newton County had two official branch libraries in operation when the *Post* reporter wrote his article.

At some point not long after the *Post* article appeared, Richard set out on a fund-raising tour, but he met with little success. Without fanfare he departed Mount Sherman in the mid-1950s and moved to Texarkana, where he married and lived a quiet life until his death in 1975.

Jansma perhaps portrayed Richmond's legacy best when she wrote, "It is clear that Ted Richmond shared with many of his hill neighbors a fierce independence and toleration of differences between people. And it is clear that, unconventional as he was, he captured the imagination of many who gave books, and many who gladly accepted and read them."

FOR MORE INFORMATION:

Cessna, Ralph. "Library in the Wilderness: Ted Richmond Tends to Reaching the Needs of Hill Folks in Arkansas Ozarks." *Christian Science Monitor*, April 5, 1947.

Jansma, Harriet. "The Book Man and the Library: A Chapter in Arkansas Library History." *Arkansas Libraries* 39 (December 1982): 28–31.

Spence, Hartzell. "Modern Shepherd of the Hills." *Saturday Evening Post*, November 8, 1952, 26, 113.